HIGHER EDUCATION OUTCOMES ASSESSMENT FOR THE TWENTY-FIRST CENTURY

D1605269

HIGHER EDUCATION OUTCOMES ASSESSMENT FOR THE TWENTY-FIRST CENTURY

PETER HERNON, ROBERT E. DUGAN,
AND CANDY SCHWARTZ, EDITORS

 LIBRARIES UNLIMITED

AN IMPRINT OF ABC-CLIO, LLC
Santa Barbara, California • Denver, Colorado • Oxford, England

Library of Congress Cataloging-in-Publication Data

Higher education outcomes assessment for the twenty-first century / Peter Hernon, Robert E. Dugan, and Candy Schwartz, editors.
    pages cm
   Includes bibliographical references and index.
    ISBN 978-1-61069-274-8 (hardcopy : alk. paper) — ISBN 978-1-61069-275-5 (ebook)
    1. Education, Higher—United States—Evaluation.   2. Educational tests and measurements—United States.   I. Hernon, Peter.
    LB2331.63.H55   2013
    378—dc23   2013001082

ISBN: 978-1-61069-274-8
EISBN: 978-1-61069-275-5

17 16 15 14 13   1 2 3 4 5

This book is also available on the World Wide Web as an eBook.
Visit www.abc-clio.com for details.

Libraries Unlimited
An Imprint of ABC-CLIO, LLC

ABC-CLIO, LLC
130 Cremona Drive, P.O. Box 1911
Santa Barbara, California 93116-1911

This book is printed on acid-free paper ∞

Manufactured in the United States of America

CONTENTS

Section II: Some Key Stakeholders

Section III: Selected Issues

Section IV: Conclusion

LIST OF FIGURES

PREFACE

In the late 20th century, the federal government and accreditation organizations (institutional and a number of program accreditation organizations) as well as the Council for Higher Education Accreditation called for evidence of student learning and expected that evidence to be associated with student learning outcomes[1] and student outcomes.[2] Within this framework and the assorted metrics advanced by these stakeholders, as well as expectations of prospective students and their parents, among others, outcomes assessment provides a richer picture of what institutions of higher education actually accomplish (and at what cost) so that they do not need to rely solely on what institutions claim they accomplish.

Higher Education Outcomes Assessment for the Twenty-First Century, which complements *Outcomes Assessment in Higher Education* and *Revisiting Outcomes Assessment in Higher Education,*[3] provides a state-of the-art review of outcomes assessment, shows student outcomes gaining in importance among key stakeholders as central to institutional effectiveness and accountability, and indicates how stakeholders intend to use and interpret those metrics. Libraries may play a partnering role in student learning outcomes, at least for certain outcomes, but librarians have not clearly articulated a role in compiling and advancing student outcomes and remain focused on course-level assessment, while stakeholders look beyond the course level. This book documents the key issues and offers strategies for libraries to put in place. Among these are depictions of student return on investment. The book also challenges current thinking about the use of library-centered inputs to demonstrate institutional effectiveness.

Divided into four parts, *Higher Education Outcomes Assessment for the Twenty-First Century* introduces trends in outcomes assessment and the increased importance of student outcomes, as well as key literature on outcomes assessment, including the identification of important websites. The second part, which builds on the foundation in the previous part, provides an extensive analysis of government as a stakeholder. Clearly, accountability is not a fad and places explicit expectations and requirements on higher education. This part, as well as part three, encourages librarians to listen to accreditation organizations and to move assessment, such as for information literacy, from the course level to the program and institutional levels.

Chapter 6 shows how stakeholders view institutional effectiveness and the type of metrics they value the most. The concept of institutional effectiveness continues to shift.

Part three also introduces assorted methods of data collection but first reminds those engaged in assessment to consider research designs and data quality. There is also a reminder that many studies of student satisfaction fail to address the Gaps Model of Service Quality and therefore do not recognize what the concept of satisfaction truly is and what related metrics could be applied.

The final part concludes the work and returns to some of the key themes of the book. The appendix is unique in its extensive listing of stakeholders within the higher education community.

The audience for this book includes faculty, administrators, and librarians at all academic institutions; accreditation organizations and associations; program officials in national educational associations; other stakeholders, including members of higher education foundations, and state and federal governments wanting to see how accountability is faring today and what key future trends are; and anyone wanting to learn more about outcomes assessment.

As academic libraries continue to change and redefine what roles and services they want to perform in the future, outcomes assessment offers many opportunities for an increased institutional role and visibility. However, for libraries, it requires a new way of thinking, one that librarians have long resisted, namely, moving their involvement in assessment from the course to the program and institutional levels. Such a movement requires planning and a new type of librarian, one grounded in learning pedagogy, evaluation and assessment research, inferential statistics, and the ability to communicate with impact and to forge new partnerships.

NOTES

1. Student learning outcomes focus on learning goals and answer the following questions: What should students learn? How does the content of one course relate to another? How well are they learning the content across a program of study? Beyond course evaluation (graded assignments and course evaluations), what evidence do institutions and programs have that learning occurred? How do programs use the evidence gathered to improve the learning process?

2. Student outcomes comprise aggregate statistics that depict graduation, retention, transfer, course, and program completion rates; job placement rates (employment rate for a graduating class); time-to-degree; affordability of higher education degrees; and so on. Such outcomes, which are really outputs, are institutional outcomes and are used to compare institutional performance. They do not measure changes in students themselves due to their college experience. They reflect what the institution has accomplished and not what or how much students learned.

3. Peter Hernon and Robert E. Dugan, *Outcomes Assessment in Higher Education* (Westport, CT: Libraries Unlimited, 2004); Peter Hernon, Robert E. Dugan, and Candy Schwartz, *Revisiting Outcomes Assessment in Higher Education* (Westport, CT: Libraries Unlimited, 2006).

Section I

INTRODUCTION

1

---•◦◦•---

OUTCOMES ASSESSMENT
TODAY: AN OVERVIEW

Peter Hernon

The term *outcomes assessment* combines two concepts, outcomes, which focus on impacts, and assessment, which is a subset of evaluation. When the term is applied to higher education, it refers to student learning outcomes, the extent to which students achieve and are able to apply pre-determined learning goals, and student outcomes, metrics that enable stakeholders to assess and compare institutions with respect to student attendance and completion rates (e.g., retention, graduation, or the length of time-to-degree). Both contexts recognize the need for higher education to address the expectations of, and requirements set by, stakeholders, one of which is the federal government. On one hand, outcomes assessment provides direction to the Council for Higher Education Accreditation (CHEA), which in turn translates that direction into policies that guide institutional and program accreditation organizations. On the other hand, it signals those metrics it wants higher education to report publicly. This chapter amplifies on this brief overview, comments on the present situation, and highlights recent developments that will guide the direction that outcomes assessment takes for the near future.

ASSESSMENT AS A SUBSET OF EVALUATION

For libraries, assessment involves partnerships between librarians and others in the institution or in the community to advance mutually shared goals and metrics. In the case of higher education, the partnership involves teaching faculty in academic departments, and those goals focus on learning as set in the institutional mission statement. Learning can be viewed from the perspective of individual courses, programs of study, and the institution and its promise for all graduates. It seems, however, that assessment for undergraduates is oftentimes confined to the general education or liberal arts component of the baccalaureate degree. That component might focus on the acquisition of knowledge through critical information gathering; the analysis, evaluation, and integration of that knowledge; making critical judgments in a logical and rational manner based on that knowledge; and explaining or communicating those judgments effectively (with impact), both in writing and orally, using accepted methods for presentation, organization, and debate particular to specific disciplines. The focus might also be on the ability of students to work collaboratively in knowledge development, making critical judgments and communicating the results; to understand international interdependence and cultural diversity; and to appreciate professional values, lifestyles, and traditions that may differ from their own. Such a component should not be confined to a degree, or part of it, and herein is the subject of assessment. Every program of academic study should have learning goals that transcend mastery of course content and identify areas that cut across courses and build student ability and skills.

Focusing on evaluation, Peter Hernon and Ellen Altman point out that it centers on 11 questions, which can be viewed singularly or in a cluster and which progress from highly quantitative to highly qualitative.[1] One of the questions "How satisfied?" might apply to both evaluation and assessment, if, for instance, accreditation organizations include satisfaction in their standards. The most critical question for both evaluation and assessment is "How well?" To answer that question, evaluation focuses on strategic plans and the extent to which goals, objectives, and targets are met, whereas assessment applies evaluation methodologies that, for instance, explore how well students master established learning goals at the program and institutional levels. Thus, an academic library might examine effectiveness from both perspectives, but when it engages in assessment, the staff agrees to learning goals that faculty finds mutually agreeable. The key phrase is *mutually agreeable*, meaning that librarians do not impose their views on others (or try to do so).

The Association of College and Research Libraries (ACRL) has developed a set of guidelines and standards for information and visual literacy.[2] These documents, in total or in part, might be shared with faculty as a discussion document and reframed as the faculty conveys its expectations at the course and program levels. That reframing, most likely, will produce a subset of goals, as those documents include too many points for meaningful examination. One document, the "Standards for Libraries in Higher Education," identifies performance indicators and a set of sample outcomes. In fact, those outcomes are outputs and tend to view librarians as creating opportunities for faculty participation and for librarians to gain recognition as helping students. Those outcomes seem to reinforce the role of librarians at the course level and do not set higher aspirations—the program or institutional level.[3]

OUTCOMES ASSESSMENT

There are two types of outcomes, student outcomes and student learning outcomes. Both are useful for the purpose of accountability and improving learning experiences. Because learning goals focus on the most important areas that transcend course and program content, they involve deep learning, which relates knowledge gained from a series of courses, centers on what is deemed important within a program of study, connects concepts, relates ideas to previous knowledge and experience, and explores links between evidence and conclusions. By contrast, surface learning includes rote learning content such as would be demonstrated by writing an essay that offers detail rather than discussion and that lists points rather than providing background or context to the work. For example, an undergraduate majoring in American history would be expected to memorize what occurred, to understand the topic from colonial to modern times, and to develop a specialty within that time frame. Learning outcomes, expressed in terms of deep learning, enhance that person's understanding of content, focus on the ability to engage in analysis and synthesis, and show to any stakeholder what a history major can do with (or how they can convey) this understanding. If an institution sets learning goals applicable to all academic programs, this does not mean that each learning goal is appropriate in all instances. For example, an institutional learning goal might relate to leadership, but is such a goal appropriate to each undergraduate major and minor?

Learning Goals (Student Learning Outcomes)

Learning goals or outcomes frame the area(s) that the faculty wants students to learn beyond mastery of course content. They focus on the knowledge, skills, attitudes, abilities, and habits of mind that students take with them from a learning experience. Institutions and programs might develop learning goals covering one or more of the following areas:

- Civic engagement
- Conflict mediation
- Creative thinking
- Critical thinking
- Ethical reasoning
- Global citizenry
- Leadership
- Literacy (information and visual)
- Problem solving
- Quantitative reasoning

Learning goals involve the transfer of knowledge to a new context and relate to high-ordered abilities defined in terms of Bloom's taxonomy. For example, as part of the cognitive domain (the recall or recognition of specific facts and concepts that serve in the development of intellectual abilities and skills), these goals relate to *analysis* (separating material or concepts into component parts so that its organizational structure may be understood, as well as distinguishing between facts and inferences) and *synthesis* (building a structure or pattern from diverse elements; putting parts together to form a whole, with emphasis on creating a new meaning or structure).[4]

Learning goals might also cover skills such as communication (written, oral, and presentation), facility with technology, foreign language communication, and intercultural skills. In such instances, students demonstrate the ability to apply what they have learned to a new context. When programs develop goals relating to communication, for instance, they build student ability to progress as effective communicators and ultimately to communicate with impact.

In summary, student learning outcomes address both types of learning goals (deep and surface) and are defined in terms of the knowledge, skills, habits of mind, and abilities that students have attained as a result of their involvement in a particular set of educational experiences. As such, they

- increase student awareness of and involvement in their own learning;
- provide a common language and framework for discussions about learning within and across departments;
- offer an approach to curriculum assessment and change;
- comprise an important first step toward clear communication of expectations to students; and
- fulfill an expectation of stakeholders, including the reporting requirements of accreditation organizations.

With the knowledge and abilities associated with Bloom's taxonomy and the acquired skill set, it is hoped that students learn to collaborate, engage in informed decision making, and work with their peers who represent diverse groups.

The assessment of student learning goals often is based on self-reports and what students or recent graduates think they have mastered. None of the goals should involve mastery of course content, which is concerned with the area of evaluation and a determination of how well instructors think students have mastered the content of the course. Where programs require completion of a test, written and/ or oral, before graduation, the intent is to gauge the extent of knowledge gained over a series of courses. Most often, evaluation per se is limited to the course level. Further, in some cases, institutions require or recommend a set of learning goals applicable across programs. Because there are degrees of mastery, goals should normally be linked to rubrics and the progression of student knowledge, abilities, and skills. It follows, then, that learning goals are best framed with verbs such as *demonstrate* or *able to synthesize*, rather than *understand* or *appreciate*.

Student Outcomes

Student outcomes are aggregate statistics on groups of students compiled at the program and, more likely, institutional levels, and they paint an overall portrait of that institution. Such data

- provide general evidence of institutional effectiveness to policymakers, accreditation organizations, and the public;
- provide insights into the return on investment in postsecondary education for individuals and families, states, and the nation at large;
- produce data to guide postsecondary policy;
- inform institutional planning, program development, and program improvement in an era of constrained resources;
- respond to concerns about whether postsecondary institutions are adequately preparing students for the workplace; and
- provide data to individuals and families to help them reach informed decisions about postsecondary institutions and programs of study.[5]

Examples of student outcomes include graduation rate, placement rate of program graduates, student retention rates, time-to-degree rate, accessibility (ability to get into a program of study), and amount of student debt accumulated. These are imperfect metrics,[6] but they are meaningful to various stakeholders that tend to ignore the imperfections. In fact, there is great interest in these metrics, and as demonstrated later in the chapter, a number of websites convey such outcomes to parents and prospective students. As discussed in Chapter 3, the federal government and some other stakeholders are shifting their focus from student learning outcomes to student outcomes associated with affordability, access to higher education, completion of a program of study, and ability to be employed based on that education. Such metrics focus on the program and institutional levels and are ones not directly linked to libraries. A question raised in following chapters is "Can libraries contribute to such metrics?"

APPLICATION OF STUDENT LEARNING OUTCOMES TO DOCTORAL STUDIES

Typically, student learning outcomes are applied to undergraduate students, and if they extend to graduate studies, they guide master's programs. It is often assumed that they have no role in doctoral studies as such programs have adequate ways to monitor progress and apply what is learned in coursework. Besides, these programs may offer a capstone experience and a written and oral examination prior to starting the dissertation. Naturally, the dissertation provides evidence of student learning and ability to engage in critical thinking and problem solving. The dissertation defense reinforces these abilities as well as communication skills. The Simmons College program in Managerial Leadership in the Information Professions is recognized as an exception to the general pattern and is guided by a conceptual model that contains 26 learning goals. In this way, the program adds another layer of assessment, one intended to identify weaknesses early in the program and correct them prior to completion of coursework.[7] Still, like with any doctoral program, the dissertation is the major learning experience, and from it, students gain a foundation on which they can build throughout their professional careers.

AREAS OF CONFUSION

An examination of the literature of library and information science discloses confusion between evaluation and assessment. Assessment is in vogue, and evaluation findings are presented as assessment studies, contrary to how this chapter views that concept. Adding to the confusion, data collection instruments developed for an area of evaluation might be relabeled as assessment instruments, but are typically not linked to mutually agreeable learning goals. The classic example is LibQUAL+™, a survey questionnaire that measures service quality, despite the multitude of articles in the literature claiming it as a way to gauge satisfaction or to engage in service quality assessment. Service quality does not form the basis of any mutually agreeable learning goals. Some self-studies that institutions submit to accreditation organizations do include data provided through this use of the questionnaire. Clearly, such reportage fails to understand the difference between service quality and satisfaction or appropriate methods for ascertaining the extent to which learning goals are met. More seriously, it may indicate that assessment teams are not comprised of individuals grounded in evaluation and assessment research.

Evidence of student mastery of course content includes grades and course evaluation forms (which typically enable students to comment on the course and the instructor as well as to suggest ways to improve course content and instructional practice). Neither grades nor course evaluations, however, address learning goals—"the foundation of meaningful assessment"[8]—other than asking students whether they were explained. Other frequently collected data points that do not address learning goals include

- percentage of time spent in active learning,
- number of student hours spent on service learning,
- number of student hours spent on homework, and
- number of student hours spent at intellectual or cultural activities related to the course.

In *Student Learning Assessment*, the Middle States Commission on Higher Education (hereafter the Middle States Commission) refers to these output metrics as indirect measures of course assessment.[9] Since such questions are self-reporting estimates that course evaluation might address, we consider them as part of evaluation, and they do not reflect on the mastery of student learning goals.

SOME TRENDS

Among the trends is movement of student learning outcomes beyond the immediate program or institution to a statewide level and greater clarity as to how government interprets student outcomes. The federal government now emphasizes student outcomes over student learning outcomes. Further, there is recognition of the weaknesses of indirect methods of gathering evidence that are not linked to particular learning goals and also recognition that different learning goals can exist at one institution. At the center of much criticism of outcomes is the National Survey of Student Engagement, which in very general terms reflects how much time students invest in their education and how the institution deploys its resources. As this section emphasizes, the trend is to embrace direct methods that reflect what students actually learn, to move away from tests or general surveys, and to center attention on certain quantitative metrics.

Statewide Assessment

The original intent of outcomes assessment was to produce evidence that course instructors, as well as faculty and administrators in programs and institutions, could use for the purpose of accountability and improvement of student learning experiences. The major criticisms of outcomes assessment tended to be that it was not always linked to a planning process, and once the results were gathered, they were not used for improving those experiences. The Association of American Colleges and Universities has formed the Liberal Education and America's Promise (LEAP) states' initiative, with funding from the Lumina Foundation, to enable students, regardless of their chosen field of study, to achieve a set of essential learning outcomes fostered through liberal education. Within eight states, the partnership focuses on the following institutions:

1. California: the state university system;
2. Kentucky: public two- and four-year universities;
3. Massachusetts: public colleges and universities;
4. North Dakota: public, private, and tribal colleges and universities;
5. Oregon: the university system;
6. Utah: the state system of higher education, public and private universities and colleges;
7. Virginia: private institutions, public institutions affiliated with the State Council of Higher Education for Virginia, and the state council; and
8. Wisconsin: the state university system and the Wisconsin Association of Independent Colleges and Universities.

The goal is to produce system-level assessment of student learning so that evidence about accountability and improvement of learning experiences extends across programs and institutions. The assessment will focus on actual curricula and student work rather than on standardized testing. In the state university systems of California, Oregon, and Wisconsin, the project builds capacity in support of academic excellence, and it emphasizes the success of students traditionally underrepresented in higher education.[10]

For Massachusetts, as one example, the Vision Project, part of the LEAP initiative, adds civic education and engagement as a key outcome; another is national leadership. The state plans to track student outcomes related to graduation rates and performance on licensure examinations and to benchmark such data to similar compilations by other states.[11]

In addition to this initiative, Florida and Missouri require students to take tests at different stages of their programs, but the institutions are not rewarded or punished based on student test scores, primarily due to uncertainty regarding test reliability, validity, and institutional resistance. In New York and Washington, outcomes assessment is encouraged as part of institutional effectiveness plans, but the states rely on aggregated data from the colleges and universities, rather than the performance of students on tests.[12]

Performance Funding

Performance funding allocates state monies to institutions based on their performance in certain areas on an annual basis; in this way, funding becomes a tool to pressure institutions of higher education to increase the number of graduates, presumably those residing within the state. One concern relates to how to reward institutions for sustaining their success, as measured by increased rates of remedial completion, retention, and graduation. In 2011, one state (Tennessee) restructured its funding model for higher education, tying all state funding for two- and four-year colleges and universities to outcomes-based metrics such as increased completion rates. Performance funding is also an effort to make institutions and their faculty more efficient and productive. Efficiency refers to the review and perhaps elimination of low enrollment programs, expansion of the availability of program credits for prior learning experiences, reduction of faculty (especially part-time or adjunct), greater collaboration in teaching general education courses, and concern for the affordability of an earned degree and the amount of student debt incurred. Effectiveness refers to retention and graduation rates as well as the alignment of high school graduation requirements with preparation for college and work upon graduation. As a result, metrics might center, for instance, on

- annual completion rates,
- graduates gaining employment in their field or enrolled in a graduate or professional program within one year of graduation,
- retention of first-year students (four-year institutions) or first-term students (community colleges), and
- student indebtedness.

   Government is shifting its focus from student learning outcomes to these types of student outcomes. At the same time, there is increased interest in quantifying faculty productivity and viewing it in terms of *how much* faculty accomplish, measured by, for example, the number of courses and students taught or advised, the amount of tuition dollars they generate (class enrollment), the number of grants received, and the number of publications produced. Relevant metrics are thus associated with outputs rather than outcomes.[13] Presumably, stakeholders take for granted the accomplishment of learning goals associated with outcomes or they see the link between such goals and student outcomes as the extent to which students gain employment in their field upon graduation and whether they are successful in those jobs. At the same time, the metrics generated from assessing student progress in accomplishing specified learning goals will be used to make comparisons across programs and institutions, as noted earlier.

Systems of Accountability

Developed in 2007, the Voluntary System of Accountability® (VSA), which began to function in 2010, is an initiative of public four-year universities to provide data on the undergraduate student experience through the College Portrait, http://www.collegeportraits.org/

   For each VSA participating institution, the College Portrait supplies basic comparable information through a common web report. Information includes student and campus characteristics, cost of attendance, success and progress rates, campus safety, class size, student experiences on campus, and student learning outcomes.[14]

For the institutions included, students and their parents find data useful in comparing and selecting a college. Among the questions, they can answer are as follows:

- How much does it cost to go to institution X?
- How does university X rank compared with other universities?
- Can I graduate in four years?
- How large are classes?
- What are the most popular majors?
- Is university X a commuter school?

The VSA and College Portrait are sponsored by the American Association of State Colleges and Universities and the Association of Public and Land-grant Universities. VSA's homepage, http://www.voluntarysystem.org/index.cfm, leads to articles from *The Chronicle of Higher Education* on student outcomes and how to improve them.

Hall of Shame

The Higher Education Act's renewal in 2008 requires that annually the U.S. Department of Education publish the Hall of Shame list. This list refers to the colleges and universities with the highest costs and biggest price increases; conversely, there is a list of those with the lowest such increases. There is no attempt to explain or place the numbers in any context. Again, the Hall is a sign of increased national focus on the cost of higher education, presuming (incorrectly) that cost correlates with the quality of the educational experience.

Complementary Websites

There are complementary websites to the College Portrait. For instance, College Results Online, http://www.collegeresults.org/, focuses on graduation rates and enables users to compare the rate among different institutions. The College Completion website of *The Chronicle of Higher Education*, supported by the Gates Foundation, shares data on graduation rates for nearly 3,800 institutions by race and gender, and over time. There is also coverage of completion per 100 students and spending per completion, articles, and commentary from *The Chronicle*, and an online discussion tool that enables users to compare their own findings with those of other readers.[15]

The U.S. Department of Education has created the College Affordability and Transparency Center, which has a website devoted to producing a college or university scorecard, http://collegecost.ed.gov/catc/Default.aspx, that enables the public to produce a report of the highest (top 5 percent) and lowest (bottom 10 percent) tuition and required fees for full-time beginning students per academic year. The report also shows net price and cost of attendance minus grant and scholarship aid. Further, the scorecard addresses graduation rate, the length of time it takes to graduate, student loan debt and student repayment of loans, and earning potential (likelihood of gaining employment upon graduation). The Obama White House sees the purpose of the scorecard as making "it easier for students and their families to identify and choose high-quality, affordable colleges that provide good value." In essence, the scorecard provides data on return on investment, defines high quality narrowly, and is a tool that parents and prospective students can use as they shop around for an institution that provides good value at an affordable price.[16]

The Display of Metrics

Texas A & M University has produced a most interesting website, https://accountability.tamu.edu/, "Measuring the Pursuit of Teaching, Research, & Service Excellence," that might serve as a model for other colleges and universities. The website covers relevant "university metrics," "college metrics," "Action 2015 metrics," "Vision 2020 metrics," "system metrics," and "reports & surveys." Action 2015, http://provost.tamu.edu/strategic-planning-2010, includes data on the adoption of the university's five-year strategic plan for fiscal years 2011–2015 and the strategic plans for the colleges and other units that build off of the university's plan. Vision 2020, http://vision2020.tamu.edu/, refers to the university's plan to gain recognition as a consensus leader among peer public institutions.

The assortment of metrics applicable to the university is most impressive and builds on the array of student outcomes widely available. One figure, for instance, displays the percentage of undergraduates who accumulated a certain percentage of credit hours, and another indicates the "first-year retention rate of first-time, degree seeking undergraduates . . . with the number of new students at [the] institution." There is a series of figures covering faculty, staff, and students. For instance, one figure relates to "student progression," and for all figures, it is possible to filter the data by appropriate categories. Filters for students might be "admitted," "enrolled," "first generation," and "retention," and, for faculty "teaching workload." For any figure, there are explanatory footnotes.

Cleverly, the website does not focus exclusively on student outcomes. There is an explanation of teaching, research, and service and what the university hopes to develop. Under teaching, we discover the university wants to:

> graduate highly recruited leaders who are critical thinkers, effective communicators, and lifelong learners with diverse and global perspectives. We will build on our historical emphasis on student leadership development to . . .:
>
> • Graduate students who are highly valued in their professions
> • Increase the number of graduates and reduce time to degree
> • Enrich the quality of life for a diverse and global campus environment
> • Enhance the integration of curricular and co-curricular experiences.[17]

From the website, therefore, readers discover the set of student outcomes and of student learning outcomes applicable to the university. However, there are no graphic displays of outcomes. Nonetheless, the website provides a standard for accountability and transparency for other institutions to model.

Finally, a new website, College Abacus, enables students to compare financial aid packages at more than 2,000 institutions of higher education. This website, https://www.collegeabacus.com/, combines the net-price calculators from the various institutions into one, easy-to-use system.

CHEA Award

In 2005, the CHEA established an Award for Institutional Progress in Student Learning Outcomes and issued its first awards the subsequent year. Through 2010, there have been 18 awards to academic institutions, colleges or schools within universities, offices of academic assessment, units of academic assessment, centers for excellence in teaching and learning, and individual projects.[18] It would be interesting to examine those grants and the websites of the recipients to identify trends and patterns. Where possible, those reports might be compared with the appropriate self-studies prepared for submission to institutional and program accreditation organizations. With the federal government emphasizing transparency, we know that many institutions fail to post their self-studies and the results of that assessment on their homepages. Given this situation, are the CHEA awards posted on the recipient's homepage? In other words, how serious are stakeholders and institutions and their programs about transparency?

OPPORTUNITIES FOR ACADEMIC LIBRARIANS

There is great concern among stakeholders about the cost of earning a degree. In 2011, the College Board Advocacy and Policy Center published a report, *Trends in College Pricing*, which shows that "increases in college prices for the 2011–12 academic year reflect the influence of a weak economy and state funding that has not kept up with the growth in college enrollments." Further, "for the fifth consecutive year, the percentage increase in average tuition and fees at public four-year institutions was higher than the percentage increase to private nonprofit institutions."[19] The cost of an education is more than just tuition; there are also room and board charges for residential students, living costs for commuter students, book and material charges, and so forth. At the same time, the

- average income in 2010 was lower than a decade earlier;
- "average net tuition and fees in-state students pay after taking grant aid from all sources and federal tax credits and deductions into consideration increased by about $170 in 2011 dollars, an annual rate of growth of 1.4% beyond inflation;" and
- state appropriations per full-time equivalent (FTE) student have declined since 2007.[20]

Given these statistics and with more stakeholders inquiring about value for money expended, more libraries might show how library use translates into a net plus, receipt of more value than money expended. On its homepage, the University of West Florida libraries, for instance, offers a calculator for students to ask the question "How can I get my tuition money's worth from the library?" They also have access to a generic form that indicates that minimal use translates into $539.90 for the academic year. A separate calculator applies at the institutional levels and enables students to see their return on investment for the following services during FY 2011:

- Studying in the library
- Borrowing books, e-books, DVDs, and laptops
- Asking reference questions or meeting with reference librarians for individual research consultations
- Conducting library instruction sessions
- Using subscription databases when off-campus[21]

Using such calculators, library managers might conduct a study, perhaps one using non-probability sampling, that asks students in different disciplines in both undergraduate and graduate programs to determine their return on investment and to comment on the value of this exercise. The results might be written as stories and provided to the institutional leadership and the press.

Academic librarians tend to focus on information literacy and collaborating with faculty members who will let them work with individual courses. As accreditation organizations focus less on the course level and more on the program and institutional level, the question becomes "How will libraries make the adjustment?" There is insufficient data on which to extrapolate to answer the question other than to say that many of them may continue to concentrate their efforts at the course level.

The Standards for Libraries in Higher Education encourages libraries to identify institutional peer groups within their Integrated Postsecondary Education Data System (IPEDS) classification and to engage in comparison benchmarking in order to enhance institutional quality and effectiveness. IPEDS data cover institutional characteristics (e.g., pricing and tuition, retention, enrollment, and budget). The standards notes that "for true 'apples to apples' comparisons, one will have to manually add more specific and descriptive parameters such as institutional governance, subcategories of general classifications (such as size of master's institution and type of baccalaureate institution), and level of research for doctorate universities."[22] Further, among other sources of data,

> . . . (ACRL) conducts an annual survey of academic libraries and offers an online service providing access to the ACRL and NCES survey data starting from 1998 and 2000, respectively. ACRLMetrics provides turn-key benchmarking templates based on ratios recommended in *Viewing Library Metrics from Different Perspective: Inputs, Outputs and Outcomes.*[23]

All of the highlighted metrics are inputs and outputs, and do not address learning goals, the institutional context, or the institutional mission. Retention, for instance, is a measure of the percentage of college students who remain at the institution and neither drop out or transfer to another institution. Some studies have investigated relationships between library use and retention. Lloyd A. Kramer and Martha B. Kramer found a positive one between library use and persistence as students who borrowed books from the library dropped out 40 percent less often than nonborrowers.[24] Elizabeth Mezick, who explored the impact of library expenditures and staffing levels on retention, found a moderate relationship between expenditures and retention.[25] Using input and output data, Mark Emmons and Frances C. Wilkinson conclude that "When controlling for race/ethnicity and socioeconomic status, a linear regression finds that a change in the ratio of library professional staff to students predicts a statistically significant positive relationship with both retention and graduation rates."[26] Other authors report that holding a campus job, such as in the library, influences student retention.[27] Still, it is commonly recognized that students in some disciplines graduate without using the library or use it only infrequently to moderately. Further, student learning outcomes and socialization issues may have an impact on retention. Clearly, the library cannot relate its contribution to any student outcome solely or largely from quantitative metrics. It needs to use qualitative means to develop stories showing any contribution. A commons—be it information, learning, or academic—offers the spaces and amenities that attract students and perhaps faculty, and may be "an environment to shift the library from the place faculty . . . [and a number of students] never have to go to the one place on campus they will always want to go."[28] Libraries need to develop stories based on indirect and perhaps direct methods of data collection. The question then becomes, "How might such metrics influence the perceptions of stakeholders about an institution?"

CONCLUDING THOUGHTS

Outcomes assessment, which has moved beyond concentration on individual courses, characterizes programs and institutions from the perspective of learning goals and a set of student outcomes. The federal government has shifted its focus from student learning outcomes to select evidence that enables parents and their college-bound children to make informed decisions about which institution to attend and to go beyond what the institution says in its effort to attract potential students. Accreditation organizations at the same time place increased emphasis on graduation rates. However, they are still concerned about how much students learn, and they now want to compare success among institutions. Success is defined in terms of graduation rate and comparative learning, however that is measured.

Student learning outcomes might produce quantitative and qualitative evidence, whereas student outcomes relate quantitative metrics that lack any qualification. As academic institutions struggle with increased accountability and how to explain themselves in terms of student outcomes, libraries must find their voice and show how they contribute to outcomes assessment beyond the course level. The problem is that websites such as the college scorecard recognize a narrow perspective on return on investment and do not really address quality or include qualitative evidence. The critical question becomes "How can libraries address their contribution to learning within such an environment?"

NOTES

1. Peter Hernon and Ellen Altman, *Assessing Service Quality: Satisfying the Expectations of Library Customers* (Chicago: American Library Association, 2010), 36–44. For additional coverage of the difference between evaluation and assessment as well as their interdependence, see Peter Hernon, Robert E. Dugan, and Danuta A. Nitecki, *Engaging in Evaluation and Assessment Research* (Santa Barbara, CA: Libraries Unlimited, 2011).

2. See American Library Association, Association of College and Research Libraries, "Guidelines and Standards" (Chicago: Association of College and Research Libraries, 2012), accessed March 24, 2012, http://www.ala.org/acrl/standards.

3. American Library Association, Association of College and Research Libraries, "Standards for Libraries in Higher Education" (Chicago: Association of College and Research Libraries, 2011), accessed March 26, 2012, http://www.ala.org/acrl/standards/standardslibraries.

4. See Benjamin S. Bloom, ed., *The Taxonomy of Educational Objectives: Cognitive Domain* (New York: David McKay Co., 1956); David R. Krathwohl, Benjamin S. Bloom, and Bertram B. Masia, *Taxonomy of Educational Objectives: Handbook II: Affective Domain* (New York: David McKay Co., 1964); and Lorin W. Anderson, and David R. Krathwohl, eds., *A Taxonomy for Learning, Teaching, and Assessment: A Revision of Bloom's Taxonomy of Educational Objectives* (New York: Longman, 2001).

5. U.S. Department of Education, National Center for Education Statistics, *Enhancing the Quality and Use of Student Outcome Data: Final Report of the NPEC Working Group on Student Outcomes from a Data Perspective* (Washington, DC: National Center for Education Statistics, 1997), 2–3, accessed March 24, 2012, http://nces.ed.gov/pubs97/97992.pdf.

6. See, for instance, "Do Graduation Rates Matter?" *Chronicle of Higher Education* LVIII, no. 27 (March 9, 2012): A1; Jeff Selingo, "The Rise and Fall of the Graduation Rate," *Chronicle of Higher Education* LVIII, no. 27 (March 9, 2012): A10, A12; Goldie Blumenstyk, "For-Profit Colleges Compute Their Own Gradation Rates," *Chronicle of Higher Education* LVIII, no. 27 (March 9, 2012): A14.

7. Peter Hernon and Candy Schwartz, "Ongoing Program Assessment in a Doctoral Program," in *Assessing for Learning: Building a Sustainable Commitment across the Institution*, 2nd ed., edited by Peggy L. Maki (Sterling, VA: Stylus, 2010), 270–71.

8. Middle States Commission on Higher Education, *Student Learning Assessment: Options and Resources*, 2nd ed. (Philadelphia: Middle States Commission, 2007), 10.

9. Ibid., 29.

10. Association of American Colleges and Universities, "Leap States Initiative" (Washington, DC: Association of American Colleges and Universities, 2012), accessed March 26, 2012, http://www.aacu.org/about/index.cfm.

11. Massachusetts Department of Higher Education, "The Vision Project" (Boston: Massachusetts Department of Higher Education, 2011), accessed March 26, 2012, http://www.mass.edu/currentinit/vpwhatsnew.asp.

12. For more information on each state, see U.S. Department of Education, Office of Postsecondary Education, "State Assessment Policy Analysis," accessed June 20, 2012, http://www.stanford.edu/group/ncpi/unspecified/assessment_states/stateReports.html.

13. See, for instance, Teresa A. Sullivan, Christopher Mackie, William F. Massy, and Esha Sinha, ed., *Panel on Measuring Higher Education Productivity: Conceptual Framework and Data Needs* (Washington, DC: National Academies Press, 2012).

14. Voluntary System of Accountability®, "About the College Portrait" (n.d.), accessed March 26, 2012, http://www.voluntarysystem.org/index.cfm?page=about_cp.

15. The Chronicle of Higher Education College Completion Website, accessed June 23, http://getideas.org/resource/the-chronicle-of-higher-education-college-complete-website/. See also "A Guide to the College Completion Site," *Chronicle of Higher Education* LVIII, no. 27 (March 9, 2012): A11.

16. White House, "College Scorecard" (Washington, DC: White House, 2012), accessed March 27, 2012, http://www.whitehouse.gov/issues/education/higher-education/college-score-card.

17. Texas A & M University, "Measuring the Pursuit of Teaching, Research, & Service Excellence," accessed May 18, 2012, https://accountability.tamu.edu/content/key-indicators-excellence-teaching-research-service.

18. For a list of the recipients and the selection criteria, see the Council for Higher Education, "2011 CHEA Awards" (Washington, DC: Council for Higher Education, 2011), accessed March 26, 2012, http://www.chea.org/chea%20award/CA_2011.02-B.html; http://www.chea.org/2012_CHEA_Award.html.

19. College Board Advocacy & Policy Center, *Trends in College Pricing 2011* (New York: College Board Advocacy & Policy Center, 2011), 3, accessed March 26, 2012, http://trends.collegeboard.org/downloads/College_Pricing_2011.pdf.

20. Ibid., 4, 15, 18.

21. See University of West Florida Libraries, Office of the Dean of Libraries, "Information . . ." (Pensacola, FL: University of West Florida Libraries, 2012), accessed March 26, 2012, http://libguides.uwf.edu/office-of-dean-of-libraries.

22. American Library Association, Association of College and Research Libraries, "Standards for Libraries in Higher Education," 13.

23. Ibid. For coverage of ACRLMetrics, see accessed June 23, 2012, http://www.acrlmetrics.com. See also Robert E. Dugan, Peter Hernon, and Danuta A. Nitecki, *Viewing Library Metrics from Different Perspective: Inputs, Outputs and Outcomes* (Santa Barbara, CA: Libraries Unlimited, 2009).

24. Lloyd A. Kramer and Martha B. Kramer, "The College Library and the Drop-out," *College & Research Libraries* 29, no. 4 (1968): 310–12.

25. Elizabeth M. Mezick, "Return on Investment: Libraries and Student Retention," *Journal of Academic Librarianship* 33, no. 5 (2007): 561–66.

26. Mark Emmons and Frances C. Wilkinson, "The Academic Library Impact on Student Persistence," *College & Research Libraries* 72, no. 2 (March 2011): 128.

27. Darla Rushing and Deborah Poole, "The Role of the Library in Student Retention," in *Making the Grade: Academic Libraries and Student Success,* edited by Maurie Caitlin Kelly and Andrea Kross (Chicago: Association of College and Research Libraries, 2002), 91–101; Stanley Wilder, "Library Jobs and Student Retention," *College & Research Libraries News* 51, no. 11 (1990): 1035–38.

28. Steven J. Bell, "Bringing Back the Faculty: The Evolution of the Faculty Commons in the Library," *Library Issues: Briefings for Faculty and Administrators* 31, no. 4 (March 2011): 1.

2

———◆-◆◆-◆———

LITERATURE ON ASSESSMENT
FOR LEARNING

Peter Hernon and Candy Schwartz

The literature of library and information science (LIS) tends to label studies of student expectations (service quality and satisfaction) and organizational effectiveness and efficiency as assessment. In fact, historically, such studies have been considered to comprise evaluation. Evaluation, a broader term, applies to the management of an organization, and it is intended to supply evidence on how well the organization is performing (meeting its mission statement and the goals set through a planning process). Assessment in higher education, on the other hand, also known as outcomes assessment, is a subset of evaluation and is typically applied by academic and other relevant stakeholders who have an active interest in understanding and improving student learning. After all, student learning is a fundamental goal of any undergraduate and graduate program, and is the focus of library educational activities related to information literacy as laid out in various guidelines and standards of the Association of College and Research Libraries (see Chapters 7 and 8). Assessment transcends what faculty in their courses measure with tests, term papers, and other graded activities designed to demonstrate student mastery of course content. The Middle States Commission points out that the academy has for a long time mistakenly "defined and assessed student learning using course-embedded assessment of student learning, such as tests, papers, projects, as well as standardized or 'customer' qualitative and quantitative measures."[1] Such a characterization views assessment and evaluation as interchangeable concepts, adds to the misunderstanding of the difference between the two concepts, and does not answer the question, "Do evaluation and assessment in higher education measure the same things?"

Both evaluation and assessment involve planning and concerns about effectiveness and efficiency. The general literature on outcomes assessment, however, focuses on these concepts in terms of student learning and assorted metrics that characterize an institution's students and graduates. Evaluation deals with other matters, as laid out in *Engaging in Evaluation and Assessment Research.*[2] The purpose of this chapter is not to either perpetuate or correct the misperception, but rather to clarify that the following discussion highlights key literature covering the assessment of student learning, especially beyond the course level. This chapter attempts not to duplicate coverage in other chapters.

This book subscribes to the definition that Linda Suskie advanced in 2004, namely, that "assessment is the ongoing process of:

- Establishing clear, measurable expected outcomes of student learning.

- Ensuring that students have sufficient opportunities to achieve those outcomes.

- Systematically gathering, analyzing, and interpreting evidence to determine how well student learning matches our expectations.

- Using the resulting information to understand and improve student learning."[3]

A number of stakeholders are interested in assessment (including prospective and enrolled students; their parents and families; the internal community of the higher education institution at all levels of governance; regional, specialized/professional, and national accreditation organizations; federal and state governments; the business community; educational associations; the mass media; and taxpayers)[4] and linkage of the evidence gathered to institutional accountability—the promises traced to the mission statement. However, accountability (as discussed in Chapters 3, 4, and 6) goes beyond learning and currently focuses on institutional productivity as defined in metrics such as retention rate, graduation rate, and placement rate for program graduates.

OVERVIEW

Peggy L. Maki relates assessment to a planning process concerned with ongoing improvement of learning, and Suskie provides an overview of student learning outcomes and appropriate data-collection methodologies.[5] However, neither of these works views data collection in terms of the type of inquiry process covered in *Engaging in Evaluation and Assessment Research*, wherein evaluation and assessment are identified with social science research, including the use of experimental and quasi-experimental designs.[6] In *Outcomes Assessment in Your Library*, an example relates a complex design involving the use of inferential statistics; however, a weakness of this example is the failure to include a rubric that can be used to track student progress from, say, novice to mastery of a particular learning goal. As students progress through a program of study toward graduation, data collection could be conducted on a repeated basis, allowing for regular monitoring and comparison.[7] These data could be either quantitative or qualitative, or both. However, one rubric typically emphasizes only one specific aspect of a course and program. While it will be an aspect that a faculty considers to be very important, one rubric cannot provide a comprehensive overview of any given learning goal, such as "communicating with impact using listening, speaking, reading, and writing skills." There are many facets to any learning goal, though faculty may not consider all facets of equal importance. New research design, methodological, reliability, and validity issues arise as assessment moves beyond the course level. These issues require a deeper knowledge of social science research than many librarians have.

ASSESSMENT FROM A STAKEHOLDER PERSPECTIVE

Figure 2.1 lists some examples of websites that provide overviews of assessment, resources, and the perspectives of different stakeholders. Perusal of an institutional assessment website such as one of these provides indications of the program values of a faculty, that is, the knowledge, skills, and abilities faculty expect their graduates to attain. It is also possible to see which learning goals institutions and programs value the most.

Launched in 2005, Liberal Education and America's Promise (LEAP), an initiative of the Association of American Colleges and Universities, offers an excellent example of a project focused on a 21st-century liberal education, drawing attention to learning outcomes and strategies for helping students to master those outcomes and be engaged in their education. (For relevant documents and links to different web pages, see http://www.aacu.org/leap/index.cfm.)

The Vision Project is affiliated with the LEAP initiative and involves states and their public institutions. Massachusetts, for example,

> is engaged in a fierce competition with other states and nations for talent, investment and jobs. The state's primary assets in this competition are the overall educational level of our people and our workforce and the inventiveness and competence of the creative individuals and organizational leaders who drive our innovation-dependent, knowledge-based economy. Nurturing these assets through education, research and creative activity is the most important contribution of the state's colleges and universities to the overall well-being of Massachusetts. The Vision Project is the vehicle through which public higher education has come together to stay focused on this work and hold ourselves accountable for results.[8]

Most interesting is the set of outcomes and metrics developed for holding the institutions accountable and making comparisons among them. The Massachusetts Department of Higher Education promises to provide the people of the state with an annual report, "comparing our work to that of peer institutions in other states," and to provide national leadership in

- College participation (college-going rates of high school graduates)
- College completion (graduation and success rates of the students we enroll)
- Student learning (academic achievements by our students on campus-level and national assessments of learning)
- Workforce alignment (alignment of our degree programs with key areas of workforce need in the state's economy)
- Elimination of disparities (achievement of comparable outcomes among different ethnic/racial, economic and gender groups) . . .
- Research activity (research activity related to economic development)
- Economic activity (economic activity derived from research)[9]

What makes the Vision Project unique is that it connects student learning to research and, through research, to economic development.

Name and URL	Content (as of 2012)
Assessments of Information Literacy http://jfmueller.faculty.noctrl.edu/infolitassessments.htm	Jon Mueller, professor of psychology at North Central College, is the author of *Assessing Critical Skills* (Linworth, 2008). He maintains an extensive and continuously updated collection of links to literacy assessment tools used in various higher education institutions.
Association for American Universities and Colleges (AAUC) Resources on Assessment http://www.aacu.org/resources/assessment/index.cfm	The AAUC resources list includes its own reports and articles, as well as those from other organizations, and highlights "featured campus examples and tools."
Council for Higher Education Accreditation (CHEA) http://www.chea.org/	CHEA makes available policy documents, talking points for use with the public, directories, papers showcasing its own research, and a range of videos and PDF files about accreditation. Recently, CHEA established the CHEA International Quality Group (CIQG), a clearinghouse and forum for global discussions of accreditation and quality assurance.
Educause Learning Initiative (ELI) http://www.educause.edu/eli	Educause is concerned with the interaction of teaching and learning, and is a good source for information on technology-based assessment tools, online learning, and analytics. ELI publishes reports, briefs, webinars, case studies, and other resources.
Lumina Foundation, http://www .luminafoundation.org/	"The mission of Lumina Foundation is to expand access and success in education beyond high school, particularly among adults, first-generation college going students, low-income students and students of color."
National Governor's Association (NGA) NGA Center for Best Practices, Education Division http://www.nga.org/cms/center/edu	The Education Division carries "provides information, research, policy analysis, technical assistance and resource development for governors and their staff in the areas of . . . postsecondary education" and contains reports such as those by the Lumina Foundation (see Chapter 6). The focus is on graduating more students to meet the workforce needs of the future.

Website	Description
National Institute for Learning Outcomes Assessment (NILOA) NILOA Learning Outcomes Resource Library http://www.learningoutcomeassessment.org/publications.html	The NILOA Library is a searchable database of publications of various types (including research papers) on assessment topics. Note especially the "Papers, Articles, and Presentations page (http://www.learningoutcomeassessment.org/papers.htm), which is a list of key papers organized by topic, including exemplars of assessment and learning outcomes.
North Carolina State University University Planning and Analysis Internet Resources for Higher Education Outcomes Assessment http://www2.acs.ncsu.edu/upa/assmt/resource.htm	This page categorizes and annotates well more than 1,300 resources, including texts and handbooks, key agencies, consultants, blogs and discussion groups, journals, conferences, data sources, tools, glossaries, the assessment pages of hundreds of college and universities, and even links to assessment humor
The Teagle Foundation, http://www.teaglefoundation.org/about/welcome.aspx	It focuses on college access, quality, and affordability.
U.S. Department of Education (1) National Advisory Committee on Institutional Quality and Integrity (NACAIE) http://www2.ed.gov/about/bdscomm/list/naciqi.html (2) College Accreditation in The United States http://www2.ed.gov/admins/finaid/accred/index.html	(1) NACAIE "advises the Secretary of Education on matters related to postsecondary (or higher education) accreditation and the eligibility and certification process for higher education institutions to participate in the Federal student aid programs." The NACAIE site includes records of the meetings and activities of the committee, as well as a small list of websites and some recommended readings. (2) The College Accreditation site carries information about accreditation, accreditation organizations, and related policy documents.
University of Hong Kong, Centre for the Enhancement of Teaching and Learning AR@HKU, http://ar.cetl.hku.hk/	AR@HKU gathers links to an impressive array of resources of all types and is described further in Chapter 11.
University of Rhode Island (URI), Office of Student Learning, Outcomes Assessment and Accreditation (SLOAA) http://www.uri.edu/assessment/	In addition to sharing slideshows and files from its own initiatives, SLOAA recommends websites and readings on a range of outcomes topics.

Figure 2.1 Useful Websites

INSTITUTIONAL WEBSITES

Perusal of search engines and online directories of assessment resources reveals that a number of guidelines, handbooks, discussions of methods of data collection, and other documents compiled by various institutions and programs are readily available on the Internet. Naturally, these writings vary in quality and utility for others seeking to engage in outcomes assessment. One of the more useful and most well-established is Alverno College's College Educational Research and Evaluation Office (ERE), which since 1976, "has been conducting ongoing research on student learning outcomes. ERE began tracking entire classes of students, from entry to graduation and up to five years after college. Alverno College studies continue to examine relationships among teaching, learning and assessment in general education and across different major fields, investigating deep and durable learning, development and performances."[10] Another good example is Kansas State University's Office of Assessment, which provides extensive guidance in the creation of rubrics and links them to different methods of data collection.[11]

Libraries also contribute to the coverage of assessment but usually from the vantage point of what they are doing as part of information literacy. Some coverage addresses data collection; for example, Project SAILS tests student knowledge and enables comparisons across institutions.[12]

JOURNALS ON ASSESSMENT

Journals in the area of assessment in higher education are listed in Figure 2.2. Most of these are indexed in the databases that cover other scholarly literature in higher education, and some are also indexed in databases in allied fields such as psychology, management, and the social sciences in general. Assessment is, of course, a very broad topic, including much more than student learning outcomes assessment, and so the range of topics included in these journals is equally broad. Even so, perusal of the tables of contents of these journals reveals research on learning outcomes using both quantitative and qualitative methods, as well as reflective essays, "how we did it good" articles, reviews, and editorials.

There are two journals devoted specifically to information literacy: *Communications in Information Literacy* (http://www.comminfolit.org/index.php? journal=cil) and *Journal of Information Literacy* (http://www.informationliter acy.org.uk/jil/). Articles on information literacy also frequently appear in journals on the topic of reference services, and occasionally in general LIS research journals such as *Library & Information Science Research* (http://www.journals .elsevier.com/library-and-information-science-research/).

RELEVANT LIS RESEARCH

One of the most important studies in this area is Laura Saunders's dissertation focusing on information literacy as reported in institutional self-studies submitted to the Middle States Committee. This research was expanded to include five additional institutional accreditation organizations.[13] One of the findings indicates that institutions are not as transparent as accreditation organizations would prefer and another is that assessment really remains at the course level and has not advanced

ASSESSMENT AND EVALUATION IN HIGHER EDUCATION

> http://www.tandfonline.com/action/aboutThisJournal?journalCode=caeh20
> Publisher: Taylor & Francis
> Peer-reviewed: Yes
> Frequency: 8 issues a year, 8-9 articles per issue
> Since: 1975
> Editorial Board: International (United States, UK, and other)

ASSESSMENT IN EDUCATION: PRINCIPLES, POLICY & PRACTICE

> http://www.tandfonline.com/action/aboutThisJournal?journalCode=caie20
> Publisher: Taylor & Francis
> Peer-reviewed: Yes
> Frequency: Quarterly, 5-7 articles per issue, often a profile of an institution
> Since: 1994
> Editorial Board: Mostly UK, some United Sates and other

ASSESSMENT UPDATE

> http://onlinelibrary.wiley.com/journal/10.1002/(ISSN)1536-0725
> Publisher: Wiley
> Peer-reviewed: No
> Frequency: Bimonthly, 6 or 7 newsy articles per issue on trends and best practices
> Since: 1989
> Editorial Board: American

EDUCATIONAL ASSESSMENT, EVALUATION AND ACCOUNTABILITY

> http://www.springerlink.com/content/1874-8597/
> Publisher: Springer
> Peer-reviewed: Yes
> Frequency: Quarterly, 4-5 articles per issue
> Since: 2009 under this title
> Editorial Board: International

PRACTICAL ASSESSMENT, RESEARCH & EVALUATION (PARE)

> http://pareonline.net/
> Publisher: Open access e-journal, supported by volunteer efforts
> Peer-reviewed: Yes
> Frequency: 15-20 articles a year uploaded continuously during the year
> Since: 1999
> Editorial Board: International, mostly United States

RESEARCH AND PRACTICE IN ASSESSMENT

> http://www.rpajournal.com/
> Publisher: Virginia Assessment Group, a network of representatives of higher education
> institutions and agencies in Virginia
> Peer-reviewed: Yes
> Frequency: Semiannual, 4-5 articles and several reviews per issue
> Since: 2008
> Editorial Board: State assessment officers and faculty in Virginia colleges and universities

Figure 2.2 Assessment Journals

beyond this level. Another body of research that should be singled out is Megan Oakleaf's work on rubrics and how librarians perceive information literacy. She reinforces the finding that information literacy activities remain predominately at the course level.[14]

CONCLUDING THOUGHTS

The literature on assessment not only reflects current trends, but is also mature enough to have a solid base that is resistant to fads. Most of the scholarly journals began in the late 1990s, many of the key texts date from the mid-2000s, and commonly used tools and methods emerged in the same time frame. With respect to information sources, one thing that has changed in the past decade is the growth on the web of rich resource collections, encouraging collaboration, sharing, and standardization. While the call for institution-wide student outcomes may be driven by concerns for fiscal responsibility and accountability, there now appears to be a large enough body of well-informed researchers and practitioners who can make sure that the focus on learning is not lost and who can look to each other around the world for support and for tested methods.

NOTES

1. Middle States Commission on Higher Education, *Student Learning Assessment: Options and Resources* (Philadelphia: Middle States Commission on Higher Education, 2007), 1.

2. Peter Hernon, Robert E. Dugan, and Danuta A. Nitecki, *Engaging in Evaluation and Assessment Research* (Santa Barbara, CA: Libraries Unlimited, 2011).

3. Linda Suskie, *Assessing Student Learning: A Commons Sense Guide* (Bolton, MA: Anker, 2004), 3.

4. Peter Hernon, Robert E. Dugan, and Candy Schwartz, *Revisiting Outcomes Assessment in Higher Education* (Westport, CT: Libraries Unlimited, 2006), 39.

5. Peggy L. Maki, *Assessing for Learning: Building a Sustainable Commitment across the Institution* (Sterling, VA: Stylus Publishing, 2004); Peggy L. Maki, *Assessing for Learning: Building a Sustainable Commitment across the Institution*, 2nd ed. (Sterling, VA: Stylus, 2010); Suskie, *Assessing Student Learning*; Linda Suskie, *Assessing Student Learning: A Common Sense Guide*, 2nd ed. (San Francisco: Jossey-Bass, 2009).

6. Hernon, Dugan, and Nitecki, *Engaging in Evaluation and Assessment Research*.

7. See Sudip Bhattacharjee and Lewis Shaw, "Enhancing Skills through Technology: A Project for Advanced Accounting Students," in *An Action Plan for Outcomes Assessment in Your Library*, edited by Peter Hernon and Robert E. Dugan (Chicago: American Library Association, 2002), 170–82.

8. Massachusetts, Department of Higher Education, "The Project Vision" (Boston: Department of Higher Education, 2012), accessed June 25, 2012, http://www.mass.edu/currentinit/visionproject.asp.

9. Ibid. For additional information on state initiatives, see Association of American Colleges and Universities, "Leap State Initiatives" (Washington, DC: American Colleges and Universities, 2012), accessed June 25, 2012, http://www.aacu.org/leap/states.cfm.

10. Alverno College, College Educational Research and Evaluation Office, "Learning Outcomes Studies Educational Research and Evaluation" (2012), accessed June 25, 2012, http://www2.alverno.edu/for_educators/ere_research.html. For additional examples, see Maki, *Assessing for Learning: Building a Sustainable Commitment across the Institution*, 2nd ed.

11. Kansas State University, Office of Assessment, "Measures, Rubrics, and Tools for Assessing Student Learning Outcomes" (Manhattan, KS: Kansas State University, 2008), accessed June 25, 2012, http://www.k-state.edu/assessment/plans/measures/index .htm.

12. Project SAILS, homepage, accessed June 25, 2012, https://www.projectsails.org/.

13. Laura Saunders, *Information Literacy as a Student Learning Outcome: As Viewed from the Perspective of Institutional Accreditation*, PhD diss. (Boston: Simmons College, 2010), UMI Number: 3452631; Laura Saunders, *Information Literacy as a Student Learning Outcomes: The Perspective of Institutional Accreditation* (Santa Barbara, CA: Libraries Unlimited, 2011).

14. See "Megan Oakleaf—Publications" (2012), accessed June 25, 2012, http:// meganoakleaf.info/publications.html.

Section II

SOME KEY STAKEHOLDERS

3

THE U.S. GOVERNMENT

Robert E. Dugan

The federal government's interest in outcomes for higher education has histori-cally focused on accessibility, the opportunity to attend college primarily through federal support for student financial aid and loans. However, as will be discussed, attention from the executive branch increasingly centers on student retention and persistence, graduation and graduation rates, and workforce readiness that should result in better jobs for graduates. Because the government invests billions in stu-dent loans and aid every year, it is expanding its right to expect and even demand quality and accountability from colleges and universities. An important benchmark of federal policy is the Higher Education Opportunity Act (PL 110–315) (HEOA) signed by President George W. Bush and enacted on August 14, 2008; it reautho-rizes the Higher Education Act (HEA) of 1965, as amended.

HIGHER EDUCATION ISSUES AND THE ROLE
OF THE FEDERAL GOVERNMENT

A catalyst for the discussion of higher education on the federal level was the forma-tion of a Commission on the Future of Higher Education, also known as the Spell-ings Commission. Margaret Spellings, the then secretary of education, charged the commission in September 2005 with recommending a national strategy for reforming postsecondary education. The commission's report, released in Septem-ber 2006, analyzed the state of higher education as well as identified the chal-lenges, in terms of access, affordability, and accountability.

The report found that access to higher education was limited, particularly for low-income Americans and minority groups. Contributing factors included inad-equate preparation of students to undertake college courses and the lack of infor-mation about college opportunities. The 1965 HEA, reinforced by the Higher Education Amendments of 1972 and subsequent amendments, symbolized the federal commitment to increase access to higher education by providing aid to undergraduate students of exceptional financial need in the form of educational opportunity grants, student loans, work-study grants, and fellowships for students

who intended to become elementary and secondary school teachers. It also ensured that the loans were portable and usable at all eligible institutions. During the
decades prior to the enactment of the HEOA of 2008, the HEA shifted its focus
on financing higher education from grants to loans and on becoming more accom-
modating to middle-income students.[1]

Access was complicated by financial issues that affect affordability, including the
rising cost of attending college, and the complexity students and their families en-
countered when navigating the financial aid system. In 2008, Senator Charles E.
Schumer (D-New York) noted that the cost of college had tripled over the past two
decades, and with many students and families struggling to keep up with the costs,
nearly two-thirds of college students were graduating with debt, often substantial,
as a result.[2]

Costs to attend college had increased for a number of reasons. Higher education stakeholders concerned with costs claimed that a link existed between
increases in federal financial aid to students and institutional increases in tuition
and fees to attend college. The HEA of 1965 enhanced student choice by providing direct financial aid to students in the hopes that expanded choice would
promote competition in the higher education market, which would increase efficiency, quality, and affordability. Student-aid increases had affected affordability
positively in the sense that low-income students were able to attend more costly
institutions, but aid increases may have had the unintended negative effect of
allowing the price of higher education to rise. Additionally, consumers increasingly viewed a college diploma as an obligatory, rather than voluntary, credential
leading to better pay, and as a result, elasticity in the price students were willing
to pay increased.[3]

Another identified problem that affected both accessibility and affordability was
that the financing system for higher education was dysfunctional and the student-
aid system was complex, confusing, and inefficient. Parents and students sought
simplification of the application process for financial aid for an array of student-aid
programs that had different eligibility requirements, regulations, and qualifying
expenses. At the same time, studies about the relationships between colleges and
private student-loan providers uncovered the improper use of incentives to attain
preferred lender status; this led to students and parents taking out expensive private
loans as a result of inadequate information.[4]

Higher education had been slow to understand the public's exasperation about
the escalating costs of higher education and the resulting debt loads carried by
graduates. Stakeholders involved in funding the costs of higher education, including students, families, taxpayers, and government officials, demanded to know
more about how the dollars were spent in addition to how much was expended.
Because institutions serve a public good and, to varying degrees, are supported
through public funds, stakeholders demanded increased accountability by the institutions as reported through the federal and state governments.[5]

Higher education had also failed to provide stakeholders with reliable and comparable information about the quality of learning, which was the real measure of
institutional performance to the Spellings Commission. The Spellings Commission identified student access, retention, learning and success, educational costs,
and productivity as benchmarks of institutional success although the commission
did not set specific standards to measure adequate learning, access, or costs. However, the Spellings report sought to require every college and university to create

databases that would allow the federal government to track students' academic whereabouts, including institutional transfers, and performance through student learning outcomes.

Exacerbating the issue of accountability was the increasing mistrust of higher education accreditors. Many stakeholders questioned the self-regulated accreditation process in which much of the information concerning the process and its results are withheld by the accreditors from public review. Stakeholders sought an expansion of the regulatory role of government with regard to accrediting organizations.[6]

The Spellings Commission report envisioned accountability not just as reporting to legislators and other policymakers, but also making information available to the general public, especially to students and their families as direct stakeholders. To that end, the commission advised the creation of sources of easily searchable and comparable consumer-friendly information on higher education.

FEDERAL EFFORTS TO RESOLVE HIGHER EDUCATION ISSUES

As a result of the publicity and discussion arising from the recommendations made in the 2006 Spellings Commission's report, and the increasing number of questions concerning the accountability of the application of federal funds, Congress accelerated its work and reauthorized the renewal of the HEA of 1965 in August 2008. The HEOA of 2008 was five years overdue when passed and had been in discussion in Congress, in one form or another, for most of the first decade of the 21st century. With more than 1,150 pages, the bill is about 20 times longer than the 1965 Act that it modified. This comprehensive piece of legislation goes beyond merely reauthorizing the 1965 law and attempted to resolve existing issues by including new and ambitious consumer-focused requirements and programs to expand access and make college more affordable, simplify the process of applying for federal student aid, and help to prepare low-income and first-generation students for college. It also attempts to pressure colleges to keep their prices in check by increasing transparency about tuition increases and other costs. Increased accountability includes requiring institutions and private lenders to adopt, publicize, and enforce a code of conduct for student lending, among other accountability procedures.[7]

The HEOA of 2008 is a policy shift toward the expansion of the federal role to increase accountability to both the federal government and to the public through a series of consumer-oriented protections that requires, and depends on, transparency from and about higher education institutions.[8] Access to college is increasingly directly linked to affordability so that higher education consumers are aware of the full and direct costs to attend college, the outcomes from attending college, and the cost of incurring debt. The HEOA increases accountability from higher education institutions by requiring them to publish and report quality information to consumers concerning their operations.

The consumer-based measures were designed to increase access to information by disseminating more information to the public than under the 1965 legislation, particularly on the cost of a college education, federal financial aid available, and student loans. The public law includes new programs to improve access to higher education through the dissemination of information such as a variety of lists and calculators to enable the consumer to receive estimates of tuition and net cost of attendance. Applying this cost information, students would be able to directly compare the costs of attendance at various colleges. Additional information concerning student financial aid is also required. As an example, the Department of Education must promote the use of its federal student financial aid website (http://studentaid.ed.gov) by displaying a link to that site from the Department's main website. To increase consumer protection concerning private student loans, the HEAO includes provisions that regulate the relationship between college financial aid officers and the private loan companies. The financial aid information provided includes nontechnical terms that will describe the various loan scenarios, including information on the different loan amounts, interest rates, and payment periods, and inform students about how much they will owe each month, including interest, in order to pay off the loan.

Additional information collected includes institutional characteristics to help inform a prospective student's decision as to which college to attend. The HEOA requires each college to provide the Department of Education with information regarding student body diversity, including the percentage of enrolled full-time students who are male or female and who self-identify as a member of a major racial or ethnic group. Additionally, each institution is required to provide information regarding retention rates for undergraduate students, disaggregated by gender, racial or ethnic subgroup, and receipt of federal aid. Reporting on alumni is also mandatory, as the college must provide the department with information regarding graduates' job placement, as well as their enrollment in graduate and professional education programs.[9]

These consumer-oriented measures serve two major objectives. First, the HEOA intends to help families gain access to college by making them more aware of its costs (tuition price and net cost), so that they can plan and save better to pay for college tuition and also apply to institutions that offer better financial aid packages; in other words, comparative shopping has been introduced. Second, as a result of the increased availability of cost information, the legislation's framers expect that informed consumers will be able to use the data to make better decisions that will ultimately pressure higher education institutions to control their costs, thereby increasing affordability and accessibility.

Specific programs and requirements selectively illustrate the HEOA's objectives. Amounts awarded and loan limits for federal student financial grants and loans were increased to promote access to postsecondary education. The maximum need-based Pell Grant award provided to low-income undergraduate and certain post baccalaureate students was incrementally increased. Another program to promote access was to streamline the Free Application for Federal Student Aid process by requiring fewer data elements and reducing the amount of financial information provided in order to determine eligibility. The borrowing limits of the Perkins Loans, which are awarded by the institutions from a pool of federal funds to students with exceptional financial need, subsidized with the federal government paying the interest during the in-school and grace periods, and linked to a favorable interest rate as well as a 10-year repayment period, were increased for undergraduate, graduate, and professional students.

Issues concerning the relationships between colleges and preferred private lenders for student loans, sometimes adversely affecting student debt, were also addressed in the legislation. Colleges and universities are required to develop, publicize, and enforce codes of conduct for their financial officers, employees, and agents that prohibit conflicts of interest with respect to private student loans. Institutions must provide borrowers with counseling, before they sign their first promissory note, regarding the average indebtedness of borrowers at the school, sample monthly repayment amounts based on a range of student indebtedness levels, starting salaries for their graduates in different fields of study, repayment options, and the likely consequences of default. Institutions that enter into preferred lender arrangements are required to make available to potential borrowers lists that include information about the preferred lenders, such as loan terms and philanthropic donations to the school; fully disclose the reason for each lender's inclusion and the students' right to choose other lenders; include at least three unaffiliated lenders and, if the school promotes or endorses private educational loans, at least two unaffiliated lenders of such loans; and prominently disclose the process used to ensure that lenders are selected on the basis of the benefits they provide to borrowers.[10]

Specific requirements and programs increasing accountability and transparency related to discovering the costs of attending college, and thereby its affordability, range from the institutional to the course level. For example, students and parents trying to estimate the cost of their education will benefit from the public availability of information concerning course textbooks and materials, providing them with information that will allow them to purchase textbooks at the lowest possible price.[11] Higher education institutions are required, to the maximum extent practicable, to list the prices and ISBN codes of the required and recommended textbooks for each course on their online course schedules used for preregistration and registration. In turn, that requires publishers to disclose certain information about textbooks and supplemental materials to faculty members as they decide what books to require. Publishers must disclose the textbook's price for all of its available formats (e.g., paperback or unbound), the copyright dates of the textbook's three previous editions, and the substantial content revisions made between the book's current and previous editions. Publishers that sell textbooks bundled with supplemental material must also make them available as separately priced unbundled items.

At the institutional level, the legislation mandates a net price calculator, which is intended to help prospective students estimate the net price of attendance at a particular institution. Net price is the average yearly price actually charged to first-time, full-time undergraduate student receiving student aid at an institution of higher education after deducting such aid. The HEOA requires the secretary of education to create a net price calculator application that can then be posted, as legislated, on the institution's website.

Supplementing the net price calculator's cost information, the HEOA required the Department of Education to create and maintain a database called the College Navigator, which allows consumers to search for colleges based on geographical area, majors, level of degree offered, or institution type. Users may review and use more than two dozen institutional characteristics such as student population, tuition and fees, admissions requirements, programs and majors, retention and graduate rates, accreditations, campus security, and student debt default rates for comparative purposes.

The legislation also requires the education secretary to create and publish, on the College Navigator website, watch lists for institutions with the lowest and highest tuition increases for the most recent year and three-year period.

The College Affordability and Transparency Center is accessible through the College Navigator's homepage. A site visitor may generate a report on the highest (top 5 percent) and lowest (bottom 10 percent) academic year charges for tuition (tuition and required fees) and net prices for each sector (public and private; four years, two years, and less than two years). Institutions that appear on watch lists for large increases must report to the Department of Education their reasons for the cost increases and the steps they are taking to reduce future increases. These explanations will be made public to consumers through an annual report.

Congress also expected the states to share the responsibility for making higher education accessible and affordable. The HEOA requires states to maintain a level of higher education appropriations equal to their previous five-year average (excluding capital and direct research and development expenses) and will withhold federal College Access Challenge Grant funds from states that fail to do so. The challenge-grant program offers matching grants intended to increase the number of low-income students who are prepared to enter and succeed in postsecondary education.

Changes to expand the information available to the public concerning the accreditation process were also legislated. The Council for Higher Education Accreditation (CHEA) found that there were significant changes in the following accreditation-related areas:

- Student Achievement. For the first time, federal law clearly affirms that colleges and universities, not government, have primary responsibility for student achievement. The law also makes explicit the long-standing partnership relationship between institutions and accreditors. Institutions are to set expectations of student achievement, and accreditors are to hold institutions accountable for both the level of expectation and the evidence that the expectations have been met.

- Transfer of Credit. Accreditors must, as a condition of federal recognition, assure that institutions have transfer policies, that these policies are published, and that they include the criteria used by the institution with regard to credit earned at another institution. Institutions are required to track some transfer activity and report this to the federal government.

- Information to the Public. Under the 1965 law, accrediting organizations have provided information to the public and government "upon request" and called on the accreditor to "notify" the U.S. secretary of education of any actions taken against an institution. The 2008 law moves "upon request" to a requirement that accreditors routinely provide information to the public and calls for a summary of actions that accreditors take. This shift in language may ultimately result in a requirement that accreditors make a good deal of additional information public, including the major work products of a review such as the self-study, team report, and other official communication between the accreditor and the institution.

- Due Process: Reviews and Appeals. The 2008 law changes the terms and conditions under which accrediting organizations can impose negative sanctions (e.g., warning, notice, show cause, termination of accreditation) on institutions. Accreditors now have to make information about the basis for a negative sanction available in writing. If an institution is appealing a negative action, this must include an opportunity to respond in writing to the accreditors' findings. And there is an opportunity, in the case of financial reasons for negative sanctions, to provide additional evidence that financial conditions have improved. Neither the requirement for action and response in writing nor the exception for evidence in financial situations was in the 1965 law. Legal counsels for institutions are able to participate in the appeals process. Finally, accreditors are required to maintain an appeals committee that is separate from the body that makes the initial decision about accredited status and are required to have a conflict-of-interest policy.

- Distance Education. The accreditation of distance education requires that an institution or program monitor student enrollment to assure that the student who registers for a course or program is the same student who participates and completes a program and obtains the academic credit.

- The Appointment and Composition of the National Advisory Committee on Institutional Quality and Integrity (NACIQI). While the 2008 law retains the federal committee that advises the U.S. secretary of education with regard to the recognition of accrediting organizations, the committee composition and appointment process have changed. The new committee will have 18 and not 15 members. Appointment authority will now be shared by the U.S. secretary of education, the House of Representatives, and the Senate, and no longer rests solely with the secretary. The new appointments are for six years, instead of the three-year appointments in the 1965 law.[12]

REACTIONS TO THE PASSAGE AND IMPLEMENTATION OF THE HEOA (2008)

An outcome of any legislation is how much it addresses the intended problems or improves the situation. The criticism of the HEOA of 2008 was immediate; President Bush's inked signature was hardly dry before the complaints commenced. Charles Miller, chairman of the Commission on the Future of Higher Education, which produced the Spelling Commission Report, commented "that the bill produced by Congress is a mishmash of new programs, new reporting requirements, and a lot of sound and fury signifying very little in the way of successful efforts to address access, affordability, or accountability."[13] In the same commentary, Barmak Nassirian, associate executive director of external relations at the American Association of Collegiate Registrars and Admissions Officers, stated that for "important issues like college costs, program integrity, predatory private-label lending, and low-income access, the legislation offers few meaningful remedies, and on virtually all of these, it ineptly or inadvertently includes provisions that are likely to make things worse rather than better."[14]

Sarah A. Flanagan, vice president for government relations and policy development at the National Association of Independent Colleges and Universities, argued that historically the renewals of the HEA, like the underlying 1965 law, have been about access to college. She finds that the HEOA of 2008 is not fundamentally about access. "It is about Congress's idea about how colleges could be better run. Traditional colleges see the utmost importance of the federal role being focused on access, and on the government's very successful partnership with colleges on en-suring access. This bill is not about a partnership with colleges; it's about Congress mandating its members' ideas on colleges."[15]

An important issue that was intended to be resolved centered on affordabil-ity and transparency. The legislation was viewed as consumer-friendly, providing those seeking financial information with the ability to find the full and net costs as well as comparative institutional data. Sandy Baum, professor of economics at Skidmore College and senior policy analyst at the College Board, comments that the bill does little to make college more affordable. For example, Baum finds that the watch lists "for institutions whose tuitions rise most rapidly may help curb the rate of increase in published prices, as colleges make small changes to avoid being publicly reprimanded. But that strategy does nothing to mitigate the fundamental pressures on tuition, and many provisions in the bill are likely to add to institu-tions' operating costs. The numerous new regulations and reporting requirements can only increase the bureaucracy and the concomitant expenses not associated with instruction."[16]

Julie Margetta Morgan, associate director of postsecondary education at The Center for American Progress, a liberal think tank, finds that the HEOA of 2008 shifts the responsibility for providing access and affordability away from the gov-ernment and institutions, and is instead placed on students and families. No matter how useful the information is concerning the cost of higher education and its net price after discounting financial aid, it is worthless if parents and students do not access it and fully understand it. She goes on to say that studies of parents' and stu-dents' access to information about cost and financial aid are sparse and limited in scope, but indicate that parents and students most often rely on guidance counsel-ors and publications from specific colleges or universities for information. Morgan echoes Baum's concern that the bill's fixes will do little to curb rising tuition prices by helping consumers make better decisions. Not only must consumers consult and understand the information distributed by the federal government, but they must also use it to make good decisions about where to apply and attend. Such a decision is presumably based on more than the full cost or net price of attendance. Instead, decisions about where to attend should involve some measure of quality, weighed against the price of attendance; that is, determining that institution gives the best value for the dollar.[17]

Critics of the legislation also found the use of the watch lists and the net price calculator to be problematic. First, the data in the net price calculator may in-clude data from more than a single year based on the information made avail-able by the institution. Colleges have also found themselves on the watch list for the largest increases in net price for tuitions, only to discover that the figure they self-reported was inaccurate based on the definition applied. The net price data favors colleges that give more money to a smaller number of students over those that award smaller amounts to more of their students, a practice different colleges follow depending on their institutional mission. Many colleges are using their fi-nancial aid to meet enrollment goals and cannot quickly change course to make it cheaper to attend. Also combining the net price calculator with the tuition and net price watch lists may confuse viewers. For example, students may notice that a college is on the watch list as having one of the highest tuitions, but may not be simultaneously on the watch list for the highest net price, raising the question as to which is the better indicator.[18]

Others have had a difficult time finding the federal information. The College Navigator, which has been promoted mostly to high school counselors rather than general consumers, does not include measures about the quality of academic programs. It does not replace consumers still having to refer to guidebooks ranking colleges on varying criteria.

Another major focus from the HEOA of 2008 was on student financing system, including student grants and loans. Student loans received the most criticism. Robert Shireman, executive director of the Project on Student Debt, has commented that students cannot learn about their options to avoid private loans because the bill does not enable the college to be notified when a student applies for a private loan. Such a notification would allow the college to counsel students better about taking unnecessary financial risks. A second missing reform is the elimination of unfair bankruptcy protections for private loan providers. Private loans have been as hard to discharge as federal loans, even though private loans exist only to generate private profits. Congress passed up an opportunity to treat private student loans more like similar forms of unsecured, high-interest consumer debt in bankruptcy.[19]

An oft-repeated criticism is that the HEOA of 2008 is only the first step of the federal government's desire and willingness to exercise significantly greater control over higher education. Two examples are the most frequently mentioned. One involves the maintenance of effort (MOE) provision that mandates that a state may not reduce higher education spending below the average of the last five years. While governors and Congress share the goal of affordable access to college, Raymond C. Scheppach, executive director of the National Governors Association, finds that this specific requirement sets a bad federalism precedent and will have negative effects on state higher education funding, other crucial state spending, and the state–federal partnership. He contends that states will be unable or unwilling to increase their MOE to make major increases or invest one-time surpluses in higher education during good times since the federal government will penalize them when they are forced to cut during economic downturns. In addition, the MOE provision mandates state spending on higher education, which, on top of Medicaid, means that the federal government will dictate how states spend almost one-third of their revenue. Scheppach points out that 49 states must, unlike Congress, balance their budgets each year. Governors, who are on the front lines every day and best understand their residents' needs, should set spending priorities, particularly during economic declines, not the federal government. The federal government should respect state sovereignty; since states raise the revenue the provision affects, states should determine its use.[20]

Higher education accreditation is another area highlighted as being subjected to federal incursion by the HEOA of 2008. Judith S. Eaton, president of the CHEA, an association of 3,000 degree-granting colleges and universities that recognizes 60 institutional and programmatic accrediting organizations, states that accreditation is being transformed from a valued self-supported, private-sector, self-regulated process over which the federal government historically has exercised limited control for more than 50 years, to a process that will be increasingly constrained by federal oversight, limiting the independent action of accrediting organizations, and may eventually penetrate the academic work of faculty members and institutions. Eaton explains that accrediting organizations must be reviewed always by an advisory committee to the secretary of education, the NACIQI, and at least every five years by the U.S. Department of Education. Additionally, the government, seeking to ensure that federal funds for student grants and loans were spent responsibly, has turned to private-sector accrediting organizations for reliable judgments about the quality of institutions and programs. This arrangement, commonly referred to as the gatekeeping role of accreditation, puts these private-sector organizations in the pivotal role of providing (or sometimes blocking) institutional or program eligibility for federal funding, which now totals about $150 billion annually. However, since the HEA of 1965 and its successive reauthorizations, particularly in 2008, Eaton claims that the federal government has started to replace both institutional and faculty judgment applied in the accrediting process concerning academic matters.[21]

Accreditation and accredited institutions were central to the Spellings Commission's deliberations concerning accountability. Accrediting bodies were subjected to severe criticism in the commission's 2006 report with findings that their processes lacked rigor, failed to address student achievement adequately, did not encourage innovation, and did not effectively inform the public about academic quality by failing to give students and the public the basis to compare institutions. The commission's report urged that accreditors take action to remedy these concerns by providing students and the public with more evidence of student achievement and institutional performance, ensuring that this evidence is easily understandable and readily accessible, and developing means to help students and the public compare institutions. The commission also recommended that accreditors and institutions produce evidence of student achievement primary in judgments about academic quality.[22]

The report's emphasis on greater accountability from accreditation found its way into the HEOA of 2008. Although there were some gains for higher education, such as specific affirmation that institutions were to set their own standards for student achievement, the act resulted in 110 new rules or reporting obligations for higher education and accreditation. These provisions for greater accountability meant both a strengthened federal interest in the academic area, heretofore the province of institutions and faculty members, and an expanded and prescriptive approach to the oversight of accrediting bodies. The impact of the law and its regulations on the academic work of institutions and faculty members appears far-reaching. For example, the federal government now has at least some legal or regulatory authority in the academic areas of transfer of credit, articulation agreements, distance learning, enrollment growth, quality of teacher preparation, and textbooks, which have traditionally been the province of the faculty and institutions. As a result, the traditional academic leadership role of the faculty and the long-standing responsible academic independence of institutions are increasingly circumscribed by federal law and regulation. This means that the core academic values that are central to the success of higher education—institutional autonomy, academic freedom, and peer and professional review—may be threatened.[23] However, the HEOA does not address student learning outcomes and, in fact, specifically reserves that review to the institutions and the accrediting bodies.

A broad criticism of the content of the HEOA of 2008 and its implementation is that it is not a definitive policy that offers a national higher education strategy. The bill is a visionless, unwieldy, sprawling mishmash of new programs and intrusive regulation composed of many specific ideas stapled together and, when summed, are incoherent as a bill supposedly reauthorizing student aid. It fails to provide the necessary federal leadership that, if higher education is to be treated as a public good, is critical for the nation to move forward with an educated populace that can compete globally.[24]

CONGRESS AND THE WHITE HOUSE INCREASE THEIR INVOLVEMENT IN LATE 2011

During nearly the first three years of Obama's presidency, his administration's higher education policy focused on getting more financial aid to needy students, including an increase in the maximum Pell Grant that accompanied the shift to direct lending in 2009 as a result of the HEOA of 2008, and a goal to have the world's highest proportion of college graduates by 2020. In November and December 2011, a flurry of policy statements and meetings accompanied a shift of federal policy to focus on what colleges can do to reduce costs and thereby increase affordability for students.[25]

Secretary of Education Arne Duncan delivered a policy speech at a higher education student financial aid conference in Las Vegas on November 29, 2011, in which he stated that the truth is "that every state and institution of higher education should be spelling out ambitious but achievable goals to substantially boost completion and control the growth in college costs," thereby reducing the burden of student debt. Additionally, he pointed out programs that included shorter degree programs and tuition freezes as good examples from some institutions to curb college costs.[26]

The following day, Representative Virginia Foxx (R-North Carolina) convened the Committee on Education and the Workforce's higher education subcommittee. Testimony at the subcommittee focused on broad trends in college pricing and specific efforts to make college more affordable. Jane V. Wellman, founder and executive director of the Delta Project on Postsecondary Costs, Productivity and Accountability, provided an overview of trends in what colleges spend to educate students and finance their operations. Wellman's research has found that a common pattern has been the combination of cost-cutting accompanied by tuition increases, with a slight decrease in the proportion of money going toward the direct cost of student instruction rather than administrative activities, technology, and other infrastructure functions. She concluded that the recession has made state public systems as well as small institutions pay closer attention to cost-cutting and productivity. Examples of productivity included a three-year degree program at Grace College and Theological Seminary in Indiana and a higher education system model based on knowledge rather than time in the classroom used by Western Governors University.[27]

On December 5, 2011, President Barack Obama convened a meeting at the White House with a small group of invited university chancellors and presidents, along with experts on higher education cost and productivity. In general, the president and the college leaders focused on a few key questions: how colleges can become more affordable while producing more graduates, and how best practices in affordability or productivity can be transplanted from one college to large state systems or the nation as a whole. Jamie Merisotis, president and CEO of the Lumina Foundation for Education, stated that the focus of the meeting was on college costs—the total cost of educating students—rather than college prices—what students pay. Merisotis added that the president understands that to increase the number of Americans with college degrees requires decreasing the cost of educating students, given limited public and other resources. Several participants said that they expect to see the administration propose financial incentives for colleges that increase degree attainment or apply new ways to cut costs and increase productivity.[28]

What were the external pressures that brought about the Obama administration and congressional activity as calendar year 2011 was coming to an end? Politicians were taking note of the rise in public outrage, intensified since September 2011 by the Occupy Wall Street movement, which had, in part, raised awareness about the price that students and families pay for colleges. When the Federal Reserve Bank of New York announced in a 2011 quarterly report that it had significantly undercounted student loans and now estimates the current total of outstanding loans at $845 billion, not $550 billion, it seemed likely only to increase the debate concerning college costs. While the Obama administration has tried to mitigate rising college prices by increasing funding for Pell grants and making it easier for students to pay back loans, it has done little to restrain the growth of college prices themselves. Federal financial aid programs and family income have not been able to keep up with increasing tuition bills. Students and families have only one recourse, namely, borrowing. Most undergraduates borrow today and leave college with an average of more than $25,000 in debt. And as the many signs displayed by the Occupy Movement attest, some graduates owe much more than that.[29] The federal efforts embodied by the HEOA of 2008 to make colleges more cost-conscious, including publishing watch lists of colleges with the highest prices and greatest price increases, as well as mandating a net price calculator so that students and families would have the information they needed to compare institutions and costs and make informed decisions, appeared to be failing three years after its enactment.

THE 2012 STATE OF THE UNION SPEECH AND THE RESULTING POLICY SHIFT

The discussions from the private meetings, Capitol Hill hearings, and Cabinet secretary speeches with higher education stakeholders conducted by the Obama administration and Congress in November and December 2011 were briefly summarized by the president in his State of the Union address in January 2012. While addressing education, he said, "Of course, it's not enough for us to increase student aid. We can't just keep subsidizing skyrocketing tuition; we'll run out of money. States also need to do their part, by making higher education a higher priority in their budgets. And colleges and universities have to do their part by working to keep costs down." He continued, "So let me put colleges and universities on notice: If you can't stop tuition from going up, the funding you get from taxpayers will go down. Higher education can't be a luxury—it is an economic imperative that every family in America should be able to afford."[30] The president called for an expansion of job-training programs at community colleges, an extension of the tuition tax credit, and a doubling of Federal Work Study jobs. He reminded lawmakers of the importance of basic research and asked them not to gut support for academic research from the federal budget, asking them to support the same kind of research and innovation that led to the computer chip and the Internet.[31]

The 2012 State of the Union marked a more public shift in higher education policy. Until the speech, the Obama administration's public appearances and private meetings centered largely on productivity—officials praised new methods of delivering higher education without attacking more traditional colleges and universities. However, in January 2012 speech, President Obama reasserted the administration's commitment to federal financial aid, but he said institutions and states would need to do their part. States should make higher education spending a higher priority while institutions should keep prices down. College affordability was joining, and perhaps even supplanting, access to college as the Obama administration's higher education focus.[32]

Although front and center because of its inclusion in this major speech, the president had addressed college affordability earlier in his administration. His 2009 stimulus plan included a temporary $2,500 tax credit for higher education expenses, which the president has now proposed making permanent. In 2010, Congress approved a bill that restructured the federal student loan program and redirected $61 billion toward postsecondary education spending.[33] However, President Obama acknowledged in the speech that the states also need to do their part by making higher education a higher priority in their budgets. Furthermore, he was not letting institutions be held blameless, stating that they have to do their part by working to keep costs down.

Although the speech did not provide details, the White House released an accompanying document titled *Blueprint for an America Built to Last*, which revealed that the president would propose to "shift some federal aid away from colleges that don't keep net tuition down and provide good value." The blueprint also stated that

- College costs are escalating at an unsustainable pace. Even after adjusting for inflation, the average published cost of tuition and fees at a four-year public university has increased by 136% in the last 20 years. This Administration has made college more affordable by continuing to increase the maximum Pell Grant award by more than $800 and creating the American Opportunity Tax Credit worth up to $10,000 over four years of college. The President called on Congress to help keep college costs within reach for middle-class families by:

  - *Keeping tuition from spiraling too high*: The President is proposing to shift some Federal aid away from colleges that don't keep net tuition down and provide good value.

  - *Preventing student loan interest rates from doubling*: The President called on Congress to stop the interest rate on subsidized Stafford student loans from doubling on July 1 of this year, so young people don't have as much debt to repay.

  - *Doubling the number of work-study jobs*: The President wants to reward students who are willing to work hard by doubling over five years the number of work-study jobs for college students who agree to work their way through school.

  - *Permanently extending tuition tax breaks that provide up to $10,000 for four years of college:* The President is proposing to make the American Opportunity Tax Credit permanent, maintaining a tax cut that provides up to $10,000 for tuition over four years of college.[34]

A few days after the State of the Union address, President Obama released a package of proposals aimed at pushing colleges and states to make higher education more affordable, effective, and consumer-friendly. In the *Fact Sheet*, the president emphasized the "responsibility shared by the federal government, states, colleges, and universities to promote access and affordability in higher education, by reining in college costs, providing value for American families, and preparing students with a solid education to succeed in their careers. Over the past three years, the Obama administration has taken historic steps to help students afford college, including reforming our student aid system to become more efficient and reliable and by expanding grant aid and college tax credits." Specifically,

- *Reforming student aid to promote affordability and value*: To keep tuition from spiraling too high and to drive greater value, the President will propose reforms to federal campus-based aid programs to shift aid away from colleges that fail to keep net tuition down, and toward those colleges and universities that do their fair share to keep tuition affordable, provide good value, and serve needy students well. This reform will reward colleges that are succeeding in meeting the following principles:

1) Setting responsible tuition policy, offering relatively lower net tuition prices and/or restraining tuition growth.
2) Providing good value to students and families, offering quality education and training that prepares graduates to obtain employment and repay their loans.
3) Serving low-income students, enrolling and graduating relatively higher numbers of Pell-eligible students.

The campus-based aid that the federal government provides to colleges through Supplemental Educational Opportunity Grants (SEOG), Perkins Loans, and Work Study is distributed under an antiquated formula that rewards colleges for longevity in the program and provides no incentive to keep tuition costs low. The president is proposing to change how those funds are distributed by implementing an improved formula that shifts aid from schools with rising tuition to those acting responsibly, focused on setting responsible tuition policy, providing good value in education, and ensuring that higher numbers of low-income students complete their education. He is also proposing to increase the amount of campus-based aid to $10 billion annually. The increase is primarily driven by an expansion of loans in the Perkins program, which comes at no additional taxpayer cost.

Colleges that can show that they are providing students with good long-term value will be rewarded with additional dollars to help students attend. Those that show poor value, or who don't act responsibly in setting tuition, will receive less federal campus-based aid. Students will receive the greatest government grant and loan support at colleges where they are likely to be best served, and little or no campus aid will flow to colleges that fail to meet affordability and value standards.

- *Creating a Race to the Top for college affordability and completion*: The president will create incentives for states and colleges to keep costs under control through a $1 billion investment in a new challenge to states to spur higher education reform focused on affordability and improved outcomes across state colleges and universities. The Race to the Top: College Affordability and Completion will reward states who are willing to drive systemic change in their higher education policies and practices, while doing more to contain their tuition and make it easier for students to earn a college degree.

- *A first in the world competition to model innovation and quality on college campuses*: The president will invest $55 million in a new First in the World competition, to support the public and private colleges and non-profit organizations as they work to develop and test the next breakthrough strategy that will boost higher education attainment and student outcomes. The new program will also help scale up those innovative and effective practices that have been proven to boost productivity and enhance teaching and learning on college campuses.

- *Better data for families in choosing the right college for them*: New actions to provide consumers with clearer information about college costs and quality will improve the decision-making process in higher education for American students and allow families to hold schools accountable for their tuition and outcomes. President Obama is proposing new tools to provide students and families with information on higher education, presented in a comparable and easy-to-understand format:

1) The Administration will create for all degree-granting institutions a College Scorecard designed to provide the essential information about college costs, graduation rates, and potential earnings, all in an easy-to-read format that will help students and families choose a college that is well suited to their needs, priced affordably and consistent with their career and educational goals.

2) There will be an updated version of the "Financial Aid Shopping Sheet," announced in October 2011, a required template for all colleges, rather than a voluntary tool, to make it easier for families to compare college financial aid packages.

3) The President is also proposing to begin collecting earnings and employment information for colleges, so that students can have an even better sense of the post-graduation outcomes they can expect.

- *Federal support to tackle college costs*: The President has already made the biggest investments in student aid since the G.I Bill through increases to the Pell Grant, and by shoring up the direct loan and income-based repayment programs. In his State of the Union Address, the President called on Congress to: keep interest rates low for 7.4 million student loan borrowers to reduce future debt, make the American Opportunity Tax Credit permanent, and double the number of work-study jobs over the next 5 years to better assist college students who are working their way through school. Specifically:

1) Keep student loan interest rates low: In the summer of 2012, the interest rates on subsidized Stafford student loans are set to double from 3.4% to 6.8%—a significant burden at a time when the economy is still fragile and students are taking on increasing amounts of debt to earn a degree. The

President is asking Congress to prevent that hike from taking place for a year to keep student debt down, a proposal that will keep interest rates low for 7.4 million student loan borrowers and save the average student over a thousand dollars.

2) Double the number of work-study jobs available: The President also proposes to double the number of career-related work-study opportunities so that students are able to gain valuable work-related experience while in school.

3) Maintain a commitment to college affordability: Over 9 million students and families per year take advantage of the Obama administration's American Opportunity Tax Credit—supporting up to $10,000 over four years of college. In his State of the Union address, the President called on Congress to make this tax credit permanent and prevent it from expiring in 2012.[35]

Secretary Duncan, speaking about the *Fact Sheet* shortly after its release, noted that "it's not just about access, it's about completion," emphasizing that the formula for calculating campus-based student-aid awards to colleges would now recognize affordability and net tuition. The campus-based student-aid programs—the Perkins Loan Program, the SEOG Program, and Campus Work Study—are those in which funds are allocated to colleges and universities to distribute, rather than flowing directly to students as is the case with Pell Grants. Along with changes in the formula for distributing campus-based aid, the administration will ask Congress to authorize an increase in Perkins Loans, to $8 billion from the current level of $1 billion. Duncan said that the administration also recognizes that state budgets are squeezed but that states have a responsibility to commit more money to higher education.[36]

Days after delivering his State of the Union speech and hours after releasing the *Fact Sheet*, President Obama brought his campaign for college affordability to students at the University of Michigan, pledging that his administration would be "putting colleges on notice" over rising costs and issuing a call for continued public support for higher education by states so that the United States does not become a nation where education is reserved for the well-to-do.[37] Referring to the theme of access to college, Obama reiterated that "We want a country where everybody has a chance." The president outlined plans to boost total federal spending on Perkins Loans, push Congress to keep interest rates low for current student loan borrowers, double the number of work-study jobs over the next five years, and establish a $55 million competition to spur new college strategies encouraging greater educational productivity and aggregate student outcomes.[38]

However, while noting that student loan debt now exceeds credit card debt, the president returned to the theme of college affordability, restating content from his State of the Union address that "higher education is not a luxury—it's an economic imperative. Higher education institutions can't assume they can increase tuition every year. We can't keep subsidizing (skyrocketing) tuition. Sooner or later we're going to run out of money." To assist states, he announced plans to push for the creation of a $1 billion competition encouraging states to contain public tuition rates, among other things. "We should push colleges to do better," he said. "We should hold them accountable if they don't."[39]

Beginning with the presentation of the State of the Union address and accompanied by the *Blueprint for an America Built to Last*, and a few days later publishing the *Fact Sheet* and then delivering the speech to students at the University of Michigan, President Obama publicly shifted his administration's policy from primarily focusing on access to college to including college affordability as another major pillar of his higher education plan. Access to college has been the driving force in federal higher education policy for decades. But the Obama administration is now pushing a fundamental agenda shift that brings a new question into the public debate: what are people getting for their money?[40]

The Obama plan's central feature is a change to the campus-based Perkins Loan Program, which provides funds to institutions to lend to their students. The White House has proposed expanding the program to $10 billion per year while also revising the distribution formula for both Perkins Loans and SEOG. The plan calls for linking federal aid not only to net price increases but also to whether colleges provide "good value" to students, which is measured by a "quality education and training that prepares graduates to obtain employment and repay their loans."[41]

Public information making it easier for students and their families to identify and choose high-quality affordable colleges that provide good value as announced in the *Blueprint* would be found in the administration's new College Scorecard located in the U.S. Department of Education's College Affordability and Transparency Center on the web. The scorecard would assist families in comparing such school statistics as graduation rates and the likelihood of getting a job after graduation, as well as serving as a shopping sheet to compare college costs and net tuitions prices with estimates of how much debt they might graduate with and estimated future payments on student loans.

This would be the third such federal government calculator/scorecard/list, joining the Paying for College worksheet available through the Consumer Financial Protection Bureau at http://www.consumerfinance.gov/payingforcollege/costcomparison/, and the watch lists available through the College Affordability and Transparency Center at http://collegecost.ed.gov/catc/Default.aspx. Increased transparency through institutional reporting concerning graduation rates, net price, and job placement is intended to help students and their families make better-informed decisions about which college to attend.

Reaction to the State of the Union and University of Michigan speeches, and to the *Blueprint* and *Fact Sheet* content, was expectedly swift. The president did not discuss how to pay for these proposals, which include extending the $2,500 American Opportunity Tax Credit, doubling the number of Federal Work Study jobs to 1.4 million, and keeping the interest rate on subsidized student loans at 3.4 percent. He also made no mention of Pell Grants, the cornerstone of the federal student-aid programs. Nor did he say how he would pressure states to prioritize education.[42] Responding to reporters on the Friday afternoon following the Tuesday State of the Union speech, Department of Education officials said that they would release information next month on how the plan could be financed, as part of the federal budget process.[43]

Concerning state funding, one possibility is requiring and enforcing the MOE and denying funds to states if they do not continue their financial support of colleges and universities at recent prior levels. Mary Sue Coleman, president of the University of Michigan, linked state funding to tuition when writing to the president in December 2011, stating that "there is no stronger trigger for rising costs at public universities and colleges than declining state support."[44] Sandy Baum, an independent analyst for the College Board, noted that the amount of money at stake—the president's plan suggests putting a total of $10 billion into campus-based aid annually—is not enough to change states' budget priorities. As public higher education institutions try to patch up their budgets, the extra aid that may be forthcoming in these campus-based programs pales in comparison with what colleges and universities could bring in by increasing tuition.[45] Al Bowman, president of Illinois State University, stated that most people, including President Obama, assume that if universities were simply more efficient, they would be able to operate with less state support. He points out that the undergraduate experience can be made cheaper, but there are tradeoffs. "You could hire mostly part-time, adjunct faculty. You could teach in much larger lecture halls, but the things that would allow you achieve the greatest levels of efficiency would dilute the product and would make it something I wouldn't be willing to be part of," he said.[46]

Much of the post-speech discussion focused on the institutional level. Terry Hartle, senior vice president for government and public affairs at the American Council on Education, thought that the administration might consider condition eligibility for campus-based student-aid programs on the rate of tuition increases. David Felder, an economist, stated that focusing on the decreasing net price that colleges charge will result in decreasing educational quality. Some people believe "that there are just million-dollar bills lying on the floors of universities all over the place," Feldman said, and that universities will find that money if threatened enough with budget cuts. But costs have not risen because higher education has become more inefficient, and budget cuts usually lead only to tradeoffs between quality and price. An oft-provided solution is to restructure federal campus-based student-aid programs rather than limiting student aid based on the rate of tuition going up.[47]

Reaction to the plan in Congress seemed to divide along party lines. "The president is saying that people can't afford to go to college anymore, and that just simply is not true," said Representative Virginia Foxx, the North Carolina Republican who is the chairwoman of the House Higher Education subcommittee. "Tuition is too high at most schools, but it isn't the job of the federal government to punish those schools. It's very arbitrary, and the president sounds like a dictator." Senator Lamar Alexander of Tennessee, a Republican and a former federal secretary of education, offered his own ideas of improving academic efficiency: "I've suggested that they could offer three-year degrees to some students. Colleges could also operate more in the summertime, which would make more efficient use of campuses and reduce their costs."[48]

David Warren, president of the National Association of Independent Colleges and Universities, suggested that "colleges, states, and the federal government must work together in a climate of mutual trust and collaboration. . . . The answer is not going to come from more federal controls on colleges or states, or by telling families to judge the value of an education by the amount young graduates earn in the first few years after they graduate." Warren also warned of unintended consequences: if colleges are forced to cut corners to reduce costs, educational quality could decline.[49]

A *New York Times* editorial (February 2012) found that the "increase in the tuition burden is largely caused by declining state support for higher education in the past three decades. In both good times and bad, state governments have pushed more of the costs onto students, forcing many to take out big loans or be priced out of once affordable public colleges at a time when a college education is critical in the new economy." While financial aid is available to some low-income students, many are driven away by tuition sticker shock. At the same time, many colleges have failed to find more cost-effective ways to deliver education and get the average student to graduation in four years. Determining what amounts to good value will be difficult, and persuading Congress to move forward on any of these ideas will be hard.[50]

Following up on the policy issues proposed in the State of the Union and University of Michigan speeches as well as the *Blueprint* and *Fact Sheet*, President Obama emphasized higher education in his proposed fiscal year 2013 budget released in February 2012. It included $8 billion for community colleges over the next three years for job training and more money for some federally-funded research. Expanded student financial aid programs included an increase for Pell Grants. Institutions may not agree with many of the president's proposals in the budget document, especially tying campus-based federal financial aid including the distribution of Work-Study funds, Supplemental Education Opportunity Grants, and Perkins Loans, to measurements of value, and administered using new formulas that attempt to reward institutions for controlling tuition increases, graduating higher percentages of students, and serving low-income and underprivileged students. Many budget watchers acknowledge that it is essentially a symbolic political document, unlikely to survive a divided, deficit-conscious Congress.[51]

PREPARING FOR THE RENEWAL OF THE 2008 HEOA IN 2013

The Department of Education's advisory board on accreditation, the NACIQI, advises the education secretary whether accrediting agencies are following federal rules and may continue to be awarded federal recognition, a status that allows them to confer on the colleges and universities they accredit the right to receive and award federal financial aid to their students. At the request of U.S. Education Secretary Arne Duncan in December 2010, a subcommittee of the NACIQI was formed to develop a set of legislative recommendations for the 2013 renewal of the HEOA. The subcommittee's charge included examining the following questions:

- How well does our current accreditation/recognition system protect the interests of the taxpayer who is underwriting that investment in education?

- If we were starting now, would we design this system? How might a system we would design differ from what currently exists?

- Should there be common standards for learning outcomes/student achievement? Who should decide on what they are? How should they be measured?

Although this subcommittee plans to focus on considering how to alter the country's decentralized system of accreditation, which has been under fire in recent years amid cries for more accountability, it plans to make legislative recommendations on nonaccreditation-related matters as well.[52]

Anne D. Neal, president of the American Council of Trustees and Alumni and a member of the NACIQI subcommittee, has made public calls for the current accreditation system to be dismantled and revamped. In an opinion piece appearing at the end of 2010, Neal questioned whether or not the Congress understands what it legislated concerning the accreditation process through the HEOA of 2008 that has resulted in members of the Senate blaming accreditors for not having protected the public interest, for allowing fraud to flourish, and for permitting institutions to persuade unprepared students to take out federally financed student loans.[53]

Neal responds that the existing accreditation system has neither ensured quality nor discovered fraud. Further, it has not done so because Congress has not intervened with legislation. If Congress truly wants to protect the public interest, it needs to create a system that ensures real accountability. Neal points out that when the accrediting system was voluntary, accreditors competed for institutional business. Colleges and universities could drop accreditation whenever they wanted, keeping accrediting associations from dictating institutional priorities. But turning accreditors into gatekeepers decades past changed the picture. In effect, accreditors now exercise substantial influence over colleges and universities since federal financial aid would not flow unless the institution received accredited status. This peer review-dependent gatekeeping system yields conflicts of interest throughout the accreditation process. The accreditation teams that visit and evaluate schools are, after all, made up of college and university personnel from other schools, not independent experts. "Peer review was intended to limit federal intrusion, but, as it turns out, it is an even better way to protect one's peer institutions—and, ultimately, one's own."[54]

The current system of accreditation is not sufficiently safeguarding the billions of dollars that flows annually to accredited colleges, and many accredited colleges are adding little educational value.[55] Neal points out that the 2006 National Assessment of Adult Literacy revealed that nearly a third of college graduates were unable to compare two newspaper editorials or compute the cost of office items, prompting the Spellings Commission and others to raise concerns about accreditors' attention to productivity and quality. In response, accreditors sought to demand more evidence of student achievement to ensure educational quality. Rather than welcoming accreditors' efforts to enhance their public oversight role, Congress told accreditors through the HEOA of 2008 to let nonprofit colleges and universities individually set their own standards for educational quality. Neal goes on to state that accreditors cannot actively discover fraud or weed out underperforming institutions because Congress has not authorized them to do so. Congress has thus produced a system that works for academic insiders, not for the public.[56]

Neal's solution is an institutional, self-certifying regimen of financial accountability, coupled with transparency about graduation rates and student success. It would require all institutions, both for-profit and nonprofit, to self-certify that they meet certain minimum academic and financial criteria in order to receive federal student aid. The certification statement would include an institutional description along with information about recruitment, admissions, student body, courses and curriculum, student complaints and student records, management, and financial capacity, including default rates over a set period, and student repayment rates. It would include information about learning outcomes, graduation and retention rates, and job placements for graduate programs and professional schools. Upon receipt of complaints or other information of concern, the U.S. Department of Education could audit a self-certified institution to see if its certification statement is accurate. The new approach would save institutions and regulators time and money. It would be institution-centered rather than imposed by regulators from above. Every institution must demonstrate an acceptable U.S. Department of Education composite financial responsibility score. Accreditation would return to its original form as a voluntary system of self-assessment and improvement, and accreditation would cease to function as the determinant of eligibility for federal funds.[57]

Shortly after receiving its charge, the NACIQI subcommittee held a series of meetings during 2011 to solicit ideas. The first draft of the subcommittee's report was released in October 2011 and focused on the current and appropriate roles of the three main stakeholders in higher education quality assurance—the U.S. government, the states, and accreditors—the extent to which those roles align or leave gaps, and whether the overlap creates an excessive data and regulatory burden that might be eased without any reduction in effectiveness. This first public draft included options and considerations rather than firm proposals and recommendations, thus illustrating the complexity of accreditation and how difficult it will be to address the accrediting process. Paralleling several of Neal's arguments, the core question continued to be whether colleges should continue to be required to gain accreditation to participate in federal financial aid programs.[58]

Sections of the October 2011 draft report argued all sides. Neal's articulation of the entanglement between the federal government and the accreditors is cited as an argument for separating accreditation from the process for gauging eligibility for financial aid programs. The fact that institutional quality and self-improvement have historically been determined by a peer-review process conducted by colleges themselves, rather than the government, has long been seen as a great strength of American higher education, but the linkage to federal financial aid has introduced an array of consequences that are neither appropriate nor desirable. On the other side, taking accreditors out of the process of determining institutional eligibility for financial aid would eliminate from the process the most experienced source of information about academic quality in the review system. It would also practically render the assessment of institutional quality a governmental decision. Keeping accreditors involved helps ensure that the quality assurance system does not subject institutions of higher education to rapid changes in how they will be judged for purposes of accreditation, and therefore, federal financial aid.[59]

Ending the linkage between accreditation and federal aid eligibility would free the accreditors of the conflict for policing financial integrity and keep the government out of questions of quality. But the panel cites arguments that financial integrity alone "is insufficient to serve the federal interest" in higher education quality, which leads it to a third option that would modify, rather than end, the link between accreditation and financial aid eligibility. Under the third option, the federal government might review colleges' compliance with baseline federal financial responsibility and performance measures. Once institutions pass this review, eligibility to participate in the financial aid programs could be attained by either satisfying specified heightened federal quantitative performance criteria or securing accreditation from an approved accrediting entity. Such an approach would, by creating a federal process that assessed colleges based on quantitative performance criteria that are not financial in nature, provide the federal government a bigger role in judging institutional quality than it has now.[60]

Reacting to the October 2011 draft report, higher education groups, accreditors, and others pushed back in written comments: accreditors believed that the link between aid eligibility and accreditation is the strongest tool they possess, while institutions feared more federal oversight. The consensus from the higher education and accrediting fields was overwhelmingly in favor of keeping the link between aid program eligibility and accreditation. During an NACIQI subcommittee meeting in December 2011, a majority of its members voted to retain the current gatekeeper link between institutional eligibility and accreditation.[61]

Committee members went on to accept many of the options presented in the October 2011 draft report, including

- setting a national minimum standard for states to follow in ensuring consumer protection in higher education,
- considering structuring accreditation so that it is judged based on institution type or mission rather than geography, and so that accreditors can more easily distinguish among colleges of varying quality, and
- defining a common set of data that the federal government would collect and share with accreditors, both to minimize reporting burden and to assure consistency. The data might include licensure, job placement, and completion data—the latter collected through a privacy-protected national unit record system.

A majority of members also supported giving accreditors more flexibility, including considering risk assessment, which would allow accreditors more options to examine institutions they consider at risk of losing accreditation; creating an expedited review process for institutions including being able to review some institutions more frequently than others, and giving accreditors a wider range of gradations of approval.[62] These recommendations were included in the second draft of the report published in early 2012.[63]

CONCLUDING THOUGHTS

The federal government's discussions on higher education are increasingly centered on national measures of affordability and quality as measured by privileging successful career and job placement over individual student learning outcomes that are, at this time, identified and delegated as institutional responsibilities. Washington's attention, which in the past has focused on accessibility to college, is now shifting to an association between public funding for higher education and aggregate institutional outcomes related to student progress to degree and prospects after graduation; in other words, there has been a shift from student learning outcomes to student outcomes. As measures relative to the cost of attendance and graduation are becoming proxies for value, the current theory is that resources are simply too precious to invest in institutions that do not yield good value and returns. As an example, Secretary Duncan pointed out after the president's State of the Union speech that, historically, federal higher education policy conversations have focused on the front end of getting students into college. However, access is just the starting point and the goal is shifting to get to the finish line, to completing college and graduating.[64]

Affordability has been adversely affected by tuition increases, which may have a strong link to declines in state taxpayer support. Additionally, as costs to attend college increase, stakeholders have pointed out that reliance on student borrowing has resulted in increased student debt that graduates and nongraduates are dealing with decades after leaving college. Dorothy Leland, while president of Georgia College & State University, stated that the "social compact is about public higher education being linked to the public good, rather than just being perceived as a private good. The more we perceive higher education as a private good and not a public good, the more likely we are to say that the funding of it is an individual responsibility, not a public responsibility."[65]

Claire Bond Potter, professor of history and American studies at Wesleyan University in Connecticut, summarized an important underlying tension. "The cost of higher education, and access to higher education, will not be addressed until the federal government and the states come to terms with what used to be common knowledge in both political parties: education is an investment. It is not a for-profit enterprise. It does not necessarily show measurable returns on that investment. It is something on which a nation agrees to lose money so that it has functioning, productive citizens down the road."[66]

The national debate concerning higher education outcomes continues. The Obama administration appears serious about affordability and college completion. It is implementing reforms to increase accountability and value by requiring higher education institutions to provide students and families with useful information to help them make informed decisions concerning which college to choose based on costs, graduation rates, job placement, and expected debt loads. However, concerned stakeholders are likely to continue to question whether or not they are receiving a return on investment in higher education or just throwing money at it. Another timely question is whether or not the current accreditation process is a valid and sustainable proxy for the quality and integrity of aggregate and student learning outcomes from higher education. Will these questions be resolved or even addressed when Congress considers renewal of the HEOA of 2008?

NOTES

1. Julie Margetta Morgan, "Consumer-Driven Reform of Higher Education: A Critical Look at New Amendments to the Higher Education Act," *Journal of Law and Policy* 17, no. 2 (2009): 541, 42, 48.

2. Senator Charles E. Schumer, "Schumer Announces Passage of Higher Education Bill with His Provisions to Protect Upstate NY Families and College Students from Soaring Tuition and Textbook Costs" (August 1, 2008), accessed February 12, 2012, http://www.schumer.senate.gov/Newsroom/record.cfm?id=301891.

3. Morgan, "Consumer-Driven Reform of Higher Education," 534, 45.

4. Ibid., 532.

5. Doug Lederman, "HEA: A Huge, Exacting Accountability Bill," *Inside Higher Ed* (August 1, 2008), accessed February 12, 2012, http://www.insidehighered.com/news/2008/08/01/hea.

6. Judith S. Eaton, "The Higher Education Opportunity Act of 2008: What Does It Mean and What Does It Do?" (Washington, DC: Council for Higher Education Accreditation, 4, no. 1 (October 30, 2008), accessed February 12, 2012, http://www.chea.org/ia/IA_2008.10.30.html.

7. Lederman, "HEA;" Rute Pinhel, "Higher Education Opportunity Act of 2008," accessed February 12, 2012, http://www.cga.ct.gov/2008/rpt/2008-R-0470.htm.

8. Maguire Associates, "The Higher Education Opportunity Act of 2008 and the Net Price Calculator: Turning the Act into Action," *Insights for a Challenging Economy* 2, no. 4

(n.d.), accessed February 16, 2012, http://www.maguireassoc.com/resource/insights_bulletin_vol2_4.html.

9. Jose Padilla, "Opportunity Knocks, and Knocks Hard: The Higher Education Opportunity Act of 2008," The Office of the General Counsel, DePaul University (winter 2008–2009), accessed February 16, 2012, http://generalcounsel.depaul.edu/news_and_events/news/archivedNews_5_1962_1463.html.

10. Rute Pinhel, "Higher Education Opportunity Act of 2008."

11. California State University, "Higher Education Opportunities Act (HEOA): Textbook Information Provision" (n.d.), accessed February 12, 2012, http://als.csuprojects.org/heoa.

12. Jan Friis, CHEA Update: "Accreditation and the Higher Education Opportunity Act of 2008" (September 19, 2008), accessed February 12, 2012. http://www.chea.org/Government/HEAUpdate/CHEA_HEA45.html.

13. Charles Miller, "The New Higher Education Act: Where It Comes Up Short," *Chronicle of Higher Education* 54, no. 48 (August 8, 2008), A19.

14. Barmak Nassirian, "The New Higher Education Act: Where It Comes Up Short," *Chronicle of Higher Education* 54, no. 49 (August 8, 2008), A19.

15. Lederman, "HEA."

16. Sandy Baum, "The New Higher Education Act: Where It Comes Up Short," *Chronicle of Higher Education* 54, no. 48 (August 8, 2008), A19.

17. Morgan, "Consumer-Driven Reform of Higher Education," 535, 72, 74.

18. Beckie Supiano and Elyse Ashburn, "With New Lists, Federal Government Moves to Help Consumers and Prod Colleges to Limit Price Increases," *Chronicle of Higher Education* (June 30, 2011), A17–8.

19. Robert Shireman, "The New Higher Education Act: Where It Comes Up Short," *Chronicle of Higher Education* 54, no. 48 (August 8, 2008), A19.

20. Raymond C. Scheppach, "The New Higher Education Act: Where It Comes Up Short," *Chronicle of Higher Education* 54, no. 48 (August 8, 2008), A19.

21. Judith S. Eaton, "Accreditation and the Federal Future of Higher Education," *Academe Online* (September–October 2010), accessed February 17, 2012, http://www.aaup.org/AAUP/pubsres/academe/2010/SO/feat/eato.htm.

22. Ibid.

23. Ibid.

24. John B. Simpson, "In a Crisis, Our Nation Must Have an Ambitious Education Strategy," *Chronicle of Higher Education* (March 20, 2009), A72.

25. Libby A. Nelson, "At the White House Roundtable," *Inside Higher Ed* (December 6, 2011), accessed February 17, 2012, http://www.insidehighered.com/news/2011/12/06/obama-meeting-focuses-cost-affordability-productivity.

26. Libby A. Nelson, "Price Back in the Spotlight," *Inside Higher Ed* (December 1, 2011), accessed February 17, 2012, http://www.insidehighered.com/news/2011/12/01/congress-duncan-focus-rising-college-prices; Kevin Carey, "Belt Tightening on College Costs," NPR (January 10, 2012), accessed February 17, 2012, http://www.npr.org/2012/01/10/144953645/new-republic-belt-tightening-on-college-costs.

27. Nelson, "Price Back in the Spotlight."

28. Nelson, "At the White House Roundtable."

29. Nelson, "Price Back in the Spotlight;" Carey, "Belt Tightening on College Costs."

30. President Barack Obama, "Remarks by the President in State of the Union Address" (January 24, 2012), accessed April 18, 2012, http://www.whitehouse.gov/the-press-office/2012/01/24/remarks-president-state-union-address.

31. Kelly Field, "Obama Highlights Education's Role in Reaching National Policy Goals," *Chronicle of Higher Education* (January 25, 2012), accessed February 17, 2012, http://chronicle.com/article/Obama-Puts-Focus-on-Colleges/130447/.

32. Libby A. Nelson, "Warnings of Unintended Consequences: Obama Plan to Tie Tuition Prices to Aid Eligibility Draws Criticism," *Inside Higher Ed* (January 26, 2012), accessed February 17, 2012, http://www.insidehighered.com/news/2012/01/26/obama-plan-tie-tuition-prices-aid-eligibility-draws-criticism.

33. Alan Silverleib and Tom Cohen, "Obama Unveils Plan to Control College Costs," *CNN Politics* (January 27, 2012), accessed February 18, 2012, http://www.cnn.com/2012/01/27/politics/obama-trip/index.html.

34. President Barack Obama, *Blueprint for an America Built to Last* (January 24, 2012), accessed April 18, 2012, http://www.whitehouse.gov/sites/default/files/blueprint_for_an_america_built_to_last.pdf.

35. White House, Office of the Press Secretary, "Fact Sheet: President Obama's Blueprint for Keeping College Affordable and Within Reach for All Americans" (January 27, 2012), accessed February 18, 2012, http://www.whitehouse.gov/the-press-office/2012/01/27/fact-sheet-president-obama-s-blueprint-keeping-college-affordable-and-wi.

36. Goldie Blumenstyk, "College Officials Welcome Obama's Focus on Higher-Education Costs, but Raise Some Concerns," *Chronicle of Higher Education* (January 30, 2012), accessed February 18, 2012, http://chronicle.com/article/Obama-Puts-College-Costs-Front/130503.

37. Goldie Blumenstyk, "Obama Calls for Control of College Costs and Renewed Support for Higher Education," *Chronicle of Higher Education* (January 27, 2012), accessed February 18, 2012, http://chronicle.com/article/Obama-Calls-for-Control-of/130496.

38. Silverleib and Cohen, "Obama Unveils Plan to Control College Costs."

39. Ibid.

40. Kimberly Hefling, "Obama's Tougher-Stance Question on Higher Education: What Are People Getting for Their Money?" GrandForksHerald.com (February 20, 2012), accessed February 25, 2012, http://www.grandforksherald.com/event/article/id/230002/.

41. Libby A. Nelson, " 'Gainful' Comes to the Nonprofits: Obama Higher Education Plan Signals Policy Shift," *Inside Higher Ed*, accessed February 18, 2012, http://www.insidehighered.com/news/2012/01/30/obama-higher-education-plan-signals-policy-shift.

42. Kelly Field, "State of the Union Speech Leaves Many Questions Unanswered," *Chronicle of Higher Education* (January 25, 2012), accessed February 17, 2012, http://chronicle.com/article/State-of-the-Union-Speech/130464/.

43. Tamar Lewin, "Mixed Reviews of Obama Plan to Keep Down College Costs," *New York Times* (January 27, 2012), accessed February 18, 2012, http://www.nytimes.com/2012/01/28/education/obamas-plan-to-control-college-costs-gets-mixed-reviews.html.

44. Field, "State of the Union Speech Leaves Many Questions Unanswered."

45. Beckie Supiano, "Aid Experts and Officials Question President's College-Affordability Plans," *Chronicle of Higher Education* (January 30, 2012), accessed February 18, 2012, http://chronicle.com/article/Aid-ExpertsOfficials/130502/.

46. Associated Press [unidentified contributed author], "College Presidents Wary of Obama Cost-control Plan," Thecabin.net: Log Cabin Democrat (January 28, 2012), accessed February 18, 2012, http://thecabin.net/news/2012–01–28/college-presidents-wary-obama-cost-control-plan.

47. Nelson, "Warnings of Unintended Consequences."

48. Lewin, "Mixed Reviews of Obama Plan to Keep Down College Costs."

49. Ibid.

50. "Editorial: Reining in College Tuition," *New York Times* (February 3, 2012), accessed February 18, 2012, http://www.nytimes.com/2012/02/04/opinion/reining-in-college-tuition.html.

51. Libby A. Nelson, "A Symbolic, but Pleasing, Budget," *Inside Higher Ed* (February 14, 2012), accessed February 19, 2012, http://www.insidehighered.com/news/2012/02/14/obama-proposes-increase-education-spending; Kelly Field, "College Groups React to Obama's Higher-Education Budget with Praise and Caution," *Chronicle of Higher Education* (February 13, 2012), accessed February 19, 2012, http://chronicle.com/article/College-Groups-React-With/130775/.

52. David Moltz, "Looking Ahead to 2013," *Inside Higher Ed* (December 3, 2010), accessed February 19, 2012, http://www.insidehighered.com/news/2010/12/03/naciqi.

53. Anne D. Neal, "Asking Too Much (and Too Little) of Accreditors," *Inside Higher Ed* (November 12, 2010), accessed February 19, 2012, http://www.insidehighered.com/views/2010/11/12/neal.

54. Ibid.

55. Eric Kelderman, "In Accreditation Proposal, Panel Pleases Neither Reformers Nor Status Quo Advocates," *Chronicle of Higher Education* (April 13, 2012), accessed May 1, 2012, chronicle.com/article/In-Accreditation-Proposals/131561/.

56. Neal, "Asking Too Much (and Too Little) of Accreditors."

57. Ibid.

58. Doug Lederman, "Quality Assurance, Rearranged," *Inside Higher Ed* (October 31, 2011), accessed February 19, 2012, http://www.insidehighered.com/news/2011/10/31/us-panels-ideas-revamping-higher-ed-accreditation.

59. Ibid.

60. Ibid.

61. Libby A. Nelson, "No Overhaul of Accreditation," *Inside Higher Ed* (December 19, 2011), accessed February 19, 2012, http://www.insidehighered.com/news/2011/12/19/committee-higher-ed-accreditation-composing-its-final-report.

62. Ibid.

63. The National Advisory Committee on Institutional Quality and Integrity, "NACIQI Draft Final Report: Higher Education Accreditation Reauthorization Policy Recommendations" (February 8, 2012), accessed May 16, 2012, http://www2.ed.gov/about/bdscomm/list/naciqi-dir/naciqi_draft_final_report.pdf.

64. Hefling, "Obama's Tougher-Stance Question on Higher Education."

65. Stephen G. Pelletier, "Stewardship in an Era of Constraint," *Public Purpose* (summer 2011): 9, accessed May 1, 2012, http://www.aascu.org/uploadedFiles/AASCU/Content/Root/MediaAndPublications/PublicPurposeMagazines/Issue/11summer_stewardship.pdf.

66. Claire Bond Potter, "What a Real Education Policy Would Look Like," *Chronicle of Higher Education* (January 27, 2012), accessed February 18, 2012, http://chronicle.com/blognetwork/tenuredradical/2012/01/extra-extra-the-white-house-announces-another-federal-education-non-policy/.

4

HIGHER EDUCATION OUTCOMES IN THE STATES AND INSTITUTIONS

Robert E. Dugan

Higher education in the United States is considered to be among the best in the world, contributing leaders, innovators, researchers, and others who have improved the quality of life and made technological and other advances. For many stakeholders (e.g., governments, businesses, and taxpayers), the expectations of those gaining a college degree are of educated and appropriately skilled people who achieve success helping to sustain an economy that competes globally, and who contributes to the general societal good. For the college graduate, completion is often seen as a means to a personally satisfying and productive life.

Over the past 20 years, the quality of the higher education system and its outcomes (the skills, values, and knowledge of its graduates) has increasingly been questioned. In fact, critics occasionally question the value of obtaining a college degree at all while others publicly wonder whether the current model of higher education is outdated and ready for transformation. The nation's youth is often advised to get a college education. A long-held perception is that such an education provides a path to a better and higher-paying job. A report from the departments of Treasury and Education found substantial evidence that receiving an education raises earnings. The median weekly earnings for a full-time, full-year bachelor's degree holder in 2011 was 64 percent higher than those for a high school graduate ($1,053 compared with $638).[1] Furthermore, it has been estimated that 61 percent of the jobs in the United States will require a higher education degree by 2018.[2] These facts would lead one to believe that those possessing a college degree will be in demand and properly compensated.

However, there is some doubt about the value of a college degree. William J. Bennett, a former secretary of education and currently a media contributor who writes about matters concerning American politics in general and higher education specifically, wrote that a college diploma may no longer guarantee high potential lifetime earnings or hold the status and significance it once did. He cites recent data from the Bureau of the Census and Department of Labor, which showed that almost 54 percent of recent graduates were unemployed or underemployed. He points out that this information does not stop an ever-increasing number of students from incurring a massive tuition debt only to end up with degrees but no jobs. He blames this on students who are ill prepared for the workforce and equipped with skills that are not aligned with current labor needs.[3] To paraphrase journalist George F. Will, today's college degree is now just an expensive signifier of rudimentary qualities, namely, the ability to follow instructions.[4] Meanwhile, staff of the Florida Department of Economic Opportunity at a conference in early 2012 estimated that, when it comes to Florida's jobs, more than 85 percent do not require a four-year degree because the state's economy is based primarily on tourism, retail, and agriculture jobs, which require less education. "[Employers] want people who have skills," said Jim Nolan, general manager for Job News, which holds job fairs in South Florida. "They might want an associate's degree or technical training." What matters most to employers is "Can you do the job?"[5]

In addition to the present-day valuing of a college degree, a significant challenge to higher education comes from the discussion concerning its near and immediate future, often focused on whether or not higher education is the next economic bubble to burst, reminiscent of the dot-com bubble of the early 2000s and the real estate bubble that is linked to the recession that officially started in December 2007. The higher education bubble is based on stakeholder concerns about

- The unsustainability of rising tuition costs and fees, which raises questions concerning ongoing access to a college education and its affordability;
- The increasing education-related, long-term personal debt loads that ultimately result in less money available to grow the economy at a time when the latest recession seems endless;
- The perception of a decrease in the economic value from obtaining a college degree, leading some to go so far as to question the need to possess it;
- Not understanding the value of higher education, which is symptomatic of institutions not telling their such stories well as that by reporting return on investments and instead maintaining a general lack of transparency;
- Overreliance on institutional inputs and outputs including productivity and efficiency measures such as faculty workloads;
- The failure of institutions to assure the fulfillment of student learning outcomes and to relate educational programs well to career prospects;
- A perceived decrease in academic rigor replaced by an increase in student amenities such as climbing walls and dormitory swimming pools;
- Problematic graduate rates and the increasing time-to-degree completion; and
- A failure to explain how information technology shapes pedagogy and affects content delivery costs.

Moody's Investors Services' outlook report for 2012 finds that a majority of colleges, those dependent on tuition or state money, will continue to face challenges throughout the year and into the first half of the next year. Those challenges will, in part, stem from the public's scrutiny of rising tuition costs and from pressures to keep those costs down. Moody analysts also expect demand to rise for admission to the largest and highest-rated institutions, while other colleges may struggle to attract students. The report addresses a key question: Is the higher education model fundamentally broken? Analysts maintain that the business model is "generally sound and long-lasting," but that higher education will have to innovate in a number of ways to remain viable. Such innovations might include collaborations among colleges, more centralized management, more efficient use of facilities, a reduction in the number of tenured faculty members, and the geographic and demographic expansion of course offerings.[6]

Predictions concerning the higher education bubble focus on traditional higher education, often symbolized as the brick-and-mortar campus with classrooms, student residences, and numerous academic and student support services. These traditional university experiences are increasingly being characterized as conveying impractical learning and having out-of-touch faculty, exorbitant tuitions, time-wasting requirements, and diminishing probabilities of employment. Frustration with traditional campus approaches to pedagogy and services leads to efforts to disrupt higher education by replacing it with different, often less costly alternatives.[7] These alternatives include online courses and programs, certificates or badges, for-profit institutions, and other experiences that are intentionally designed to be more collaborative, social, virtual, and peer-to-peer. For example, the Massachusetts Institute of Technology's MITx (https://www.edx.org/university_profile/MITx) self-service learning system lets students take online tests and earn certificates after watching free course materials posted by the university. StraighterLine, which offers self-paced introductory courses online (http://www.straighterline.com), provides students with access to the Collegiate Learning Assessment (CLA) and other similar tests, allowing them to take results to employers or colleges to demonstrate their proficiency in certain academic areas. A hurdle for many of these new course-delivery ideas is the monopoly that traditional colleges currently possess, as they have the legal ability to provide federal government student aid; this ability results from the requirements of a federally approved accreditation.

The traditional campus and its model of content delivery may be viewed as an "industrial production line" in which the raw materials (students) enter and are converted by processes (teaching) and time into something that is inspected and subject to some local quality control (tests and other outcomes) although not standardized within the industry (each institution has a unique mission statement recognized by the accreditation process). Two characteristics of the aforementioned alternatives to the traditional college experience are its individualized approach and its mobility in that students can consume content at any time from any place when they are connected to the Internet. It is evident, then, that the root of the disruption is the ubiquitous application of technology. George L. Mehaffy, vice president of Academic Leadership and Change at the American Association of State Colleges and Universities, finds that higher education is moving toward an age where information is created, aggregated, and disseminated in powerfully different ways. The industrial model of the university as a collection of experts, the model of teaching that requires expert knowledge, and the model of an institution that requires the physical presence of attendees is being called into question. As a result of the declining funding for public higher education from state government, the growing expectation of stakeholders is for colleges and universities to produce more skilled graduates to contribute to the national economy and successfully compete globally, and the ubiquitous deployment of mobile technologies, new ways to organize and deliver instruction, structure and sequence the curriculum, and design and assess learning environments. This will alter the traditional college experience.[8]

The outcomes frequently discussed (college completion, affordability, institutional productivity, transparency, and quality) provide substantial challenges to higher education and will be discussed in this chapter. The challenge when reduced to its core elements is simply "how do higher education institutions educate more students, to higher levels of learning outcomes, with less money?"[9]

COLLEGE COMPLETION

An outcome that has gained significant attention over the past few years is college completion. According to the U.S. Chamber of Commerce, U.S. workers rank 15th out of 34 industrialized countries in the percentage of the adult-age population with a college diploma. Although the United States has been successful at getting more people to start college, few finish a degree: 70 percent of high school graduates move on to some form of postsecondary education, but fewer than half of those who enroll finish a degree or certificate within six years.[10] President Barack Obama set a goal in 2009 that by 2020, the United States would, once again, have the highest proportion of college graduates in the world.[11] A private foundation dedicated to increasing students' access to and success in postsecondary education, the Lumina Foundation, includes "Goal 2025" as part of its mission to increase the percentage of Americans who hold high-quality degrees and credentials to 60 percent by 2025.[12] Lumina's third annual report tracking progress toward that goal found that 38.3 percent of working-age adults held at least a two-year degree in 2010, which is up from 37.9 in 2008. However, at that pace, less than 47 percent of Americans will hold a degree by 2025, leaving the workforce short by 23 million needed degree holders.[13]

College completion is both an output and an outcome. As an output, it is a measurable activity—the number of students who obtain a degree who have enrolled in a college and the length of time it takes them to do so. It is also a student outcome and a student learning outcome. The college completion metric can be aggregated by institution and within the institution by organizational unit (e.g., program and school), and by discipline or major. As a student learning outcome, completion is a proxy for quality; if students complete an academic program and graduate, it is assumed that they possess the knowledge required by the program to satisfy the graduation criteria and requirements, especially if the institution has been accredited by a regional accreditation organization.

In addition to the national completion goals set by the Obama administration and the Lumina Foundation, the "American Freshman" poll, conducted by the University of California at Los Angeles (UCLA) since 1966, found that the nation's current college freshmen, having seen their parents' struggle with unemployment and other money worries, are therefore concerned with the latest economic crisis and increasingly view completing a bachelor's degree as a necessary requirement to gain better jobs. Nearly 86 percent of first-year students surveyed across the country stated that being able to land a good job is a very important reason for attending college. That is the strongest response to that question in the 40 years it has been asked and is higher than the 70.4 percent reply in 2006, before the recession began. Not completing college could lead to economic insecurity.[14]

States are also concerned about the lack of college completion. Indiana, for example, views degree completion as a means to further the state's economic competitiveness with other states.[15] A task force of students, professors, business leaders, and college presidents organized by the Higher Education Policy Commission and West Virginia Council for Community and Technical College Education took a year to review education statistics and prepare a plan to increase the state's chronically low 40 percent college completion rate. The report, released in June 2012, recommended five steps to increase the state's college completion rate:

1. Create a statewide and campus-wide culture including senior leadership, faculty and staff, in which college graduation is a priority over enrollment;
2. Reduce the time it takes students to earn their degrees by reducing the cumbersome transition between remediation courses and credit courses;
3. Improve remediation education courses;
4. Increase adult completion rates; and
5. Transition to more of an outcomes-based funding model where part of a college's state financing is related to ensuring students graduate.[16]

The City Colleges of Chicago have linked graduation rates to the formal job responsibilities of the chancellor, presidents, and trustees. If the 7 percent graduation rate does not improve, Chicago Mayor Rahm Emanuel has stated that the system's leaders could lose their jobs.[17]

University of Utah graduation rates do not measure up against comparable institutions, undermining the state's competitiveness and depressing tax revenues, according to a legislative audit released in May 2012. "Graduation rates are an important consideration if Utah is going to produce the number of people with bachelor's degrees necessary to meet 2018 job needs," said state auditor Janice Coleman. She points out that a 5 percent increase in the bachelor's-degree-holding population may increase tax revenue by as much as $24.5 million a year. The University of Utah conducted a study to identify barriers to college completion and to learn why only 58 percent graduate within six years of starting. Factors underlying poor graduation rates were complex and often beyond universities' control. For example, three-fourths of University of Utah students work at least 30 hours a week, usually off-campus. Another key reason is that many students progress slowly through college because they are earning credits that do not advance them toward graduation. Additionally, there is a measurable lack of college readiness among incoming freshmen, requiring more than 50 percent of the students to enroll in some form of remedial education, particularly in math and science. It was found that too many high school seniors were exercising "work release options" rather than taking serious courses, according to William Sederburg, Utah's commissioner of higher education.[18]

Recent research identifies some of the factors that contribute to student success and college completion. A 2012 report from the Higher Education Research Institute at UCLA found that, while an institution's size and cost to attend were factors in college completion, students who visit a college before enrolling, live in on-campus housing, participate in clubs, school rituals, and other activities, and those who have used the Internet for research and homework are more likely to complete a degree earlier than others.[19] These factors align with student engagement, often measured over the past decade by the National Survey of Student Engagement, administered by the Indiana University Center for Postsecondary Research, sponsored in part by the Carnegie Foundation for the Advancement of Teaching, and paid for by the participating colleges. The institutionally administered, self-reported student survey evaluates participating institutions' performances in five categories: level of academic challenge, active and collaborative learning, student–faculty interaction, enriching educational experiences, and supportive campus environment.[20] Institutions may use the reports generated from the survey to improve undergraduate education and, as an extension, provide information that can be used to increase college completion.

Those traditional higher education institutions that take college completion seriously as both an output and an outcome are exploring and implementing alternatives to increase their graduation rates. One approach is for not-for-profit institutions and state public higher education systems to offer flexible degree options. Flexible degree options, popularized by the online Western Governors University, enable students to demonstrate competencies that they have gained from previous coursework or in nontraditional ways (e.g., on-the-job training, independent study, work, volunteer, and military experience) and earn credit for meeting certain levels of knowledge, not for completing traditional courses.

Competency-based learning furnishes working adults who never attended or finished college with the degrees necessary to pursue more advanced jobs. A research brief from the Council for Adult and Experiential Learning described students who received credits for prior learning as being two-and-a-half times as likely to graduate as those who did not earn such credits. Students typically earn prior-learning-assessment credits for on-the-job training, as well as work, volunteer, and military experience.[21]

In several states, including Texas, Indiana, and Washington, students may attend a state-sanctioned partnership with Western Governors University, which provides access to customized academic programs. However, the state university system in Wisconsin plans to build its own flexible degree program offering undergraduate and graduate degrees in fall 2013. Tuition rates have not been finalized, but current planning is that a competency-based course would cost the same as a course in one of the system's online degrees. Students may also just take the competency exam in lieu of the entire self-paced course, which would be less expensive. University of Wisconsin administrators will work with faculty to determine competency levels that match up with colleges' existing courses and how students can demonstrate those competencies. The new program will prioritize the courses of study that are most needed to prepare Wisconsin students for relevant and available jobs in fields such as business and management, health care, and information technology. The flexible program will be centrally administered, but degrees will be granted from one of the system's 26 institutions. For example, if a student passes competency courses from the University of Wisconsin–Green Bay, the degree will come from Green Bay, not the flexible degree program itself.[22]

Another strategy to increase college completion is to encourage students to earn a degree faster. A state law passed in 2012 requires Ohio's 14 public universities to show, by October 2012, how 10 percent of their baccalaureate programs can be completed in three years and how 60 percent of degrees will meet that time-to-completion by 2014. Jim Petro, chancellor of the Ohio Board of Regents, stated that the longer it takes a student to finish, the less likely it is that person will finish. He also points out that, while 70 percent of high school graduates in Ohio enroll in higher education, less than half will ever earn a degree. Statewide, just 56 percent of students enrolled from any location (not just Ohio) finish in six years. Ohio's requirement will not reduce the number of credit hours required for degrees. Instead, it calls on universities to illustrate how a student could graduate a year sooner by attending college in the summer, testing out of classes with advanced placement assessments for high school students, taking college courses during high school with the postsecondary enrollment program or through an early college high school, or applying for college credit for career-technical experience. Students can also take more courses than a typical full-time student. Ohio's law does not create any goals for how many students actually earn their degree in three years. University officials, however, say they expect the numbers to rise as schools create websites showing students how it can be done.[23]

Another popular strategy to increase graduation rates is for a traditional institution to offer online courses and programs, which may be a hybrid of face-to-face classes along with synchronous and asynchronous online content delivery, fully synchronous or fully asynchronous online delivery. Programs may include a few online courses to supplement traditionally delivered courses for an academic program or the entire program may be delivered online. More recently, traditional institutions have begun to offer massive open online courses, usually referred to as MOOCs. MOOCs are courses offered online to tens of thousands of students or members of the general public worldwide, usually with no fees, though in some cases fees may pertain if a credential is sought. They are not limited to public higher education institutions; several private universities such as Harvard, Princeton, MIT, and Stanford have been at the forefront of experiments with the format. Institutions may eventually form federations or networks in which they use "the best of MOOC's" to provide courses they do not offer, cannot afford to provide online, or as may be needed by students to meet degree requirements for college completion at their local campuses.[24]

An emerging alternative outcome to a college degree is the awarding of certificates or badges. In late 2011, MIT announced that it will create MITx, a self-service learning system offering a portfolio of its courses for free to a virtual community of learners around the world. Students can take online tests, and if they prove that they have learned the material for select courses, MITx will, for a small fee, provide them with a certifying credential.[25] Other educational endeavors across the web are adopting systems of "badges" to certify skills and abilities. At the free not-for-profit online-education provider Khan Academy, for instance, students get a "Great Listener" badge for watching 30 minutes of videos from its collection of thousands of short educational clips. With enough of those badges, paired with badges earned for passing standardized tests administered on the site, users can earn the distinction of "Master of Algebra" or other "Challenge Patches."[26]

Mozilla, the group that developed and maintains the Firefox web browser, is designing a framework to let anyone with a web page (colleges, companies, or even individuals) issue education badges designed to prevent forgeries and give potential employers details about the distinctions by clicking on a descriptive link. Some employers may prefer badges to college diplomas that provide no details about what the degree recipient learned. Students using Mozilla's proposed badge system might display dozens or even hundreds of merit badges on their online résumés detailing what they studied. Further, students can immediately display the badges as they earn them rather than waiting four or more years to earn a diploma.[27]

At least one higher education provider is adopting a different strategy concerning completion outcomes other than certificates and badges. StraighterLine enables students to take as many for-credit college courses as they want in nearly 40 online courses, in science, humanities, English, math, and business, for $99 a month plus a per-course registration fee. Students take online self-paced college courses and transfer passed courses for full credit when enrolled in one of StraighterLine's accredited partner colleges. Partner colleges include Albany State University, La Salle University (PA), Concordia University Chicago, Liberty University (VA), and the University of the Incarnate Word (TX).

In early 2012, StraighterLine announced agreements with the Education Testing Service (ETS) and the Council on Aid to Education (CAE) to provide competency test materials online to students. StraighterLine's students, for a fee, will be able to take the ETS iSkills test, which measures their ability to navigate and critically evaluate information from digital technology, and the CLA through CAE that presents realistic problems requiring students to analyze complex materials and determine the relevance to the task and credibility. Students' written responses to the CLA tasks are evaluated to assess their abilities to think critically, reason analytically, solve problems, and communicate clearly and cogently. StraighterLine's students can tell employers how they did on the CLA and iSkills test, strong predictors of future positive work performance.[28]

Students earning certificates or badges, or having access to nationally normed tests usually offered by traditional higher education institutions, may validate gaining skills and knowledge without completing a college degree. It is unknown at this time whether or not these alternatives will be viewed as acceptable to meeting the completion goals set forth by the Obama administration and the Lumina Foundation. The question may become, what is more important: the skills needed to do the job, or the completion of a program and the awarding of a degree?

COLLEGE AFFORDABILITY

To many stakeholders, a measurable and unwanted student outcome is education-related personal debt. While long a theme of higher education, public anxiety over college costs and affordability is at an all-time high. "The affordability of a college degree—whether it is affordable—is becoming a third rail in the national conversation about higher education," said Jamie P. Merisotis, president of the Lumina Foundation for Education.[29]

As college costs continue to increase, Ronald G. Ehrenberg, director of Cornell University's Higher Education Research Institute, finds that Americans increasingly view higher education as a private good, not as a wider societal benefit.[30] Because it is considered a personal option, the costs associated with attending college should not be considered a state or federal government entitlement. This public perception toward higher education adversely affects the longtime goal of equitable access to a college degree for anyone wanting one.

Higher Education Costs

The College Board, a not-for-profit membership organization representing nearly 6,000 colleges, universities, and schools, annually publishes *Trends in College Pricing*. It is useful to this discussion to list several of the facts concerning affordability and higher education:

- Over the decade from 2001–2002 to 2011–2012, published tuition and fees for in-state students at public four-year colleges and universities increased at an average rate of 5.6 percent per year beyond the rate of general inflation. This rate of increase compares with 4.5 percent per year in the 1980s and 3.2 percent per year in the 1990s.

- Over the decade, published tuition and fees at private nonprofit four-year institutions increased at an average rate of 2.6 percent per year beyond inflation. This rate of increase compares with 4.8 percent per year in the 1980s and 3.1 percent per year in the 1990s.

- Published in-state tuition and fees at public four-year institutions average $8,244 in 2011–2012, $631 (8.3 percent) higher than that in 2010–2011. Average total charges, including tuition and fees and room and board, are $17,131, up 6 percent from 2010–2011.

- Published tuition and fees at public two-year colleges average $2,963, $236 (8.7 percent) higher than that in 2010–2011.

- Published tuition and fees at private nonprofit four-year colleges and universities average $28,500 in 2011–2012, $1,235 (4.5 percent) higher than that in 2010–2011. Average total charges, including tuition and fees and room and board, are $38,589, up 4.4 percent from 2010–2011.

- In 2011–2012, full-time undergraduates receive an estimated average of about $5,750 in grant aid from all sources and federal tax benefits at public four-year institutions, $15,530 at private nonprofit four-year institutions, and $3,770 at public two-year colleges.

- State appropriations per full-time equivalent (FTE) student declined by 9 percent in inflation-adjusted dollars between 2007–2008 and 2008–2009, by 6 percent in 2009–2010, and by 4 percent in 2010–2011. Average tuition and fees at public four-year colleges rose by 9 percent beyond inflation in 2009–2010 and by 7 percent in 2010–2011.

- State funding per FTE student for higher education institutions was 23 percent lower in inflation-adjusted dollars in 2010–2011 after increasing by 6 percent in the 1980s and by 5 percent in the 1990s.

- At all types of public institutions, the average share of revenues coming from net tuition increased between 1998–1999 and 2008–2009, while the share coming from state and local appropriations decreased.

- Over the entire income distribution in the United States, average income was lower in 2010 at all levels of the income distribution than it had been a decade earlier. Declines ranged from 16 percent in inflation-adjusted dollars for the bottom 20 percent of families, and 11 percent for the top 5 percent, to 3 percent for families in the 60th–80th percentiles.

- Total enrollment in public four-year colleges and universities was 27 percent higher in fall 2009 than in fall 2000. Enrollment increased by 24 percent at public two-year colleges and by 22 percent at private nonprofit four-year institutions over that time period.

- Total faculty compensation, including health insurance and other fringe benefits, has risen more rapidly over the past two decades than faculty salaries, but much more slowly than published tuition and fees.[31]

These facts may be briefly summarized: tuition has risen faster than inflation, the ratio of state funding appropriated to support public higher education tuition has decreased, inflation-adjusted family incomes are lower for those in the lowest income brackets, and enrollment at public higher education institutions has increased.

Discussion in the news media of the drivers of cost increases for higher education tends to focus on compensation for institutional employees (staff, faculty, and administration), including health insurance and other fringe benefits; interinstitutional competition; and declining state funding allocated to higher education institutions. Higher education is labor intensive, with courses taught by faculty, support services provided by staff, and administration coordinating the activities of faculty and staff. As a result, compensation costs usually comprise a majority of the annual operating costs of higher education institutions. When a parent at a town hall meeting asked Vice President Joseph R. Biden Jr., in 2012, why college costs keep rising, he cited faculty pay. "Salaries for college professors have escalated significantly. They should be good, but they have escalated significantly." However, first, the American Association of University Professors (AAUP) maintains that faculty pay is not the cause of rising college costs. Full-time faculty salaries rose 1.8 percent during the 2011–2012 academic year, which coexisted with a 3 percent inflation rate; therefore, faculty salaries actually fell by an average of 1.2 percent. Second, AAUP points out that tuition has increased at a much faster rate than full-time faculty salaries. The faculty association also notes that between 2006–2007 and 2010–2011, median presidential salaries jumped by 9.8 percent, when adjusted for inflation, while median full-time faculty salaries rose by less than 2 percent.[32]

In another study, the Education Department's National Center for Education Statistics (NCES) found that the average salary of full-time (i.e., 9–10 month) faculty at four-year colleges and universities for the period 1993–2003 increased 10.7 percent in constant dollars. For the executive/administrative/managerial category, the corresponding increase was higher, at 17.7 percent. Similarly, the Higher Education Price Index, which is an inflation metric customized to institutions of higher education, showed a significantly higher increase for administrative salaries than for faculty salaries from 2002 to 2010. The compensation cost is a longitudinal matter of not only average salary but also the total size of full-time faculty. According to the NCES, the size of the full-time faculty has increased, but at a lesser rate than the student body. Specifically, the number of full-time faculty at four-year private and public institutions of higher education rose 16 percent from 1993 to 2003, while the colleges' student enrollments increased 19 percent. In comparison, during this same period, the corresponding growth rate for part-time faculty was 54.8 percent, and for the executive/administrative/managerial category, it was 29.8 percent. Thus, faculty salaries are not solely responsible for the increased cost of college education caused by compensation. Because the overall expenditure ratio for full-time faculty members' salaries is approximately three times larger than that for administrators' salaries, the faculty factor is more visible to the public and to Vice President Biden.[33]

A second cause of college cost increases has to do with interinstitutional competition. In the for-profit business sector, competition encourages companies to take the risks necessary for innovation and efficiency. However, competition in higher education often discourages risk taking and may lead colleges and universities to make overly cautious short-term decisions, even promoting a need to keep up with their peer and aspirant institutions. To become more attractive to potential students and their families, institutions build new facilities that directly contribute to its educational program, but they may also undertake ambitious physical plant expansions, including campus residences, athletic and fitness centers, and student centers.[34]

Although institutions scoff at the importance attached to school rankings such as the *U.S. News and World Report* survey and others, administrators and their boards are always looking for ways to gain advantage. Some institutions compete for academic talent such as faculty who will bring prestige to graduate programs and help attract private and government grants. This may also mean that institutions will have to increase salaries to retain their best people. A visible result of this type of interinstitutional competition is the emergence of seven-figure salaries for university presidents, formerly reserved for university athletic coaches.[35]

In analyzing the complex picture concerning higher education costs, most experts, such as Jane V. Wellman (when she was affiliated with the Delta Cost Project) have concluded that the biggest driver of increasing tuition costs for public colleges and universities has been the decline in state appropriations.[36] Her last Delta Project Cost report, in 2011, found that the increases in tuition are a result of the loss of state financial support. Additionally, Delta found that health-care costs are a "double whammy," sapping public treasuries even as they force public universities to hike spending. As a result, public colleges now rely on tuition money to pay more than half their costs for the first time in history.[37]

Health-care increases were not the only state funding problem in Illinois. Public higher education funding increased there by 12 percent, from $3.2 billion in fiscal year 2011 to $3.6 billion in fiscal year 2012. However, the increase is not going to benefit students. Instead, the additional funding for fiscal 2012 went to the State Universities Retirement System (SURS), which is responsible for the pensions of the state's university employees and is facing an unfunded liability of $17.2 billion, according to its 2011 annual report. The increase in the amount of money being given to SURS seeks to make up for decades of chronic underfunding by governors and legislators, and shrinking returns on investments because of the stagnant economy.[38]

A 2012 report from the State Higher Education Executive Officers (SHEEO) found that state funding for higher education fell to a quarter-century low for the second consecutive year in fiscal year 2011, 2.5 percent less than in fiscal year 2010, while public institutional enrollments continued their climb to record highs. From the beginning of the recession, in the 2008 fiscal year, through the 2011 fiscal year, college enrollment increased nationally by 12.5 percent, to 11.5 million students, the report says. However, state and local appropriations decreased by $1.3 billion over the same period. To make up for the loss of state dollars, tuition revenue per student reached $4,774 in 2011, an all-time high, according to the report. Over the past 25 years, the percentage of educational revenue supported by tuition nationally has climbed steadily, from 23.2 percent in 1986 to 43.3 percent in 2011.[39] It is this cumulative public divestment by state governments, not campus extravagances such as recreational centers, that is primarily responsible for rising tuitions at state institutions, which enroll three out of every four college students.[40]

The cutbacks in state funding come at a time when many states—and the country as a whole—are striving to increase the number of people they educate and the number of degrees, certificates, and other credentials they award. As a result, "the tension between the nation's attainment objectives and drive and our fiscal condition is put in stark relief," said Paul Lingenfelter, president of the national association of SHEEO. Added James C. Palmer, who directs the Illinois State University's Center for the Study of Education Policy: "The question is how do we meet our stated goals for increased educational attainment in an era marked by stagnant or diminishing economic growth. It seems like we aren't going to be able to meet them by increased state funding for higher education at least in the near term."[41]

States can be penalized by the Department of Education for failing to comply with a federal rule enacted as part of the 2008 reauthorization of the Higher Education Act, which requires states to spend at least as much on colleges and universities each year as they spent on average in the previous five years. States that fail to meet this "maintenance-of-effort" requirement can lose their eligibility for College Access Challenge Grants, a $150-million program that provides financial aid, academic counseling, and other assistance to students from low-income families.

Alabama and Michigan were penalized, in 2011, for state spending cuts in fiscal year 2009, and their appeals for reversal were rejected. Michigan will use $2 million of state funds to make up for some of the lost grants and has balked at replacing the roughly $59 million in state higher education spending that would be required to meet the federal maintenance-of-effort standard. State officials in Alabama, which is losing a little more than $2 million, have responded similarly, saying that the state cannot afford the additional $36 million it would need to spend on higher education to meet the federal requirement.[42] During a conference call with reporters in June 2012, Education Secretary Arne Duncan cited state budget cuts as the most important factor in tuition increases in recent years, directly blaming state legislatures and governors for cutting back on higher education.[43]

Shifting Costs

The decline of state funds allocated to support the costs of higher education signals a change in the pattern of paying for public higher education. For at least the past 15 years, an ever-larger share of college costs has shifted from taxpayers to students and their families. In Minnesota, for instance, a modest increase in tuition of less than $1,000 does not seem steep unless the student is working and increasingly dependent on loans to fund attendance. On average, Minnesota students graduate with $29,000 in college-related debts. Debt will inhibit purchasing homes and cars and starting families, which, in turn, slows that state's recovery from the 2007 recession. It may also have the effect of graduates opting for lower-income careers in public service or teaching. In the long run, the trend to increase tuition that results in increased personal debt puts at risk developing Minnesota's best economic asset, its well-educated workforce.[44]

A similar trend of shifting the costs of operating public colleges and universities from state taxpayers to students and their families is occurring in other states. University of South Florida students will pay more than half of the cost of their college education in academic year 2012–2013 as tuition rises and the state's contribution continues to decline. In 1990, general tax revenues funded 71 percent of per-student costs in Florida while tuition covered 18 percent. In 2010, taxes funded 49 percent of per-student costs while tuition covered 40 percent.[45] Missouri state appropriations paid 55.4 percent of costs in fiscal year 2001, while students paid just more than one-third through tuition. In 2012, according to a report given to the House Appropriations—Education Committee by the Missouri Coordinating Board for Higher Education, students will shoulder 54.7 percent of operating costs while the state share will be less than one-third.[46] In response to declining state fiscal support, Iowa's public universities and community colleges have raised tuition charges. Between 2001 and 2010, state per capita personal income increased by about 8 percent (in constant dollars), but undergraduate tuition at the University of Iowa increased by about 99 percent. During a period when higher education is more important to economic growth and prosperity than ever because of the current unstable financial situation, state leaders in Iowa have chosen to reduce sharply state investment in higher education.[47] Echoing Iowa, the University of South Florida provost Ralph Wilcox told members of the university's board of trustees, in June 2012, that there "appears to be no interest in meaningful investment in higher education in the state of Florida."[48]

As state funding has decreased, public higher education institutions have raised tuition and, when there is still a gap between revenues and expenditures, reduced training for skilled jobs the economy needs most. As a result, state colleges in Nebraska, Nevada, South Dakota, Colorado, Michigan, and Texas have eliminated entire engineering and computer science departments.[49] However, in North Carolina, state funds are being used to train workers at local companies, essentially diverting the funds from supporting higher education. According to the state, North Carolina spent about $9.4 million to train workers as part of projects that created nearly 4,500 jobs during fiscal year 2011. As an example, the state is paying about $1 million to help nearly 400 workers acquire specific work-related technical skills for Caterpillar, a maker of industrial equipment, while a community college has committed to develop a custom curriculum valued at about $4.3 million. Although the sums spent on training are usually small compared with the tax breaks and other credits paid out by states, some critics question the tactic. "The question is, why shouldn't the company pay for this training?" asked Ross Eisenbrey, the vice president of the liberal Economic Policy Institute, a nonprofit, nonpartisan think tank in Washington, DC. "It's for their benefit." However, state officials posit that such programs are necessary to attract businesses to the state, and business executives argue that government-subsidized training is a fair payoff given that the companies bring jobs to the state.[50]

This pattern of state disinvestment and increasing costs threatens the future well-being not just of individual students, but also of the nation's long-standing commitment to equal access to higher education regardless of one's socioeconomic background, as increasing costs are pricing low-income students out of an education. It also threatens the future economic health of states, as insufficient financial support contributes to low rates of college completion, depriving states of the educated workforces needed to thrive in the 21st-century economy. State government leaders may consider the following recommendations when considering state investments in public higher education:

- Invest more wealth in higher education, especially given the current growth in student enrollments.
- Reform the tax system to ensure that funding for higher education will not continue to get squeezed out of their budgets.

- Recognize that any specific percentage reduction in state aid requires much larger percentage rises in tuition. Such increases price low- and moderate-income students out of higher education.[51]

Mark B. Rosenberg, president of Florida International University, may have summed it up for many public higher education institutional leaders when he stated that "in the end, if higher education is viewed by most states as a cost and not an investment, then it's inevitable that this kind of cost shifting will continue to occur."[52]

Education-Related Debt

Until recently, a college degree was considered affordable, especially if a student was willing to work and to attend an in-state public school. In the past decade, the cost of a college education has risen faster than inflation. As tuition and fees increase, more students are taking out loans; it is estimated that two-thirds of students graduate with debt, and the current average is $25,000 per student. The Federal Reserve Bank of New York's study of student loan debt estimated that cumulative student loan debt surpassed $1 trillion in 2012 for the first time, more than that is owed on credit cards or car loans.[53]

Patrick Callan, president of the Higher Education Policy Institute, a nonpartisan organization focused on higher education issues, has stated that it is difficult to single out any one reason for assessing blame concerning the decrease in college affordability and its impact on debt. Among the contributing factors are

- Budget cuts from state legislatures, and public higher education institutions are making up for much of it by raising tuition. In many instances, public colleges now get more money from tuition dollars than from the state; this is a reversal of the traditional setup.

- A gradual shift of responsibility for payment from government to students and their families.

- A "seller's market" in which colleges can raise tuition without repercussions. Students remain willing to pay, concluding that to forgo a college degree would be worse for them in the long term. Many colleges, especially the best ones, are still flooded with applications.

- Traditional universities are inefficient, with high fixed costs: lots of buildings, big campuses, and large faculties and staffs. Containing costs is usually not a priority. Most colleges are not in session year round, and most retain the traditional model of a college class, with a professor teaching a roomful of students.[54]

Some critics see another culprit in the rising cost of higher education, which is the wide availability of federal loans. Often called the Bennett hypothesis, for former education secretary William Bennett, the controversial argument is that federal financial aid allows schools to raise tuition because it shifts costs from schools to the government and the families who are borrowing.[55] Vice President Joe Biden essentially concurred that the hypothesis may have some value when, in a response to a question at a Twitter town hall in spring 2012, he stated that the trillion dollars of loan debt, the rising defaults on these loans, and the increasing tuition prices are all worth it as the price for increased access to a college degree. Refusing to pay this higher price would be against the national interest. Americans, at least for the short term, likely will continue to borrow for college as long as government-subsidized loans are available.[56]

The current student financial aid system has also been identified as part of the cause for the increased debt loads. Loan commitments grow with tuition increases; limiting loan commitments to some maximum amount would curb the desire and ability of colleges to raise tuition and fees. Additionally, most grant aid is disbursed without any reward for academic excellence; it was once estimated that for every Pell Grant recipient who graduates, almost two drop out.[57] Rather than disburse aid based only on financial need or academic achievement, grants should be awarded to students who have some need and who are likely to succeed because of that financial incentive. This would require students to make progress toward completing their degrees as an outcome, not just to maintain a certain grade-point average as an output, in order to continue receiving financial aid.[58]

Additionally, student debt has grown because, as tuition rates have risen and the costs shift more onto the students and their families as state support decreases, parents are struggling to make up the difference. Paula Knudson, dean of students at the University of Wisconsin-La Crosse, finds that as a result of this latest recession, more parents have lost jobs and seen their credit ratings and home equity plummet, rendering them less able to help out their children financially. "Families are hurting as the economy has hit home," as she notes. "Often times, students will end up taking out additional loans because the family can't help."[59] However, a 2012 white paper published by the nonprofit research group Institute for Higher Education Policy challenges the assumption that colleges are pricing themselves out of reach of many Americans who are, in turn, burying themselves deeper in debt to try to afford a postsecondary education. The authors, economists Sandy Baum and Saul Schwartz, reframe the discussion about higher education funding away from questions such as what colleges are charging, how much of students' and families' incomes they are spending to earn their degrees, and whether increasing numbers of students are accumulating large levels of student loan debt. They find that "although many students and families have very real difficulties paying for college, the perception of college affordability is often worse than the reality" because many people overestimate how much colleges actually charge and "do not understand the extent to which the net price they will actually pay is lower than the published price." Baum and Schwartz also argue that consumers and others should think of postsecondary education more as a long-term investment than as a good they consume. "Paying for college is usually framed in terms of the annual out-of-pocket cost for the few years the student is in school, even though the benefits are enjoyed over a longer period. The difference is not so much in the nature of the expenditure as in the way it is framed," they continue. "It is possible that education would seem more affordable if people thought about it as a fundamental need and as an investment to be paid for over time, much as they think of housing."[60]

As discussed earlier in this chapter, the national discussion is shifting from access to college to the rising cost of college education. Terry Hartle, a senior vice president at the American Council on Education (ACE), states that while some college students put a value on the traditional college experience of a physical campus and dorms, more college goers are looking at costs, wanting a good degree for less money and incurring less debt. He finds that, unlike the past in which every generation has paid for the bulk of the education costs of the generation that came behind it, through taxes or parental support, it is now the case that because the individual benefits from the education, it is expected that individuals will pay for their education on their own and out of future earnings.[61]

Solutions Offered to Increase Affordability

Students are not the only ones that have gone deeper into debt; so have colleges and universities as they build new residence halls and recreational facilities, and add other amenities that, in some cases, add little to learning outcomes. The debt taken on by colleges has risen 88 percent since 2001, to $307 billion. In the hindsight of a deep and lasting recession, decreasing state funds, increasing financially needy students, and competition to traditional campus-based education from the for-profit sector, it is not surprising that the current college cost model is unsustainable and needs to be transformed.[62] Leadership at higher education institutions, as a result of pressure from their numerous stakeholders and constituents, needs to make every effort to rein in cost increases. The good news is that there are many suggestions for increasing affordability in higher education.

Policies in higher education are a place to start. Colleges and universities should make an effort to reduce the number of wasted college credits. Many students take more than the necessary credits required for a bachelor's degree that thereby increases the cost of the degree, partly because of students changing majors and partly because colleges often refuse to accept credits from other institutions. However, one-third of students transfer from one college to another before earning a degree. Colleges make transferring credits difficult, often in the name of protecting academic quality.[63]

Another cost-saving policy change is consolidating campuses and eliminating governing boards. Public higher education systems in Georgia and New York have already combined campuses under a single president. Reforming accreditation policies will reduce institutional costs. Those critiquing and evaluating accreditation organizations view them as protective, run as voluntary associations of existing institutions that appear to be dedicated to keeping newcomers out. Acquiring and retaining accreditation is expensive: including faculty and staff time along with the opportunity cost, a five-figure price tag for an accreditation site visit is a reasonable cost estimate. This does not include considerable efforts spent to support ongoing assessment, processes for continuous improvement, and collecting the documentation required by accreditors prior to the physical site visit. Gaining regional accreditation status provides the institution with access to government financial aid—money not available to unaccredited organizations and individuals. As a result, competition is reduced because of the entry cost of gaining accreditation.[64]

The California state senate introduced legislation to limit executive raises at the California State University system within two years of a tuition increase or no increase in the allocation it receives from the state.[65] In response, the Board of Trustees of the California State University System approved a new policy in early 2012 that caps the amount of state dollars campuses can direct toward compensation for new presidents at 10 percent more than their predecessors received. This is a political more than financial policy since presidential compensation in the California State system, even for the highest paid presidents, does not amount to even 1 percent of any campus's budget.[66]

The cost of textbooks has become a popular media topic. The average college textbook in 2010 cost $104, a 24 percent increase from five years before. Between 1986 and 2004, textbook prices rose 186 percent, double the inflation rate. Students can expect to spend more than $1,100 a year on books.[67] While reducing the price of textbooks will not make up for the tuition increases, it would be a start.

Universities are considering several approaches to reduce the cost of textbooks substantially. One is for consortia of universities to purchase e-textbooks in bulk. This model ends the need for students to buy their own books each semester by requiring them to pay a course materials fee to the university, which would use the money to purchase e-textbooks at deeply discounted prices.[68] Another approach uses digital open-source textbooks; textbook material is housed in a cyberspace repository that is freely accessible to faculty and students. By clicking, cutting, copying, and composing, professors can customize their own textbooks. As an alternative, they can select a generic course book, free of copyright restrictions. Rice University's repository, created by Richard Baraniuk, an electrical engineering professor, houses 1,100 open textbooks. The e-textbooks are free, and students may purchase printed copies for less than $30.[69]

Students want to save money on course materials that often cost hundreds of dollars, and open-source textbooks—generally available free online or cheaply in print—accomplish that affordability goal. Free texts, however, are usually difficult to find and are often not peer-reviewed. The University of Minnesota launched an online catalog in 2012 of open-source books to make them easier to find. Further, the project will pay Minnesota professors $500 each time they post an evaluation of one of those books. The University is not creating any of the books, but just assembling the best of what has been published elsewhere. The material posted in the catalog must have an open license, be a complete book, have a print version, and be adoptable outside the author's institution. The project is meant to address two faculty critiques of open-source texts: they are hard to locate and they are of indeterminate quality.[70]

A growing number of institutions are increasing affordability by holding down the cost of tuition. One approach is to freeze tuition, a rare occurrence before the 2007 recession. According to the National Association of Independent Colleges and Universities, which represents more than 950 private colleges, 15 have announced tuition freezes for the 2012–2013 school year.[71] However, not every college has the financial resources to freeze tuition. Several are considering other strategies to reduce the tuition bill for students hard-pressed to afford college educations. For example, Duquesne University in Pittsburgh is reducing tuition by 50 percent for freshmen who enroll in the school of education in 2012. The price cut is good for four years for students who stay in the program. Jacksonville University in Florida, Medaille College in New York, and Midland University in Nebraska offer four-year "graduation guarantees" in which the school pays the additional tuition if a full-time student fails to graduate in four years. Beginning in fall 2012, Baldwin-Wallace College in Ohio will cover the extra cost no matter how long it takes to obtain a degree.[72] Kettering University in Michigan will offer a fixed-tuition guarantee for all undergraduate students beginning in 2012 as well as eliminate all academically related fees, removing the guesswork as to the students' cost to attend.[73]

High-achieving freshmen who enrolled at Seton Hall University by December 15, 2011, received a tuition discount of $21,000—or 66 percent—for the

2012–2013 school year. The same deal is being considered for freshmen enrolling in the 2013–2014 school year. According to a 2012 report released by Moody's Investors Service, of 257 of the higher education institutions whose creditworthiness it rates, nearly 54 percent of the private colleges increased their discount levels between the fall of 2010 and the fall of 2011 and 22 percent of the institutions increased the discount rate by more than 2 percent. For the same period, 42 percent of public universities increased their discount rates, reaching an average discount of 32.4 percent. Moody's finds that discounts "are becoming increasingly important in attracting and retaining students in light of growing pricing sensitivity."[74]

Another evolving approach is to offer a degree at a set cost. In 2011, Texas Governor Rick Perry challenged the state's university systems to develop a bachelor's degree that only costs $10,000. One program that begins in 2013 involves the Texas State University System. This degree opportunity is available to high school students who graduate with at least a 2.5 Grade Point Average (GPA) and complete at least 30 hours of college credit. Students then spend a year at the junior college before completing their degrees at Sul Ross State University Rio Grande College. The total cost is capped at $10,000 through deferred scholarships—worth $2,122—that students earn provided they maintain at least a 3.00 GPA and take 15 hours of classes each semester, allowing them to graduate in three years.[75]

The three-year degree, as proposed by the Texas State University system to meet the governor's request for a $10,000 bachelor degree, is another strategy to increase affordability, along with flexible degrees. Other schools, including Ashland University in Ohio, Thomas More College in Kentucky, the Wentworth Institute of Technology in Massachusetts, and Wesleyan University in Connecticut are introducing three-year bachelor's degree programs.[76] A three-year degree accelerates the pace of completion, eliminates most or all of that fourth-year tuition, and potentially puts the student in the job market a year early. Yet the three-year option has been slow to catch on, first, as some students now undertake a second or even a third major, convinced that this will make them look better to prospective graduate schools or employers. Second, public universities have not offered many three-year degrees.[77]

Flexible degrees commonly allow students to begin classes any time they want, work at their own pace, and earn credit for what they already know. Popular with for-profit institutions, Wisconsin was one of the first public higher education systems to offer a flexible degree beginning in 2012. The goal of the degree program is to make it cheaper and easier to earn a degree, particularly for the roughly 700,000 Wisconsin adults who have some college credits and want to advance in their career, but do not want to take classes on a physical campus. Wisconsin Governor Scott Walker touted the program as a way to increase employment, particularly by ensuring employers who post job openings are able to find qualified applicants, and to meet the need of state residents who do not have the time or money to attend a traditional college program. University of Wisconsin System President Kevin Reilly noted that the states that have a higher proportion of people with college degrees have higher per capita income and that 25.5 percent of Wisconsin's population has a bachelor's degree, two points less than the national average. The governor expects the flexible degree program to help the state close the skills gap at an affordable price.[78]

Another common strategy to reduce costs is to expand the use of technology in the classroom. The National Center for Academic Transformation, a nonprofit organization dedicated to the effective use of information technology to improve

student learning outcomes and reduce the cost of higher education (http://www
.thencat.org/), has redesigned courses on more than 200 campuses, cutting costs
by an average of 37 percent, by using instructional software to reduce burdens
on professors and frequent low-stakes online quizzes to gauge student progress.[79]
Computer grading is also suggested as a cost saver and may, in fact, increase reliability over humans.[80]

Oftentimes, technology in higher education is associated with the institution
offering more courses online. Online learning may resolve several issues that affect the costs of attending college. First, the online availability of courses may
become a means of enrolling more students into a course with less expenditures,
especially if the online version of a course replaces the need to use or even build
traditional physical classroom space, which can be costly. Second, online learning
allows students to take courses that may be harder to find or get into, because of
faculty reductions and reduced course availability, enabling students to maintain
their progress toward completion.[81] It has also been suggested that institutions
could eliminate their lowest quality courses and related costs, replacing them with
the best courses offered by other institutions through loose federations or formal
networks. This is the idea behind the New Paradigm Initiative, a group of 16 liberal arts colleges in the South that have joined together to offer online and hybrid
courses to students on any campus in the group.[82]

Other cost-saving ideas include the use of volunteer faculty to teach courses
and outsourcing grading. Using volunteers to teach classes would incur immediate implications concerning institutional accreditation. As to outsourcing, Western
Governors University hires graders for whom both the student and the faculty
member remain anonymous, and who are required to calibrate their work against
other graders to ensure consistency.[83]

While many of these ideas would reduce costs, some stakeholders expect states
to increase allocations to public institutions to decrease the tuition increases directly affecting affordability. An example is Michigan. Higher education is a concern for Business Leaders for Michigan (http://www.businessleadersformichigan
.com/) because its members know that to remain competitive they need an educated workforce and nearly 1 million more two-year or four-year graduates by
2025. The recession in Michigan has decreased state allocations to its public higher
education institutions. As a result, state residents have experienced rising tuition
rates that make it increasingly difficult for them to afford the education they need
to compete in the modern economy. While Michigan spends $1.1 billion a year on
public universities, North Carolina provides $2.5 billion. Not surprisingly, a public
university education in North Carolina is more affordable than it is in Michigan.
Michigan's Grand Valley State University President Thomas Haas noted that his
institution received $2,365 per student in state funding in fiscal year 2012 while
the University of North Carolina gets $11,000. According to the SHEEO, it costs
an average of $38,125 in tuition and fees to earn a four-year degree at a public
university in Michigan, compared with $18,877 in North Carolina, which, in turn,
produces more college graduates. As Michigan's economy recovers and a little
more money becomes available to state government, the business leaders expect
Michigan Governor Rick Snyder and the State Legislature to direct more money
to public universities.[84]

Michigan may want to follow the University of Central Arkansas's (UCA) lead
and conduct an economic impact study to learn how higher education institutions

contribute to local commerce, using a return on investment to demonstrate higher education's value. The UCA study applied financial language to a student, graduate, and local taxpayers' perceived pay-out in regard to the university and found that, for every dollar a student invests in UCA, he or she receives a cumulative $5.30 in higher future income over the course of a working career. Additionally, the study found that for every dollar of state tax money invested in UCA, an individual will see a cumulative return of $2.40 in the form of higher tax revenues and avoided social costs. Social costs, as defined by the study, include welfare, unemployment, and costs associated with crime. Furthermore, the study found that UCA students expand the state's economic base through higher incomes, while the businesses that employ them also become more productive through the students' added skills. Those benefits, together with associated multiplier effects, contribute an estimated $87.7 million in taxable income to the Arkansas economy each year.[85]

INSTITUTIONAL PRODUCTIVITY

Another outcomes issue concerns productivity and its application to improve institutional efficiencies and effectiveness. A multiplicity of stakeholders wants assurances that the personal and governmental investments in higher education are not wasted. Legislators and governors are increasingly demanding data proving that money given to colleges is well spent. States spend about 11 percent of their general-fund budgets subsidizing higher education. This productivity/accountability movement is driven as well by educational statistics, which reveal underperformance. Just over half of all freshmen entering four-year public colleges will earn a degree from that institution within six years, according to the Department of Education.[86] The message to higher education leaders is simple: "If you want more money, prove you deserve it."[87]

Institutional productivity is focused on improving efficiencies and effectiveness. This includes efficiencies and funds needed to administer and support the institution's infrastructure for day-to-day operations, and the effectiveness of the institution's outputs and outcomes. One of the most contentious productivity issues concerns the inputs, outputs, and outcomes of institutional faculty: how much they are paid, how many hours they work, and what they produce including research, publications, and graduates. An exchange through the media illustrates this point. Davis C. Levy, president of the education group at Cambridge Information Group, former president and director of the Corcoran Gallery and College of Art and Design, and a former chancellor of the New School University, contributed an opinion piece in *Washington Post* in March 2012. He points out that college costs have risen faster than inflation for three decades and, at roughly 25 percent of the average household's income, now strain the budgets of most middle-class families and impose an unprecedented debt burden on graduates. He contends that faculty compensation and faculty teaching schedules facilitate the rising costs for college. Faculty salaries are now equal to those of most upper-middle-class Americans working outside of higher education a minimum of 2,000 hours yearly (40 hours a week for 50 weeks) while, for the most part, faculty only work 9–15 hours per week for 30 weeks, spending only 360–450 hours per year in the classroom. And, he notes, this includes faculty at institutions whose primary mission is teaching, not research. He proposes that if higher education institutions were to adjust their schedules and semester structure so that teaching faculty clocked a 40-hour week (roughly 20 hours of class time and equal time spent on grading, preparation, and related duties) for 11 months, the enhanced efficiency could be the equivalent of a dramatic budget increase. Many colleges would not need tuition raises in the near future. The vacancies created by attrition would be filled by the existing faculty's expanded teaching loads—from 12 to 15 hours a week to 20, and from 30 weeks to 48, thereby increasing teachers' overall classroom impact by 113 percent to 167 percent.[88]

Jill Kronstadt, an associate professor of English at Montgomery College, wrote a rebuttal challenging Levy's reasoning, stating that using the average salary of a full professor to illustrate his argument was misleading because only about half of the teaching faculty at Montgomery College, the institution Levy used as an example, are full-time and, of them, only a few are full professors. She also contested Levy's interpretation of the faculty workload, saying that professors spend another 13–20 hours a week grading papers, with additional time spent on office hours and preparing for classes.[89] Marybeth Gasman, a professor of education at the University of Pennsylvania Graduate School of Education, wrote a response to Levy in *Chronicle of Higher Education*. As to Levy's assertion that faculty work no more than 15 hours a week for 30 weeks, she replies that, if a faculty member teaches three or four classes a semester, it might appear on the surface that she is working only 9–15 hours a week. However, that professor is also preparing the lectures and class activities for each of those courses. Most faculty members spend at least three hours preparing for each class each week. In addition, although a faculty member might list only two to three office hours on his syllabus, he is typically meeting with students outside of those office hours. As to research, she adds that more and more colleges and universities are requiring their faculty to conduct research—even those institutions with a teaching focus. Of course, the requirements are not at the level required by a research-focused institutions, but it means that even at teaching colleges, faculty are required to do research on top of their heavy teaching loads and tend to do their research at night, on the weekends, and during the 22 weeks, Levy claims, they have for vacations. She also points out that faculty members serve on countless committees and provide service throughout colleges and universities, interact with individual students, advise student groups, give pro bono lectures on campus, and are expected to present at conferences and to be active in national organizations.[90]

Critics see an education system in which some tenured professors only teach two or three classes a year, sometimes on obscure topics that mesh with their research but not necessarily with student needs. At the same time, more instruction is handled by part-time lecturers, who now make up at least 50 percent of the nation's higher education faculty, up from 30 percent in 1975, according to the AAUP.[91] However, in a working paper, two University of Wisconsin at Madison professors test the relative costs and benefits of popular student success measures, such as reducing student–faculty ratios. The goal of the study was to encourage colleges to base resource allocations decisions on actual effectiveness, rather than on what sounds good or what has usually been done. The researchers found that a college will improve its productivity by replacing adjuncts with full-time faculty more than by reducing class sizes and that replacing adjuncts with full-time faculty appears to produce more degrees per dollar than colleges do now on average.[92]

Contentiousness of faculty productivity is based on the conflicting application and the resultant accountability of input, output, and outcome metrics. States, as stakeholders, are beginning to resolve the conflict amid a national drive to assess more rigorously what, exactly, public universities are doing with their students, and their tax dollars. The governors of Texas and Florida have advocated for efforts to measure faculty productivity and to promote teaching at the expense of research stating, in effect, that instructors, lecturers, graduate students, and non-research faculty members subsidize the reduced teaching schedule of productive, research-active scholars.[93]

Nowhere has the productivity movement taken hold more firmly than in Texas. A law that took effect in 2010 requires public universities to post online the budget of each academic department, the curriculum vitae of each instructor, full descriptions and reading lists for each course, and student evaluations of each faculty member. The law, the first of its kind in the nation, requires the information to be accessible within three clicks of the college's homepage. In September 2010, the chancellor of the Texas A&M University system released a 265-page spreadsheet that amounted to a profit-and-loss statement for each faculty member, weighing annual salary against the number of classes and students that they teach, tuition generated, and research grants obtained. One metric divides a faculty member's salary by the number of students that he or she teaches. The range found some nontenured lecturers earn less than $100 for each student they instruct, while some professors are teaching such small classes that their compensation works out to more than $10,000—in a few cases, more than $20,000—per student.[94]

The concept of Texas's productivity spreadsheet came from a state university summit in May 2008, which suggested several reforms with a common theme: enable taxpayers to view and review outcomes at every public institution from their perspective. Other state examples include the Minnesota state college system, which has created an online accountability dashboard for each campus. Bright, gas-gauge-style graphics indicate how many students complete their degrees; how run-down (or up-to-date) facilities are; and how many graduates pass professional licensing exams. The California State University system, using data from outside sources, posts online the median starting and mid-career salaries for graduates of each campus, as well as their average student loan debt. F. King Alexander, president of California State University, Long Beach, states that this information helps students and their families derive a good estimate of their rate of return.[95]

Performance Funding

One means to increase institutional productivity has been application of performance funding by state government. In its simplest form, performance funding is a shift from rewarding higher education institutions for their increases in inputs such as enrollment, to that of valuing outcomes, such as student progress toward completion, and the number of degrees and credentials awarded. Typically, state appropriations to an institution are driven by enrollment with funding based on the number of students enrolled, and, as a result, colleges have a financial incentive to boost enrollment at the start of the term rather than make sure students successfully complete classes and earn degrees. Rewarding such performance with additional state funding as an incentive, such as degree completion, allows states to align their fiscal policies with statewide goals for workforce development and economic prosperity.[96]

Stakeholder attention to degree completion is directly related to the need for more college graduates who can find jobs, support the workplace needs for skills to compete globally successfully, and pay off the education-related personal debt accrued while attending college. Proponents of state-based performance funding include the Complete College America, a national nonprofit organization established in 2009 to increase educational attainment in the United States, the Lumina Foundation, Bill and Melinda Gates Foundation, the College Board, and the Education Commission of the States. The Obama administration has also recommended that states explore performance-based funding to improve college completion.[97] Julie Davis Bell, education group director for the National Conference of State Legislatures, stated that her group is a proponent of performance-based funding because the state legislators are frustrated by a lack of completions, excessive transfers, and students taking six or seven years to graduate.[98] The National Governors Association (NGA) also supports the use of performance based funding for higher education. "The post-secondary system is not often accountable to the real world," John Thomasian, director of the NGA's Washington-based Center for Best Practices said. He added, "Governors are recognizing we are investing in these systems. We need to make sure they are performing to the level we need them to."[99]

The approach to performance funding varies by state in its implementation:

- Goals generally consist of state or institutional priorities, such as increasing the number of college graduates and improving outcomes for low-income students;
- Measurement tracks campus outputs and progress toward these goals and typically reflect state priorities and campus mission; and
- Incentives in the form of financial or regulatory rewards are given to stimulate action on improving measurements to meet the goals. While incentives are often in the form of state appropriations, they can also consist of changes in campus autonomy, such as greater tuition-setting authority.

The three prevalent performance-based funding models that link state funding to campus outcomes are

1. Output-based systems, that is, funding formulas linking state funding and outputs, such as the number of students meeting credit milestones and completing college;
2. Performance contracts negotiated between states and institutions that serve as documents representing customized, campus-centric approaches to improving performance to achieve results; and
3. Performance set-asides, which are separate portions of state funding designed to improve campus performance by being awarded to institution campuses on a competitive nature based on campus results.[100]

The concept of linking institutional performance with state appropriations has been met with praise and skepticism from stakeholders in higher education, leading to its mixed success over the past 30 years. It was especially popular during the 1990s when abundant state coffers provided performance funds for colleges and universities.

As state revenues declined during the early half of the 2000s, many performance-based funding systems were considered extraneous and eliminated from state budgets. Between 1979 and 2007, 26 states enacted performance funding, while 14 abandoned their programs. Only a handful of states currently have performance funding, many of these link only a small portion of state funding to performance.[101] For the 2013 fiscal year, for its statewide competitive performance program, Illinois allocated $6.5 million, which is only half a percent of the state's $1.3 billion higher education budget. The Missouri plan recommends that no more than 3 percent of a school's budget should be awarded based on performance.[102] Indiana's 2013 fiscal year performance funding comprises 5 percent of the state's $1.2 billion higher education budget, or about $61 million. In fiscal year 2014, performance funding will make up 6 percent of the state allocation, rising to 7 percent for the 2015 fiscal year.[103]

The key advantages to performance-based funding have been

- Greater awareness of performance of college campuses that facilitates discussions about resource allocation, mission, and priorities;
- Improved delineation of state and institutional priorities by allowing governors and state legislatures to set priorities for public higher education and attach funding to them, shifting the focus from institutional needs to state priorities;
- Enhanced transparency and accountability by delineating key state and institutional priorities while allowing stakeholders to evaluate institutional performance; and
- Increased institutional productivity gains for campuses, leading to a better value for students, parents, and state residents.

By contrast, the key disadvantages include

- A limited portrait of university performance because institutions operate in a multifaceted, varied, and complex environment;
- Mission distortion if institutional leaders abandon, distort, or manipulate the university's core mission and responsibilities in order to inflate performance metrics or change inputs to influence outcomes; an example would be limiting access to students from disadvantaged backgrounds;
- Quality reduction because performance-based funding may not capture gains in student learning or skills acquired, in other words, reducing program rigor to achieve better outcomes;
- Lack of program support from faculty members and others who may object to market principles being integrated into academic operations, believing that evaluating performance based on a few metrics is antithetical to academic freedom and campus autonomy; and
- Increased inequality and instability because focusing on outcomes may hurt institutions that need the most help, especially those serving disadvantaged populations, because the lack of resources, not university efforts, may be the driver behind poor performance.[104]

The metrics proposed or used by the states implementing performance-based funding are usually centered on completion of degree programs and measurable progress toward completion. Examples of degree completion metrics include

- Total undergraduate degrees: total number of bachelor's degrees awarded by an institution in a given year;
- Credentials awarded: students completing an associate degree, certificate, or apprenticeship;
- Time-to-degree factor: total bachelor's degrees multiplied by the school's six-year graduation rate, to encourage timely completion;
- The percentage of students who graduate on time;
- Institutional mission factor: degrees divided by full-time student equivalents and multiplied by 100; this aggregate measure adjusts for part-time and transfer students, providing a common framework for comparing degree productivity among institutions with different missions and student bodies;
- Cost-to-degree factor: degrees weighted using cost-based weights to compensate for the varying costs associated with differing degree types;
- Critical fields factor: degrees awarded in fields identified as critical workforce needs, such as computer science, engineering, math, physics, nursing, allied health and teaching certificates for math and science; and
- At-risk factor: degrees awarded to students who meet the federal criteria for being at high risk for non-completion; indicators are being a federal Pell Grant recipient, part-time student, General Educational Development recipient, or entering higher education at age 20 or older.

Examples of metrics for the successful progress toward completion include

- Persistence factor: students who complete 30, 60, or 90 credit hour at the four-year institutions; 15, 30, and 45 credit hours at two-year institutions; and 30 and 60 credit hours at four-year, non-research institutions;
- College credit hour attainment: completion of first 15 college credits; first 30 college credits; and the core curriculum;
- Developmental education: completion of development education in math, reading, and writing;
- Gateway courses: completion of a first college-level math and college-level English course; and
- Transfers to a four-year institution: students transferring to a general academic institution after completing 15 hours of coursework.[105]

There are problems with performance-based funding. The research literature does not provide firm evidence that performance funding significantly increases rates of remedial completion, retention, and graduation. When performance claims are made, they are not based on data that control for other possible causes of changes in student outcomes beyond performance funding. In fact, the few multivariate quantitative analyses of the impacts of performance funding on institutional retention and graduate rates uniformly fail to find statistical positive results. The research literature also documents various unintended impacts of performance funding. They include increased costs for compliance, narrowing of institutional missions, grade inflation and lowering of academic standards, restrictions on student admissions, and diminished faculty voice in academic governance.[106] As an example, George Wasson, president of St. Louis Community College's Meramec campus, cautioned that performance-based funding could put too much emphasis on too few areas of performance, prompting schools to neglect things (e.g., community service activities) that do not have a direct impact on the state's preferred completion and progress measures.[107]

Additional research has found several common factors that played a role in the demise of performance funding, including

- A sharp drop in higher education funding;
- A lack of support by higher education institutions for the continuation of performance funding;
- The loss of key supporters of performance funding; and
- Weak support by the business community; and the establishment of performance funding through a budget proviso rather than a statute.[108]

Several of these factors surfaced during budget discussions in Louisiana. As the fiscal year 2013 higher education budget was being developed, Randy Moffett, the president of the University of Louisiana system, asked the state's top higher education board to scrap its method for divvying up dollars among the state's public colleges, saying the formula was inappropriate to use with budget cuts because it was designed when state funding for higher education was increasing by creating incentives for campuses to improve their performance. Performance funding was not designed to reduce funding for schools. The commissioner of higher education, Jim Purcell of the Board of Regents, showed no interest in suspending use of the performance-based system, even with budget cuts. Louisiana intends to split about $1 billion in state funding across the four individual university systems based on the state's formula, which considers graduation rates, skills training for high-need job areas and other benchmarks, rather than appropriating funds solely on student enrollment. Moffett said that the formula divisions do not recognize differences in campus roles and missions, do not account for the greater risks of cuts at small schools, and do not acknowledge differences in tuition rates compared with peer institutions. Purcell said credit hours are weighted in the formula based on the type of school and program to assure adequate and proper funding for schools. He said the formula includes a provision that seeks to protect schools with declining enrollments or a shrinking share of funds that he said kept many of the University of Louisiana System campuses from deeper cuts in the most recent budget cycle.[109]

TRANSPARENCY

An important outcomes issue concerns the transparency of information available from, and about, higher education institutions. The Higher Education Opportunity Act of 2008 has increased higher education transparency through its implementation of the College Affordability and Transparency Center at the Department of Education (http://collegecost.ed.gov/catc/Default.aspx), which includes the watch lists for the higher education institutions with the highest and lowest tuition as well as the highest and lowest net process. This cost information is helpful as potential college attendees begin the process of deciding to which college to apply for admission. However, costs are not the only information needed when choosing a college. Additional desirable information would include postgraduate annual earnings, assessment of student learning outcomes, and incurring education-related debt. Furthermore, genuine transparency is more than simple disclosure. The information should also be provided in a summary that is in an easy-to-read form that also discussed the implications of the information and in an understandable context, tailored to a specific and identified audience.[110]

As an example, the lifetime wage premium that accompanies a college degree has long been a selling point for postsecondary study; college graduates earn more than high school graduates. It is also known that not all colleges or majors are equal when it comes to postgraduate annual earnings. However, it is difficult, if not impossible, for consumers to get information about how much a graduate in a specific major from a particular university earns. This may be one of the best measures of the return on investment in higher education. With tuition prices continuing to increase, the most recent economy recovery being slow, and the media-generated publicity concerning the debt incurred, families are increasingly demanding more information about investing the money and time concerning the graduate's outcome from a degree as well as a specific institution.

It was reported in early 2012 that Virginia was creating a public database to give families access to median salaries for the graduates of hundreds of academic programs across every public institution and some private colleges in the state.[111] However, the implementation and availability of the database had stalled. In the meantime, consumers are turning to Payscale (www.payscale.com) to learn about median salaries arranged by occupation or salary by degree or major.

The availability of institutional assessment information on student learning outcomes appears to be as elusive as wage information of college graduates. A 2012 report on the availability of student learning outcome information found that colleges and universities are posting more information on their websites about whether their students are learning, but the report noted that most assessment information was on the web pages geared to internal audiences, such as the offices of institutional research and chief academic officers. Furthermore, assessment information is often hidden or not presented effectively in a form that prospective students and parents could understand and use to make their college choices.[112] The report also pointed out that

- Accreditation seems to matter in terms of encouraging transparency as those public institutions and institutions accredited since 2008 showed more assessment information than did independent institutions and institutions not recently accredited;

- Institutions are reporting more information about student learning on their websites than found previously, but the information appears to represent only a fraction of the assessment activity underway;

- Assessment results are most often found only on internal institutional research web pages not routinely searched by prospective students, parents, and other interested parties;

- Even when institutions share the results of student learning assessments, rarely is the information presented in an easy-to-read form or tailored to a specific audience;

- While more than half of all institutions posted the results of student learning outcomes assessment on their websites, only a third offered examples of how they are using results;

- Institutions participating in national transparency initiatives, particularly those in Voluntary System of Accountability and Transparency by Design, tended to make more assessment information public than did nonparticipating institutions; and

- None of the colleges and universities examined presented information about whether the assessment results led to improved student learning following changes in teaching and learning approaches or policies and other practices.[113]

Information concerning education-related debt is not as transparent as consumers want. The lack of readily accessible, accurate information about borrowing at specific colleges means that prospective students cannot factor the information in their decisions about whether to apply. It also makes it more difficult for colleges to compare their own students' indebtedness with that of students at other institutions—a process that could lead to changes in financial aid policy at colleges where students carry an abnormally high debt load. As a result, no one knows how much, on average, students borrow at every institution to attend college. That has possible consequences for students who cannot consider average debt early in the college selection process before they have applied for and received financial aid, and for colleges themselves, which do not have a complete and accurate way to compare themselves with their peers.[114]

The Obama administration is adding a "College Scorecard" to the Department of Education's College Affordability and Transparency Center to provide prospective students and their families a one-page picture of a college's tuition prices and financial aid policies for comparing colleges including

- Costs: average net price after grants and scholarships compared with other institutions;
- Graduation: percentage of full-time students who graduate within six years compared with other institutions;
- Student loan repayment: percentage of total loan amounts being repaid by former students compared with other institutions;
- Student loan debt: the average amount of loans students borrow to get a degree as compared with other institutions; and
- Earnings potential.[115]

While the federal government is trying to increase transparency through its watch lists and scorecards, institutions and the state public higher education systems are leading the effort to increase transparency as part of being accountable to its numerous stakeholders and constituencies to demonstrate productivity, efficiency, and impact. A good example is the dashboard found at the University of Texas system. This is a business intelligence system, a suite of web-based applications including an information delivery portal and reporting application for viewing, exploring, and sharing data related to performance across all mission areas of the University of Texas system and its institutions. The dashboard includes 10 core indicators that provide a high-level overview of system and institutional performance, including, for instance,

- Enrollment;
- Degrees awarded;
- Graduation rates;

- Post-graduation success (percentage of baccalaureate graduates who are employed and/or enrolled in graduate school);
- Average teaching load credits (faculty workload);
- Gross revenue from intellectual property (tech transfer);
- Delta cost: Education and related expenses (per degree and per FTE student); and
- Endowments.

The purpose of the dashboard is to

- Improve data access and transparency;
- Improve data consistency;
- Provide customized, user-built views of the data;
- Report data on metrics that assess productivity and impact;
- Support decision- and policy-making;
- Track progress toward institutional- and system-level goals; and
- Provide performance comparisons with relevant benchmarks and peer groups.[116]

Minnesota State colleges and universities also provide a set of state-based higher education system dashboards. The series of dashboards include financial, enrollment, facilities, licensure exams pass rates, student persistence and completion, and tuition and fees information. Results are shown for the system as whole, separately for four-year universities and two-year colleges, and for each institution. The website states that that system's board of trustees and system institutions use this information to improve their services to students and to the citizens of Minnesota.[117]

An example of a comprehensive institutional dashboard can be found at Texas A&M University. This dashboard, which sets a high bar for transparency and accountability, provides access to system, university, and college metrics, including, for instance,

- Undergraduate progression;
- Graduate progression;
- First-year retention rate of first-time college students;
- State appropriations per student FTE;
- Average tuition and fees for resident undergraduates;
- Total enrollment;
- Faculty demographics with teaching workload;
- Student demographics;
- Student degrees awarded;
- Staff demographics; and
- High-impact educational practices.[118]

Lastly, institutional expenditures are another area for which states are seeking transparency. The Arkansas legislature passed an act, during the 2011 session, requiring all state institutions of higher education to provide transparency and accountability for the people of Arkansas by making available expenditure data on a website operated by the state-supported institution, and eventually showing at least 10 years of information.[119] The University of Arkansas staff completed the OpenUA website to display its FY2012 expenditure records for its Fayetteville campus and other entities of the UA System whose accounting records are maintained at Fayetteville. They include the (Division of Agriculture) Agricultural Experiment Station, Arkansas Archeological Survey, Criminal Justice Institute, Clinton School of Public Service, and System Administration. Information includes university salaries by individuals and expenditures to vendors supporting university operations.[120]

QUALITY

A critical higher education outcome is quality, a topic that covers, among other things, courses and programs, the administration of the institution, and the components of the institution's infrastructure. For this chapter, quality is an outcome applied to the college graduate. What has the graduate learned, and what can they do as a result of their time and experiences in higher education? Furthermore, stakeholders expect accreditation organizations, as one of their primary responsibilities, to set high standards concerning the quality of the institution and its most important outcomes (graduates), ensuring credibility by holding institutions accountable for meeting the standards. However, stakeholders are critical of the self-regulating membership-driven accrediting process; they claim that accreditation organizations are self-protective of the member institutions they are charged with critically reviewing and evaluating.

The Need to Measure Quality

The state and federal higher education agendas in the past focused on making college as accessible as possible for anyone who wanted to attend, facilitating access with financial aid tools such as scholarships and loans. In late 2011, there was a shift on the federal level (see Chapter 3) toward making college more affordable, specifically tuition costs, as a means of increasing and ensuring accessibility. State government leaders have been focusing on tuition costs for public higher education institutions as well. Additionally, the shift in discussion concerning affordability has been accompanied with pressure to increase the number of graduates and the rate by which college students complete their degrees, and the ability for graduates to get jobs and contribute to the economy as well as to begin paying off their education-related personal debts. However, there is little mention about whether or not students learn anything, and what knowledge or skills are students acquiring in exchange for the tuition they pay? Richard Arum and Josipa Roksa tracked more than 2,300 undergraduates at 24 U.S. universities who took the CLA, an essay test that measures critical thinking, complex reasoning, and written expression. They found that 45 percent of the undergraduates did not significantly improve their reasoning or writing skills during the first two years of college. And after four years, 36 percent of the students did not improve significantly between their freshman and senior years. Further, college students spend about 12 hours a week studying, on average, and one-third of them report studying less than five hours per week. More than half the students said that they had not taken a single class in the semester before they were surveyed that required a total of 20 pages of writing. The main culprit for lack of academic progress of students, according to the authors, is a lack of rigor.[121]

In spring 2011, Arum and Roksa, joined by Esther Cho and Jeannie Kim, surveyed more than 900 of the students to follow up on their progress since graduation: whether they were employed, enrolled in graduate school, what their living arrangements were, and how civically engaged they were. Their report found a positive correlation between poor performance on the CLA—the test used to measure gains over the students' time in college—and unemployment, credit card debt, and the likelihood of living at home.[122] Graduates who scored in the bottom 20 percent on the CLA fared far more poorly on measures of employment and lifestyle when compared with those who scored in the top 20 percent. The students scoring in the bottom quintile were three times more likely than those in the top quintile to be unemployed (9.6 percent compared with 3.1 percent), twice as likely to be living at home with parents (35 percent compared with 18 percent), and significantly more likely to have amassed credit card debt (51 percent compared with 37 percent).[123]

Phil Gardner, director of research for the Collegiate Employment Research Institute at Michigan State University, was not surprised that students who scored low on the CLA are not doing as well in the job market. He finds that many students going through college today do not come out much different than when they started. They do not have a sense of why they are there, and they do not do the things that they need them to do in order to be employable. Students do not have to put as much effort into college as they used to and are not held accountable.[124] The findings from the Arun et al. reports are not good news for higher education institutions and systems trying to make the case for public financial support and lessening governmental oversight. Higher education leaders have long stated that the rising costs to attend college, the increasing debt students accrue, and the high dropout rates are unavoidable as a result of maintaining high academic standards when graduating students. Further, both of these studies surveyed only college graduates.[125]

Richard Hersch and Richard Keeling propose that, while national debate over the value of a college education has focused on the cost, the more critical issue is whether students are acquiring the skills that have long been associated with a college degree including critical thinking and analytical skills, mastery of their field of study, and the development of a moral perspective and sense of personal and social responsibility.[126] They argue that colleges and universities need to focus more urgently on identifying high-quality standards and assessments that measure and define student learning outcomes based on their missions, adopting and implementing assessment methods, and providing evidence through reports to stakeholders that they add value to a student's knowledge and skills while attending college.[127]

The Association of American Colleges and Universities launched the Liberal Education and America's Promise (LEAP) in 2005 as a national advocacy, campus action, and research initiative, which recognizes that college graduates need higher levels of learning and knowledge as well as strong intellectual and practical skills to navigate the demands of the 21st century successfully and responsibly. LEAP proposes that beginning in school, and continuing at successively higher levels across their college studies, students should prepare for 21st-century challenges by gaining these essential learning outcomes:

- Knowledge of human cultures and the physical and natural world
  - Through study in the sciences and mathematics, social sciences, humanities, histories, languages, and the arts and practiced extensively, across the curriculum, in the context of progressively more challenging problems, projects, and standards for performance
- Intellectual and practical skills, including
  - Inquiry and analysis
  - Critical and creative thinking
  - Written and oral communication
  - Quantitative literacy
  - Information literacy
  - Teamwork and problem-solving and practiced extensively, across the curriculum, in the context of progressively more challenging problems, projects, and standards for performance
- Personal and social responsibility, including
  - Civic knowledge and engagement—local and global
  - Intercultural knowledge and competence
  - Ethical reasoning and action
  - Foundations and skills for lifelong learning and anchored through active involvement with diverse communities and real-world challenges
- Integrative learning, including
  - Synthesis and advanced accomplishment across general and specialized studies and demonstrated through the application of knowledge, skills, and responsibilities to new settings and complex problems[128]

The New Leadership Alliance for Student Learning and Accountability, a coalition of higher education groups, released guidelines, in January 2012, which called for higher education institutions to gather evidence systematically of student learning and release the results. The guidelines do not explicitly advocate standardized tests as a means of gathering evidence. Guideline advocates argue that the point is not to measure how each college's students perform after four years, which depends heavily on the caliber of students it enrolls in the first place, but to see how much they improve along the way. For example, it is less about measuring knowledge of chemistry or literature than about harder-to-define skills like critical thinking and problem solving. The coalition acknowledges that many colleges use standardized tests that vary widely in what they test, how, and when. Examples of these tests include the ETS Proficiency Profile, from Educational Testing Service; the Collegiate Assessment of Academic Proficiency, produced by ACT; and the CLA, from the Council for Aid to Education, a research group. And the coalition recognizes that most institutions keep the results from standardized tests to themselves.[129]

Accreditation

A tension point concerning quality involves the role of accreditation organizations. The federal government has delegated much of the reviewing and/monitoring of quality in higher education to a group of accreditation organizations that are operated by the colleges and universities themselves as member institutions. To stakeholders (e.g., parents), accreditation organizations and their oversight processes should be responsible for ensuring, even guaranteeing, the high-quality outcomes of the institution and its graduates.

John C. Cavanaugh, chancellor of the Pennsylvania State System of Higher Education, states that to have legitimacy, accreditation must focus on the core issue of student learning. The institution or the state system should define what students are supposed to know, referred to as the Common Core, and should be able to demonstrate attainment of these outcomes at various levels of educational attainment. Accreditation organizations should take the defined outcomes, create accreditation standards and metrics that reflect the outcomes, and certify that students actually learn and that what they learn matches the stated objectives of a course, academic program, or specific set of objectives. In short, accreditation would transition from certifying that an institution claims that it is doing what it is supposed to do to certifying that students are learning and progressing in their acquisition of knowledge/competence.[130] As an example of implementation, Indiana's Commission for Higher Education has called for the state to implement a common core curriculum for colleges that requires at least 30 hours of credit in core subjects.[131]

An example of the transition to measuring student quality is the Western Association of Schools and Colleges (WASC), a regional accreditor. WASC approved a new set of policies in 2011 aimed at giving it a greater role in assuring the academic quality of its members. WASC will begin external reviews of the retention and graduation rates of the colleges it accredits and will post the action letters and team reports that result from its every-five-year reviews. The agency will also require all institutions to show that their graduates have achieved institutionally defined levels of proficiency in written and oral communication, quantitative skills, critical thinking, and information literacy, and to define the learning outcomes of each degree it offers.[132]

Some stakeholders view the voluntary accreditation process as a conflict of interest and an obstruction to competition in higher education, which would surely improve the effectiveness of the institution as well as the outcomes quality of its graduates. However, changes to the accreditation process are not easy to propose or implement. In 2010, Molly Corbett Broad, president of the ACE, told a group of accreditors and campus administrators that as pressure mounted on colleges to keep prices down and productivity up, higher education leaders had better reform the voluntary accreditation system that serves as the enterprise's quality control mechanism or change would be imposed from the federal government with potentially serious consequences for the current accrediting organizations' governance structure. Broad appointed a panel of college presidents and other higher education leaders to see how much of this reform could be agreed on by member institutions.[133]

The panel, whose own members were frequently at odds, focused its deliberations on reaching agreement about the principles that should guide a system of voluntary accreditation and a set of recommendations to better accomplish them.

The report of the ACE's National Task Force on Institutional Accreditation offers insights of just how fractious an issue accreditation is, and how difficult it might be to win agreement within higher education for the sort of major change that board suggested might be necessary or that politicians might eventually impose. Among the panel's recommendations to strengthen the current accreditation framework are the following:

- Keep rather than dismantle the regional structure through which the institutional accreditors operate;
- Maintain the link that makes accreditation the main gatekeeper for colleges to gain access to federal financial aid funds;
- Do not give the government more direct responsibility for some of the roles that now fall to accreditors;
- Increase the transparency of the accreditation process, in large part by making public more information about its outcomes;
- Focus more on student success and educational quality;
- Take stronger, quicker action against clearly failing institutions;
- Increase the involvement of college presidents and other senior officials in accreditation; and
- Impose differing levels of scrutiny and oversight on institutions with different profiles; a streamlined but in-depth review of data and documents for institutions with a sustained record of good performance, while less established or thriving institutions might require a comprehensive traditional review.[134]

A system to ensure the high quality of the institution and its educational outcomes is necessary to sustain/ensure the public good of higher education. If there is any doubt as to the credibility and effectiveness of the quality assurance system, then the current voluntary system of accreditation will be replaced with alternatives offered by the marketplace. For example, employers may begin to accept badges to certify an individual's skills and abilities. Belle S. Wheelan, president of the Commission on Colleges of the Southern Association of Colleges and Schools, a regional accrediting organization, stated in early 2012 that accreditors have not yet reviewed the issue of badges. She points out that college "used to indicate that not only did you have a skill set in a particular area, but that you gained a body of knowledge that made you a well-rounded person. People don't care about being well-rounded anymore, they just want to get a job."[135] StraighterLine announced that, in the fall of 2012, it was making versions of instruments that are most commonly used as institutional measures (ETS's Proficiency Profile and iSkills assessments, and the CAE's CLA) available to individuals. Individuals would, in turn, use the outcomes from these tests to prove their abilities to think critically, solve problems, or do the other things the tests measure. It is StraighterLine's plan that employers will eventually accept the outcomes of these tests in lieu of a college-awarded credential.[136] Of course, the most common alternative to the traditional higher education institution is the for-profit education provider, such as the University of Phoenix and Western Governors University.

Stakeholder pressure is increasing for the vast majority of traditional higher education institutions to demonstrate that they add value to student learning in light of rising tuition and other costs to attend college, increasing education-related personal debt, increasing times to graduate if students graduate at all, and anecdotes of graduates unable to find employment. Prospective parents and students want to know if their experience will be of high quality and rigorous enough to justify the cost and will result in sufficient financial rewards in the job market.[137]

CONCLUDING THOUGHTS

The pressures on higher education, particularly state-funded public higher education institutions, concerning aggregate and individual student outcomes, are numerous and focused. States are undertaking efforts to stem rising tuitions and thereby increase college accessibility and affordability, increase graduation rates and the number of students completing degrees, increase institutional productivity, and ensure that institutions are graduating high-quality individuals with the appropriate skills to sustain and grow the workplace in an increasingly competitive environment. The new normal is centered on generating more output with fewer input resources especially dollars and to hold institutions accountable for these outcomes in an understandable and transparent manner for a multiplicity of stakeholders with varying political, financial, social, and business agendas.

College completion, affordability, institutional productivity, transparency, and quality as outcomes affect both the individual and the institution. As well, the outcomes are interrelated, illustrating the complexity of higher education. For example,

- Increasing affordability may increase completion. A less expensive-to-attain college degree may increase completion rates.

- Increasing productivity may increase affordability. If institutional productivity increases, the year-after-year trend of rising college costs exceeding inflation rates may decrease thereby increasing individual affordability.

- Increasing productivity may decrease quality. Guided by the mantra of doing more with less, increasing class sizes to increase productivity by lowering the cost of teaching per student may decrease the quality in course delivery.

- Decreasing affordability may decrease completion. An example is the decline in the number of students attending summer sessions during 2012, the first year since 2008 in which summer Pell Grants were not available. Without the financial aid available, students may take longer to complete their degrees.[138] If a state and federal objective is to improve time-to-degree completion, then affordability is a direct outcome that must be considered.

- Decreasing transparency may decrease affordability. With little or outdated institutional, financial, and demographic information available concerning degree offerings and student success, parents and prospective students may make poor decisions concerning the appropriate institution to attend, resulting in accruing additional and unnecessary debt, not graduating, or transferring before graduation, thus delaying completion.

If the penultimate higher education outcome is a successful graduate with the values, knowledge, and skills to be productive in the workplace and a contributor to the good of society, then the traditional education system that fits all individual needs must be challenged. It may be that these individual outcomes are achieved in a traditional college setting and experience, while the asynchronous learning environment may be best for another individual, and yet another person may find the blending of the traditional and online to be the most rewarding as well as productive. Others seek to reduce higher learning to a quickly earned diploma and reduce higher education outcomes to a mere transaction as opposed to a life-changing transformation.[139] If the outcomes identified (college completion, affordability, institutional productivity, transparency, and quality) are to be realized by individuals and institutions, then planned and sufficiently supported approaches to attain the desired increases for each of these outcomes should be the goals of higher education in this millennium's second decade.

NOTES

1. U.S. Department of the Treasury, *New Report from Treasury, Education Departments: The Economic Case for Higher Education* (June 21, 2012), accessed July 12, 2012, http://www.treasury.gov/press-center/press-releases/Documents/The%20Economics%20of%20Higher%20Education_REPORT%20CLEAN.pdf.

2. Anthony Carnevale, Nicole Smith, and Jeff Strohl, *Help Wanted: Projections of Jobs and Education Requirements through 2018* (June 2010): 15, accessed July 10, 2012, http://www9.georgetown.edu/grad/gppi/hpi/cew/pdfs/HelpWanted.FullReport.pdf.

3. William J. Bennett, "Do We Need a Revolution in Higher Education?" *CNN* (June 13, 2014), accessed June 14, 2012, http://www.cnn.com/2012/06/13/opinion/bennett-higher-education/index.html.

4. George F. Will, "'Higher Education Bubble' Is about to Burst," *BostonHerald.com* (June 10, 2012), accessed June 18, 2012, http://bostonherald.com/news/opinion/op_ed/view.bg?articleid=1061137890.

5. Marcia Heroux Pounds, "Most Florida Jobs Don't Require Bachelor's Degree," *Sun Sentinel* (January 21, 2012), accessed May 26, 2012, http://articles.sun-sentinel.com/2012-01-21/business/fl-bachelor-degree-florida-20120116_1_job-fairs-annual-openings-fort-lauderdale-job.

6. Scott Carlson, "Outlook for Higher Education Remains Mixed, Moody's Says," *Chronicle of Higher Education* (January 23, 2012), accessed May 28, 2012, http://chronicle.com/article/outlook-for-higher-education/130434/.

7. Bill Fischer, "Disruption: Coming Soon to a University near You," *Forbes* (January 19, 2012), accessed May 28, 2012, http://www.forbes.com/sites/billfischer/2012/01/19/disruption-coming-soon-to-a-university-near-you/.

8. George L. Mehaffy, "Medieval Models, Agrarian Calendars, and 21st-Century Imperatives," *Teacher-Scholar: The Journal of the State Comprehensive University* 2, no. 1 (fall 2010): 6, 13.

9. Ibid., 6.

10. The Institute for a Competitive Workforce, *Leaders & Laggards: A State-by-State Report Card on Public Postsecondary Education* (June 2012), accessed July 4, 2012, http://icw.uschamber.com/reportcard/files/Leaders-and-Laggards-2012.pdf.

11. President Barack Obama, "Remarks by the President on the American Graduation Initiative" (July 14, 2009), accessed July 4, 2012, http://www.whitehouse.gov/the_press_office/Remarks-by-the-President-on-the-American-Graduation-Initiative-in-Warren-MI/.

12. The Lumina Foundation, "About Us," accessed July 4, 2012, http://www.luminafoundation.org/about_us/.

13. Paul Fain, "Not Quite Complete," *Inside Higher Ed* (March 27, 2012), accessed May 26, 2012, http://www.insidehighered.com/news/2012/03/27/lumina-reports-slow-progress-completion-push.

14. Larry Gordon, "More College Freshmen See Getting Good Job as Key Goal, Poll Finds," *Los Angeles Times* (January 26, 2012), accessed May 26, 2012, http://articles.latimes.com/2012/jan/26/local/la-me-0126-freshman-20120126.

15. Bill McCleery, "More Hoosiers Need College Degrees, Commission Says," *Indianapolis Star* (March 11, 2011), accessed May 26, 2012, http://www.courier-journal.com/article/20120310/news02/303100054/.

16. Amy Julia Harris, "Task Force Sets Plan to Increase College Completion," *Charlestown Gazette* (June 1, 2012), accessed June 13, 2012, http://wvgazette.com/News/201206010169.

17. Paul Fain, "Price of Success," *Inside Higher Ed* (January 16, 2012), accessed May 26, 2012, http://www.insidehighered.com/news/2012/01/16/improving-graduation-rates-job-one-city-colleges-chicago

18. Brian Maffly, "U. of Utah Graduation Rate Sags in Face of Poor College Readiness," *Salt Lake Tribune* (November 30, 2011), accessed May 26, 2012, http://archive.sltrib.com/article.php?id=18260596&itype=storyID.

19. Carla Rivera, "Keys to College Students' Success Often Overlooked, Report Says," *Los Angeles Times* (November 28, 2011), accessed May 26, 2012, http://articles.latimes.com/2011/nov/28/local/la-me-college-retention-20111129.

20. Sara Lipka, "Engineering Majors Hit the Books More Than Business Majors Do, Survey Finds," *Chronicle of Higher Education* (November 17, 2011), accessed May 26, 2012, http://chronicle.com/article/who-hits-the-books-more-study/129806/.

21. "Prior-Learning Assessment Confers a Semester's Worth of Credits, Study Finds," *Chronicle of Higher Education* (September 7, 2011), accessed July 17, 2012, http://chronicle.com/blogs/ticker/prior-learning-confers-a-semesters-worth-of-credits-study-says/36003.

22. Elise Young, "Another State to Assess Skills," *Inside Higher Ed* (July 9, 2012), accessed July 17, 2012, http://www.insidehighered.com/news/2012/07/09/wisconsin-seeks-competency-based-degree-program-without-help-western-governors.

23. Meagan Pant, "Public Colleges Told to Outline 3-Year Grad Plan," *Dayton Daily News* (July 9, 2012), accessed July 17, 2012, http://www.daytondailynews.com/news/public-colleges-told-to-outline-3-year-grad-plan-1402608.html.

24. Jeff Selingo, "MOOC's Aren't a Panacea, but That Doesn't Blunt Their Promise," *Chronicle of Higher Education* (July 11, 2012), accessed July 17, 2012, http://chronicle.com/blogs/next/2012/07/11/moocs-arent-a-panacea-but-that-doesnt-blunt-their-promise/.

25. Kevin Carey, "MIT Mints a Valuable New Form of Academic Currency," *Chronicle of Higher Education* (January 22, 2012), accessed May 28, 2012, http://chronicle.com/article/MIT-mints-a-valuable-new-form/130410/.

26. Kahn Academy, "About Khan Academy," accessed August 10, 2012, http://www.khanacademy.org/about.

27. Jeffrey R. Young, " 'Badges' Earned Online Pose Challenge to Traditional College Diplomas," *Chronicle of Higher Education* (January 8, 2012), accessed May 28, 2012, http://chronicle.com/article/badges-earned-online-pose/130241/.

28. Richard Vedder, "Beware: Alternative Certification is Coming," *Chronicle of Higher Education* (January 23, 2012), accessed May 28, 2012, http://chronicle.com/blogs/innovations/beware-alternative-certification-is-coming/31369.

29. Karin Fischer, "Crisis of Confidence Threatens Colleges," *Chronicle of Higher Education* (May 15, 2011), accessed May 28, 2012, http://chronicle.com/article/a-crisis-of-confidence/127530/.

30. Ibid.

31. Jennifer Ma and Sandy Baum, *Trends in College Pricing 2011* (Advocacy & Policy Center of the College Board 2011), accessed July 19, 2012, http://trends.collegeboard.org/sites/default/files/analysis-brief-trends-by-state-july-2012.pdf.

32. Audrey Williams June, "Professors Seek to Reframe Salary Debate," *Chronicle of Higher Education* (April 8, 2012), accessed May 29, 2012, http://chronicle.com/article/faculty-group-says/131432/.

33. Perry A. Zirkel and Jean Johnson, "Buying the Professor a BMW," *Inside Higher Ed* (December 16, 2011), accessed June 18, 2012, http://www.insidehighered.com/views/2011/12/16/essay-explores-rising-college-prices-and-whether-professors-benefit.

34. Mark C. Taylor, "How Competition Is Killing Higher Education," *Bloomberg* (May 17, 2012), accessed June 19, 2012, http://www.bloomberg.com/news/2012–05–17/competition-is-killing-higher-education-part-1-.html.

35. Neil deMause, "The Soaring Cost of College Has Multiple Causes and No Easy Solution," *Village Voice* (January 4, 2012), accessed June 18, 2012, http://www.villagevoice.com/2012–01–04/news/the-soaring-cost-of-college-has-multiple-causes-and-no-easy-solution/.

36. Perry A. Zirkel and Jean Johnson, "Buying the Professor a BMW," *Inside Higher Ed* (December 16, 2011), accessed June 18, 2012, http://www.insidehighered.com/views/2011/12/16/essay-explores-rising-college-prices-and-whether-professors-benefit.

37. deMause, "The Soaring Cost of College Has Multiple Causes and No Easy Solution."

38. Andrew Thomason, "12 Percent Increase in State Higher Education Funding Goes to Pensions," *Rock River Times* (January 25, 2012), accessed June 19, 2012, http://rockrivertimes.com/2012/01/25/12-percent-increase-in-state-higher-education-funding-goes-to-pensions/.

39. Eric Kelderman, "State and Local Spending on Higher Education Reached a New 25-Year Low in 2011," *Chronicle of Higher Education* (March 16, 2012), accessed June 18, 2012, http://chronicle.com/article/statelocal-spending-onr/131221/.

40. Catherine Rampell, "Where the Jobs Are, the Training May Not Be," *New York Times* (March 1, 2012), accessed June 18, 2012, http://www.nytimes.com/2012/03/02/business/dealbook/state-cutbacks-curb-training-in-jobs-critical-to-economy.html.

41. Doug Lederman, "State Support Slumps Again," *Inside Higher Ed* (January 23, 2012), accessed June 18, 2012, http://www.insidehighered.com/news/2012/01/23/state-funds-higher-education-fell-76-2011-12.

42. Eric Kelderman, "Federal Officials Penalize 2 States for College-Spending Cuts," *Chronicle of Higher Education* (March 14, 2012), accessed June 18, 2012, http://chronicle.com/article/us-penalizes-2-states-for/131150/.

43. Elise Young and Libby A. Nelson, "'Hall of Shame,' Year Two," *Inside Higher Ed* (June 13, 2012), accessed June 18, 2012, http://www.insidehighered.com/news/2012/06/13/education-department-focuses-state-role-cost-increases-annual-lists.

44. Editorial Board, "Editorial: Tuition Cost Shift Hurts State's Future," *StarTribune* (May 29, 2012), accessed June 16, 2012, http://www.startribune.com/opinion/editorials/155494335.html.

45. Kim Wilmath, "Tuition Hike Means USF Students Paying for Greater Share of Their Education Than State," *Tampa Bay Times* (April 20, 2012), accessed June 16, 2012, http://www.tampabay.com/news/education/college/tuition-hike-means-usf-students-paying-for-greater-share-of-their/1225959.

46. Rudi Keller, "Higher Education Leaders Describe Effect of State Cuts," *Columbia Daily Tribune* (February 2, 2012), accessed June 16, 2012, http://www.columbiatribune.com/news/2012/feb/02/higher-education-leaders-describe-effect-of-state/.

47. Tom Mortenson, "Reverse Tactic of Shifting Costs to Students," *Gazette* (March 18, 2012), accessed June 16, 2012, http://thegazette.com/2012/03/18/reverse-tactic-of-shifting-costs-to-students/.

48. Wilmath, "Tuition Hike Means USF Students Paying for Greater Share of Their Education Than State."

49. Rampell, "Where the Jobs Are, the Training May Not Be."

50. Motoko Rich, "Private Sector Gets Job Skills; Public Gets Bill," *New York Times* (January 7, 2012), accessed June 16, 2012, http://www.nytimes.com/2012/01/08/business/states-pay-to-train-workers-to-companies-benefit.html?pagewanted=all.

51. John Quinterno, *The Great Cost Shift: How Higher Education Cuts Undermine the Future Middle Class*, (2012): 1–3, accessed June 18, 2012, http://www.demos.org/sites/default/files/publications/thegreatcostshift_0.pdf.

52. Rampell, "Where the Jobs Are, the Training May Not Be."

53. Amanda Paulson, "Student Debt: What's Been Driving College Costs So High, Anyway?" *Christian Science Monitor* (June 6, 2012), accessed June 14, 2012, http://www.csmonitor.com/USA/Education/2012/0606/Student-debt-What-s-been-driving-college-costs-so-high-anyway.

54. Ibid.

55. Ibid.

56. Thomas K. Lindsay, "Fool for Higher Education," *Inside Higher Ed* (May 17, 2012), accessed June 15, 2012, http://www.insidehighered.com/views/2012/05/17/us-should-curtail-student-loans-help-taxpayers-and-students-essay.

57. Richard Vedder, "Obama, Higher-Education Costs, and Student Aid," *Chronicle of Higher Education* (January 30, 2012), accessed June 14, 2012, http://chronicle.com/blogs/innovations/obama-higher-education-costs-and-student-aid/31432.

58. Eric Kelderman, "State Student-Aid Grants Should Focus on Completion, Not Just Merit, Report Says," *Chronicle of Higher Education* (May 8, 2012), accessed June 14, 2012, http://chronicle.com/article/state-student-aid-grants/131821.

59. Patrick B. Anderson, "UW System Students Facing Greater Debt," *LaCrosse Tribune.com* (March 11, 2012), accessed June 15, 2012, http://lacrossetribune.com/news/local/uw-system-students-facing-greater-debt/article_4752d952–6b2d-11e1–8596–001871e3ce6c.html.

60. Doug Lederman, "College Isn't So Unaffordable," *Inside Higher Ed* (July 12, 2012), accessed July 20, 2012, http://www.insidehighered.com/news/2012/07/12/report-college-isnt-really-so-unaffordable.

61. Paulson, "Student Debt: What's Been Driving College Costs So High, Anyway?"

62. Jeff Selingo, "Fixing College" (Opinion Pages), *New York Times* (June 25, 2012), accessed June 27, 2012, http://www.nytimes.com/2012/06/26/opinion/fixing-college-through-lower-costs-and-better-technology.html?_r=1.

63. Ibid.

64. Daniel Jelski, "A Free College Education for All," *Forbes* (January 19, 2012), accessed June 16, 2012, http://www.forbes.com/sites/ccap/2012/01/19/a-free-college-education-for-all/.

65. Nanette Asimov, "Yee Bill Is 2nd Effort to Cap CSU Executive Pay," *SFGate* (January 14, 2012), accessed May 29, 2012, http://www.sfgate.com/cgi-bin/article.cgi?f=/c/a/2012/01/13/BAB71MPBCV.DTL#ixzz1wGRRsuIP.

66. Kevin Kiley, "A Cap on Pay (and Bad Press)," *Inside Higher Ed* (January 26, 2012), accessed May 29, 2012, http://www.insidehighered.com/news/2012/01/26/california-state-approves-cap-salary-increases-incoming-president.

67. George Skelton, "Let's Make Textbooks Affordable," *Los Angeles Times* (December 12, 2011), accessed June 16, 2012, http://articles.latimes.com/2011/dec/12/local/la-me-cap-textbooks-20111212.

68. Jeffrey R. Young, "5 Universities to Test Bulk-Purchasing of E-Textbooks in Bid to Rein in Costs," *Chronicle of Higher Education* (January 18, 2012), accessed June 16, 2012, http://chronicle.com/article/5-universities-to-test/130373.

69. Skelton, "Let's Make Textbooks Affordable."

70. Mitch Smith, "Textbook Alternative," *Inside Higher Ed* (May 10, 2012), accessed June 16, 2012, http://www.insidehighered.com/news/2012/05/10/university-minnesota-compiles-database-peer-reviewed-open-source-textbooks.

71. The group includes two well-known, selective schools, Mount Holyoke College and Sewanee, the University of the South. See Editorial Board, "Welcome Trend in College Tuition," *New York Times* (March 5, 2012), accessed June 16, 2012, http://www.nytimes.com/2012/03/06/opinion/welcome-trend-in-college-tuition.html.

72. Tony Pugh McClatchy, "Some Private Colleges Offering Deals for Students," *New Hampshire SentinelSource.com* (May 20, 2012), accessed June 19, 2012, http://www.sentinelsource.com/features/education/some-private-colleges-offering-deals-for-students/article_bdd10238–84d8–59d7–9e13–3e92823908e2.html.

73. Matt Roush, "Kettering Offers Fixed Tuition Guarantee for 10 Semesters," *CBS Detroit* (March 13, 2012), accessed June 16, 2012, http://detroit.cbslocal.com/2012/03/13/kettering-offers-fixed-tuition-guarantee-for-10-semesters/.

74. Lawrence Biemiller, "While Tuition Revenue Climbs, Discounts Do Too, Moody's Says," *Chronicle of Higher Education* (January 4, 2012), accessed June 16, 2012, http://chronicle.com/article/while-tuition-revenue-climbs/130210/.

75. Reeve Hamilton, "Texas State University System Has $10,000 Degree Plan," *Texas Tribune* (July 12, 2012), accessed July 20, 2012, http://www.texastribune.org/texas-education/higher-education/texas-state-university-system-unveils-10000-degree/.

76. Tony Pugh McClatchy, "Some Private Colleges Offering Deals for Students," *New Hampshire SentinelSource.com* (May 20, 2012), accessed June 19, 2012, http://www.sentinelsource.com/features/education/some-private-colleges-offering-deals-for-students/article_bdd10238–84d8–59d7–9e13–3e92823908e2.html.

77. Daniel de Vise, "New Momentum for the Three-Year Degree?" *Washington Post* (May 30, 2012), accessed June 16, 2012, http://www.washingtonpost.com/blogs/college-inc/post/new-momentum-for-the-three-year-degree/2012/05/30/gJQAh6801U_blog.html.

78. Matthew DeFour, "UW System to Offer New 'Flexible Degree' Program," *Wisconsin State Journal* (June 19, 2012), accessed June 20, 2012, http://host.madison.com/news/local/education/university/uw-system-to-offer-new-flexible-degree-program/article_a8b6ba54-ba1c-11e1-85a7-001a4bcf887a.html.

79. Selingo, "Fixing College."

80. Jelski, "A Free College Education for All."

81. Neil Nisperos, "Public Universities Expand Web Education Offerings," *Sun* (San Bernardino and the Inland Empire) (May 27, 2012), accessed June 18, 2012, http://www.sbsun.com/ci_20714014/public-universities-expand-web-education-offerings.

82. Selingo, "Fixing College."

83. Jelski, "A Free College Education for All."

84. Editorial Board, "Restore Public Funding of Universities," *Traverse City Record-Eagle* (May 19, 2012), accessed June 19, 2012, http://record-eagle.com/opinion/x1321933601/Restore-public-funding-of-universities/print.

85. Courtney Spradlin, "UCA, Higher Education Major Players in Local Economy," *thecabin.net* (March 3, 21012), accessed June 19, 2012, http://thecabin.net/news/local/2012-03-03/uca-higher-education-major-players-local-economy#.UQk0yh2Yu9E.

86. Stephanie Simon and Stephanie Banchero, "Putting a Price on Professors," *Wall Street Journal* (October 22, 2010), accessed May 26, 2012, http://online.wsj.com/article/SB10001424052748703735804575536322093520994.html.

87. Tim Barker, "Colleges to Prove Worth for State Funds," *stltoday.com* (April 17, 2012), accessed May 26, 2012, http://www.stltoday.com/news/local/education/colleges-to-prove-worth-for-state-funds/article_fc67a932-685c-5435-a2b6-133fd9deec95.html.

88. David C. Levy, "Do College Professors Work Hard Enough?" *Washington Post* (March 23, 2012), accessed May 29, 2012, http://www.washingtonpost.com/opinions/do-college-professors-work-hard-enough/2012/02/15/gIQAn058VS_story.html.

89. Kaustuv Basu, "And the Livin' Is Easy?" *Inside Higher Ed* (March 27, 2012), accessed May 29, 2012, http://www.insidehighered.com/news/2012/03/27/newspaper-op-ed-sets-debate-over-faculty-workload-and-faculty-bashing.

90. Marybeth Gasman, "Yes, Faculty Members Work Hard Enough!," *Chronicle of Higher Education* (March 30, 2012), accessed May 29, 2012, http://chronicle.com/blogs/innovations/yes-faculty-members-work-hard-enough/32070/.

91. Stephanie Simon and Stephanie Banchero, "Putting a Price on Professors," *Wall Street Journal* (October 22, 2010), accessed May 26, 2012, http://online.wsj.com/article/SB10001424052748703735804575536322093520994.html.

92. Jack Stripling, "Unconventional Wisdom," *Inside Higher Ed* (December 10, 2010), accessed May 26, 2012, http://www.insidehighered.com/news/2010/12/10/productivity.

93. Gary A. Olson, "How Not to Measure Faculty Productivity," *Chronicle of Higher Education* (December 7, 2011), accessed May 26, 2012, http://chronicle.com/article/how-not-to-measure-faculty/130015/.

94. Simon and Banchero, "Putting a Price on Professors."

95. Ibid.

96. Garrison Walters, "It's Not So Easy: The Completion Agenda and the States," *Liberal Education* 98, no. 1 (Winter 2012), accessed May 26, 2012, http://www.aacu.org/liberaleducation/le-wi12/walters.cfm.

97. Thomas L. Harnisch, *Performance-Based Funding: A Re-Emerging Strategy in Public Higher Education Financing* (June 2011): 2, accessed May 26, 2012, http://www.congressweb.com/aascu/docfiles/Performance_Funding_AASCU_June2011.pdf.

98. Barker, "Colleges to Prove Worth for State Funds."

99. Amanda J. Crawford, "Governors Call for Linking University Financing to Performance," *Bloomberg* (July 15, 2011), accessed on May 26, 2012, http://www.bloomberg.com/news/2011-07-15/u-s-governors-push-performance-based-support-for-colleges-1-.html.

100. Harnisch, *Performance-Based Funding*, 2.

101. Ibid., 3, 6.

102. Barker, "Colleges to Prove Worth for State Funds,"

103. Kevin Kiley, "Performance Anxiety," *Inside Higher Ed* (December 16, 2011), accessed May 26, 2012, http://www.insidehighered.com/news/2011/12/16/indiana-revamps-performance-funding-focusing-first-year-completion.

104. Harnisch, *Performance-Based Funding*, 6–8.

105. Reeve Hamilton, "Outcomes-Based Higher Ed Funding Plans Move Forward," *Texas Tribune* (March 20, 2012), accessed May 26, 2012, http://www.texastribune.org/texas-education/higher-education/outcomes-based-higher-ed-funding-plans-moving-forw/; Kevin Kiley, "Performance Anxiety," *Inside Higher Ed* (December 16, 2011), accessed May 26, 2012, http://www.insidehighered.com/news/2011/12/16/indiana-revamps-performance-funding-focusing-first-year-completion.

106. Kevin Dougherty and Vikash Reddy, *The Impacts of State Performance Funding Systems on Higher Education Institutions: Research Literature Review and Policy Recommendations* (December 2011): 43–44, accessed May 26, 2012, http://ccrc.tc.columbia.edu/DefaultFiles/SendFileToPublic.asp?ft=pdf&FilePath=c:\Websites\ccrc_tc_columbia_edu_documents\332_1004.pdf&fid=332_1004&aid=47&RID=1004&pf=Publication.asp?UID=1004.

107. Barker, "Colleges to Prove Worth for State Funds."

108. Kevin Dougherty and Rebecca Natow, *The Demise of Higher Education Performance Funding Systems in Three States* (May 2009), accessed on May 26, 2012, http://ccrc.tc.columbia.edu/DefaultFiles/SendFileToPublic.asp?ft=pdf&FilePath=c:\Websites\ccrc_tc_columbia_edu_documents\332_694.pdf&fid=332_694&aid=47&RID=694&pf=Publication.asp?UID=694.

109. Melinda Deslatte, "UL System Leader Urges Reworking of College Cuts," *Bloomberg Businessweek* (June 12, 2012), accessed June 13, 2012, http://www.businessweek.com/ap/2012-06/D9VBL3C80.htm.

110. Natasha A. Jankowski and Staci J. Provezis, *Making Student Learning Evidence Transparent: The State of the Art* (November 2011): 25, accessed May 26, 2012, http://www.learningoutcomesassessment.org/documents/TransparencyOfEvidence.pdf.

111. Jeff Selingo, "Taking Some of the Guesswork Out of the Value-of-College Question," *Chronicle of Higher Education* (February 20, 2012), accessed May 26, 2012, http://chronicle.com/blogs/next/2012/02/20/taking-some-of-the-guesswork-out-of-the-value-of-college-question/.

112. Collin Eaton, "Colleges' Data on Student Learning Remain Largely Inaccessible, Report Says," *Chronicle of Higher Education* (November 21, 2011), accessed May 26, 2012, http://chronicle.com/article/Colleges-data-on-students/129853/.

113. Natasha A. Jankowski and Staci J. Provezis, *Making Student Learning Evidence Transparent: The State of the Art* (November 2011), accessed May 26, 2012, http://www.learningoutcomesassessment.org/documents/TransparencyOfEvidence.pdf.

114. Libby A. Nelson, "What We Don't Know about Debt," *Inside Higher Ed* (May 18, 2012), accessed June 15, 2012, http://www.insidehighered.com/news/2012/05/18/what-we-dont-know-about-college-student-debt.

115. The White House, "College Scorecard," accessed July 15, 2012, http://www.whitehouse.gov/issues/education/scorecard.

116. The University of Texas System, "Welcome to the UT System Dashboard," accessed May 26, 2012, http://www.utsystem.edu/osm/dashboard/homepage.html.

117. Board of Trustees, Minnesota State Colleges and Universities, "Accountability Dashboard," accessed July 15, 2012, http://www.mnscu.edu/board/accountability/index.html.

118. Texas A&M University, "Measuring the Pursuit of Teaching, Research and Service Excellence," accessed July 15, 2012, https://accountability.tamu.edu/.

119. Lindsey Tugman, "University Expenditures Now Available Online," accessed July 15, 2012, http://www.todaysthv.com/news/story.aspx?storyid=216749.

120. University of Arkansas, "OpenUA," accessed July 15, 2012, http://openua.uark.edu/.

121. Jonathan Zimmerman, "Are College Students Learning?" *Los Angeles Times* (January 31, 2012), accessed May 26, 2012, http://articles.latimes.com/2012/jan/31/opinion/la-oe-zimmerman-are-college-students-learning-20120131. See also Richard Arum and Josipa Roksa, *Academically Adrift: Limited Learning on College Campuses* (Chicago: University of Chicago Press, 2010).

122. Richard Arum, Esther Cho, Jeannie Kim, and Josipa Roksa, *Documenting Uncertain Times: Postgraduate Transitions of the Academically Adrift Cohort* (New York: Social Science Research Council, 2012).

123. Dan Berrett, "'Adrift' in Adulthood: Students Who Struggled in College Find Life Harsher after Graduation," *Chronicle of Higher Education* (January 25, 2012), accessed May 26, 2012, http://chronicle.com/article/Adrift-inadulthood-/130444/; Allie Grasgreen, "Alumni Adrift," *Inside Higher Ed* (January 25, 2012), accessed May 26, 2012, http://www.insidehighered.com/news/2012/01/25/next-phase-academically-adrift-research-links-low-cla-scores-unemployment.

124. Grasgreen, "Alumni Adrift."

125. Kevin Carey, "'Academically Adrift': The News Gets Worse and Worse," *Chronicle of Higher Education* (February 12, 2012), accessed May 26, 2012, http://chronicle.com/article/academically-adrift-the/130743/.

126. Richard Hersch and Richard Keeling, *We're Losing Our Minds: Rethinking American Higher Education* (New York: Keeling and Associates, LLC, 2012); Julie Mack, "U.S. Colleges Put Low Priority on Student Learning, Say Authors of 'We're Losing Our Minds,'" *mlive.com* (May 20, 2012), accessed May 26, 2012, http://www.mlive.com/education/index.ssf/2012/05/us_colleges_put_low_priority_o.html.

127. Richard Kahlenberg, "A Better Way to Evaluate Colleges—and Improve Education?" *Chronicle of Higher Education* (April 8, 2012), accessed May 26, 2012, http://chronicle.com/blogs/innovations/a-better-way-to-evaluate-colleges-and-improve-education/32156.

128. The National Leadership Council for Liberal Education & America's Promise, *College Learning for the New Global Century* (2007), accessed May 26, 2012, http://www.aacu.org/leap/documents/GlobalCentury_final.pdf.

129. Richard Pérez-Peña, "Trying to Find a Measure for How Well Colleges Do," *New York Times* (April 7, 2012), accessed May 26, 2012, http://www.nytimes.com/2012/04/08/education/trying-to-find-a-measure-for-how-well-colleges-do.html.

130. John C. Cavanaugh, "Accreditation in an Era of Open Resources," *Inside Higher Ed* (December 14, 201), accessed May 26, 2012, http://www.insidehighered.com/views/2011/12/14/cavanaugh-essay-how-accreditation-must-change-era-open-resources.

131. McCleery, "More Hoosiers Need College Degrees, Commission Says."

132. Scott Jaschik, "Western Accreditor Adopts Reforms on Academic Quality," *Inside Higher Ed* (November 15, 2011), accessed May 26, 2012, http://www.insidehighered.com/quicktakes/2011/11/15/western-accreditor-adopts-reforms-academic-quality.

133. Doug Lederman, "ACE Panel Calls for Sustaining but Changing Regional Accreditation," *Inside Higher Ed* (June 7, 2012), accessed June 12, 2012, http://www.insidehighered.com/news/2012/06/07/ace-panel-calls-sustaining-changing-regional-accreditation.

134. Ibid.

135. Jeffrey R. Young, "'Badges' Earned Online Pose Challenge to Traditional College Diplomas," *Chronicle of Higher Education* (January 8, 2012), accessed May 28, 2012, http://chronicle.com/article/badges-earned-online-pose/130241/.

136. Doug Lederman, "Firms to Offer Standardized Tests to Individuals through StraighterLine," *Inside Higher Ed* (January 20, 2012), accessed June 16, 2012, http://www.insidehighered.com/quicktakes/2012/01/20/firms-offer-standardized-tests-individuals-through-straighterline.

137. Jeff Selingo, "The Value Gap," *Chronicle of Higher Education* (January 11, 2012), accessed May 28, 2012, http://chronicle.com/blogs/next/2012/01/11/the-value-gap/.

138. Libby A. Nelson, "A Summer without Pell," *Inside Higher Ed* (August 2, 2012), accessed August 4, 2012, http://www.insidehighered.com/news/2012/08/02/colleges-worry-about-elimination-summer-pell-grant.

139. Richard Guarasci, "The Crisis in Higher Education: How Civic Engagement Can Save Higher Education (Part I)," (June 27, 2012) *HuffPost*, accessed July 20, 2012, http://www.huffingtonpost.com/richard-guarasci/civic-engagement-programs_b_1630919.html.

5

OUTCOMES AND THE NATIONAL PARTY PLATFORMS IN THE 2012 PRESIDENTIAL ELECTION

Robert E. Dugan

Higher education outcomes impacting the individual and the institution (college completion, affordability, institutional productivity, transparency, and quality) are frequently discussed in the media and by a multiplicity of higher education stake-holders. As addressed in Chapter 3, the federal government's discussions, which in the past had focused on accessibility to college, have shifted to affordability and graduation as proxies for value, measured by successful career and job placement, as well as manageable levels of education-related debt. Discussion concerning individual student learning outcomes is far less prevalent. This chapter provides a brief review of the higher education outcomes discussed in the Republican and Democratic 2012 party platforms as approved at their respective conventions and are likely to point to the direction that the next president and Congress are likely to take.

Colleges and universities received specific attention in the Republican Party's 2012 platform; the party criticized them on several fronts. It alleged that political and scientific biases are found in college classrooms. Because debt-saddled graduates cannot find jobs owing to President Barack Obama's failed economic policies, the Republican platform called for changes to the student loan program and discussed its alternatives to traditional four-year colleges.[1] The Democratic Party's 2012 platform, on the other hand, was less detailed concerning higher education. It outlined the party's vision, which describes higher education as the "surest path to the middle class" and an economic necessity vital to national competitiveness. It also reviewed the administration's accomplishments since the president took office, while reasserting his goal that the United States would have the world's highest proportion of college graduates by 2020.[2] Both platforms stated that accessibility to college would be improved by increasing college affordability for students and their families. The means to realizing affordability, however, differs between the two parties.

THE PARTIES' GENERAL PERSPECTIVE
ON HIGHER EDUCATION

The Republican platform recognized that U.S. "universities, large and small, public or private, form the world's greatest assemblage of learning. They drive much of the research that keeps America competitive."[3] However, pages earlier, the platform document stated that since "1965 the federal government has spent $2 trillion on elementary and secondary education with no substantial improvement in academic achievement or high school graduation rates (which currently are 59 percent for African-American students and 63 percent for Hispanics)." Furthermore, college costs "are on an unsustainable trajectory, rising year by year far ahead of overall inflation. Nationwide, student loan debt now exceeds credit card debt, roughly $23,300 for each of the 35,000,000 debtors, taking years to pay off. Over 50 percent of recent college grads are unemployed or underemployed, working at jobs for which their expensive educations gave them no training."[4]

Representative Paul Ryan, confirmed by the convention as the Republican Party's vice presidential nominee, echoed the platform's text stating in his acceptance speech that this country's economic prosperity has been slowed by debt-burdened and unemployed college graduates.[5] Of the "millions of young Americans" who have graduated from college during the past four years, he said, "half of them can't find the work they studied for, or any work at all." Continuing he added, "College graduates should not have to live out their twenties in their childhood bedrooms, staring up at fading Obama posters and wondering when they can move out and get going with life."[6] A prominent solution offered in the platform was for higher education institutions "to get back to basics" with "programs directly related to job opportunities."[7]

The text in the Democratic platform addressed college affordability and student debt as issues directly related to college access, finding that our "work is far from done. A crisis this deep did not happen overnight and it won't be solved overnight. Too many parents sit around their kitchen tables at night after they've put their kids to bed, worrying about how they will make a mortgage payment or pay the rent, or how they will put their children through college."[8] In the months leading up to the convention, the issue of college affordability was often mentioned in the president's campaign speeches. The Democrat's platform highlighted President Obama's successes concerning college affordability over the past four years: ending the federal bank-based student loan program, doubling the federal investment in Pell Grant scholarships, creating the American Opportunity Tax Credit worth up to $10,000 over four years of college, and establishing more lenient policies for repaying federal student loans. The platform restated several of the points the president made in his State of the Union address in January 2012, including encouraging colleges to keep their costs down by reducing federal aid for those that do not, investing in colleges that keep tuition affordable and provide good value, doubling the number of work-study jobs available to students, and continuing to ensure that students have access to federal loans with reasonable interest rates.[9]

During the Democratic convention in Charlotte, NC, the mayor of Newark, NJ, Cory Booker, who was the chairman of the party's platform committee, reiterated the importance of education in his speech. "Our platform and our president state it clearly: our nation cannot continue to be the world's No. 1 economy if we aren't committed to being the world's No. 1 educator."[10]

THE PLATFORMS OFFER DIFFERENT SOLUTIONS

Solutions concerning college affordability were addressed by the adopted platforms or in campaign speeches. The Republicans view the consumer right of choice as an important part of their affordability solution.[11] Supporting consumer choice, the Republican platform stated that "efforts should be taken to provide families with greater transparency and the information they need to make prudent choices about a student's future: completion rates, repayment rates, future earnings, and other factors that may affect their decisions."[12] Governor Willard Mitt Romney suggested in campaign speeches that consumers should "shop around" for the "best education they can afford."[13] The Democratic platform chastised Governor Romney for this suggested solution and often referred to the remark as an example of the have-and-have-not economic differences between the two nominees.[14]

Student financial aid and debt were also addressed by the approved party platforms. The Republican platform was direct with its assessment: "federal student aid is on an unsustainable path."[15] This was clearly directed at two of the Obama's higher education financial aid policies concerning student lending and Pell Grants. In 2010, the Obama administration replaced banks with a direct federal loan program, making the government the prime lender for student loans and eliminating the federal subsidies the commercial lenders collected by acting as the middleman in the college loan process. The Republican platform supported ending the federal direct-loan program. "The federal government should not be in the business of originating student loans; however, it should serve as an insurance guarantor for the private sector as they offer loans to students. Private sector participation in student financing should be welcomed."[16]

With the savings generated from converting the student loan process from banks to the federal government, the Obama administration doubled funding available for Pell Grants and raised the amount of each award by more than 10 percent. The Pell Grant is the cornerstone of federal financial aid, and the Obama administration has resisted budget-cutting pressure by accepting several tradeoffs to preserve the maximum grant award of $5,550 as a budget priority. Those tradeoffs involved not only cuts to other federal financial aid programs, but also changes to the Pell Grant Program itself. Eligibility changes that took effect during the summer 2012 cut more than 100,000 students from the program, including some part-time students and those who have been enrolled for more than six semesters. Congress eliminated year-round Pell Grant funding; 2011 was the last time Pell Grants were available for summer semester enrollment at colleges and universities to students who are full-time in fall and spring semesters. Despite these tradeoffs, and particularly in recognition of the federal deficit, the Republican 2013 budget proposal created by Ryan as the chairman of the House Budget Committee would lower the income level at which students qualify for an automatic maximum Pell Grant, create a maximum income to be eligible for a grant, reduce the maximum grant award, and make students attending school less than half-time ineligible for grants.[17] An outcome of the Ryan budget plan would be to direct working class and financially needy students toward private loans.[18]

Pell Grants, however, might not be such an appealing target for federal budget reductions because the federal government spent $2.2 billion less on Pell Grants in the most recent fiscal year (which ended on July 1, 2012) compared with the previous year. The decrease in spending also occurred while the number of Pell recipients increased by 58,000. That means, more of the almost 9.7 million lower-income students who received the grants last year got smaller awards. One reason for that could be more students attending college part-time, because part-time enrollment status reduces Pell award amounts. Another probable cause for the decrease in expenditures is the elimination of the year-round, or summer, Pell Grant, which allowed students to qualify for two awards in a year.[19] Another higher education financial aid program is the Post-9/11 Veterans Education Assistance Improvements Act, also known as the Iraq/Afghanistan GI Bill. This affordability effort pays all public school in-state tuition and fees for veterans and creates a cap of $17,500 for those enrolled in a private or foreign school. The Iraq and Afghanistan Veterans of America, represented by Tom Tarantino, the group's chief policy officer and an Iraq War veteran, attended both party conventions to talk with party leaders and delegates about the future of the program. Given the country's bleak budget outlook, Tarantino said members fear possible cuts to the GI Bill. And while both platforms pledged to make good on government commitments to educational benefits earned by service members, Tarantino said that both parties may be tempted to cut the GI Bill because of the federal deficit.[20]

The burden of student loans is part of the Republican Party's broader economic narrative.[21] Ryan referred to student debt in his acceptance speech at the August Republican convention, and as mentioned earlier, Governor Romney has urged students to exercise their freedom of choice to seek the best deal they can and to shop around in campaign speeches. The Republican platform also addressed those in the federal civil service who fail to repay their student loans, stating that a "Republican Administration will make enforcement among its own employees a priority and, unlike the current Administration, will name to public office no one who has failed to meet their financial obligations to the government and fellow taxpayers."[22]

As a solution to the increasing education-related student debt, the Obama campaign launched a website with information about an income-based student loan repayment program, along with a calculator, which would be implemented in a second Obama administration (http://www.barackobama.com/education-calculator). The "Pay As You Earn" program caps monthly federal student loan repayment at 10 percent of monthly discretionary income, meaning that a student may choose the college they want to attend based on their career goals and not only the price of tuition. Families can know that as long as students make their payments on time, they will not owe more than they can reasonably afford each month.[23]

The Republican platform stated that new "models for acquiring advanced skills will be ever more important in the rapidly changing economy of the twenty-first century, especially in science, technology, engineering, and math." The plank found that "the status quo is not working" and that public policy should therefore advance "the affordability, innovation, and transparency needed to address all these challenges." The platform calls for "new systems of learning" to compete with traditional four-year colleges. That system centers on "expanded community colleges and technical institutions, private training schools, online universities, life-long learning, and work-based learning in the private sector." Additionally, the Republicans opposed efforts to regulate the for-profit colleges.[24]

The Democrats' platform also supported community colleges, calling "for additional partnerships between businesses and community colleges to train two million workers with the skills they need for good jobs waiting to be filled, and to support business-labor apprenticeship programs that provide skills and opportunity to thousands of Americans."[25] However, the Democratic platform singled out for-profit colleges for criticism. The Obama administration has sought to tighten rules for for-profit colleges, which, the administration says, squander federal student aid by poorly preparing students for well-paying jobs but leaving them with big debts.[26]

Additionally, the Democratic platform directly challenged the Republican nominee concerning military veterans and his support for proprietary education programs. "We Democrats have focused on making sure taxpayer dollars support high-quality education programs, but Mitt Romney is a staunch supporter of expensive, for-profit schools . . . that prey on our service members and veterans."[27] The platform referred to an executive order, signed by the president in April 2012, which directed the Department of Veterans Affairs to trademark the term "GI Bill," making it easier for the government to track down for-profit groups that deceptively use the term to enroll veterans. It also required the 6,000 colleges that participate in the GI Bill to provide veterans a "Know before You Owe" document that more transparently explains how much debt they will take on to complete their degree. It would also make it easier for cheated service members to register their complaints and for institutions that have been subject to repeated allegations of abuse to be kept off military installations.[28]

Two other planks related to higher education appeared in the Republican platform. Republicans expressed concern about a liberal "ideological bias" that is "deeply entrenched within the current university system." "Whatever the solution in private institutions may be," trustees at public institutions "have a responsibility to the public to ensure that their enormous investment is not abused for political indoctrination." It urged state officials to "ensure that our public colleges and universities be places of learning and the exchange of ideas, not zones of intellectual intolerance favoring the Left."[29] The Democratic Party platform was silent concerning ideological bias and higher education.

Both platforms proposed allowing more foreign students with American degrees to stay here to work. The Republicans found that the United States "can accelerate the process of restoring our domestic economy—and reclaiming this country's traditional position of dominance in international trade—by a policy of strategic immigration, granting more work visas to holders of advanced degrees in science, technology, engineering, and math from other nations. Highly educated immigrants can assist in creating new services and products. In the same way, foreign students who graduate from an American university with an advanced degree in science, technology, engineering, or math should be encouraged to remain here and contribute to economic prosperity and job creation. Highly skilled, English speaking, and integrated into their communities, they are too valuable a resource to lose. As in past generations, we should encourage the world's innovators and inventors to create our common future and their permanent homes here in the United States."[30] The Democratic Party plank, while somewhat shorter, came to the same conclusion: "And to make this country a destination for global talent and ingenuity, we won't deport deserving young people who are Americans in every way but on paper, and we will work to make it possible for foreign students earning advanced degrees in science, technology, engineering, and mathematics to stay and help create jobs here at home."[31]

CONCLUDING THOUGHTS

The parties' platforms expressed their respective ideology and vision supporting their long-held philosophies about the role of government in the lives of individuals. Text about higher education in the Republican Party's platform reflected a philosophy of the individual having choice to make decisions in the market of alternatives. Government has little to no role to play because higher education is a commodity, not a public good. For-profit education programs should be supported in the marketplace as alternatives to traditional four-year colleges, encouraged to thrive by removing federal regulations and unnecessary oversight that have hindered some private-sector education providers. Students should shop around for the best education they can afford and attend the program that may have a lower price where one can get a good education while reducing the need to accrue unmanageable education-related debt. Private banks and other lenders should be more involved in the financing and delivery of education, not less. The award available for Pell Grants will be reduced, if still available, because of the need to address the country's unsustainable federal debt. And do not expect the federal government to forgive the debt that one may assume in furthering their education.

Democrats viewed education as a public good in their platform; the way to upward mobility is through self-improvement, and the way to self-improvement is through education. The platform document focused on what President Obama had accomplished since 2009 and his long-range goals through 2020. Improvements were needed to student loan programs that were addressed when direct federal lending removed the middle man in the college loan process by making the government the prime lender for student loans. To make college more affordable and accessible so that all can attend the college of their choice rather than what they can minimally afford, the Democrats sought to protect the Pell Grants program from past and future budget reductions as well as continue to increase the individual award amounts. And to assist with the debt accrued by attending college, the Democrats wanted to improve the income-based repayment program for student loans whose debt is high relative to their incomes.

Both parties supported greater transparency about products and services to better inform the student's understanding of the costs of higher education as an outcome. And both parties favored enabling foreign students with American degrees to remain in the United States to help bolster the economy.

NOTES

1. Paul Fain, "Heard but Not Seen," *Inside Higher Ed* (August 30, 2012), accessed September 10, 2012, http://www.insidehighered.com/news/2012/08/30/student-debt-and-profit-issues-largely-absent-tampa.

2. Democratic National Committee, "Moving America Forward: 2012 Democratic National Platform," 36 (September 2012), accessed September 9, 2012, http://assets.dstatic.org/dnc-platform/2012-National-Platform.pdf.

3. Republican National Committee, "We Believe in America: 2012 Republican Party Platform," 37 (August 2012), accessed September 9, 2012, http://www.gop.com/wp-content/uploads/2012/08/2012GOPPlatform.pdf.

4. Ibid., 35, 37.

5. Michael Stratford, "On Republican Convention's Last Night, Fleeting Nods to Student Debt," *Chronicle of Higher Education* (August 31, 2012), accessed September 10, 2012, http://chronicle.com/blogs/decision2012/2012/08/31/on-republican-conventions-last-night-fleeting-nods-to-student-debt/.

6. Lee Gardner, "In Scant References to Higher Ed, Ryan Digs at Obama," *Chronicle of Higher Education* (August 30, 2012), accessed September 10, 2012, http://chronicle.com/blogs/decision2012/2012/08/30/in-scant-references-to-higher-ed-ryan-digs-at-obama/.

7. Republican National Committee, "We Believe in America," 37.

8. Democratic National Committee, "Moving America Forward," 33.

9. Ibid., 36–37.

10. Michael Stratford, "Aid for Students and Veterans Gets a Spotlight at Democrats' Convention," *Chronicle of Higher Education* (September 5, 2012), accessed September 10, 2012, http://chronicle.com/blogs/decision2012/2012/09/05/aid-for-students-and-veterans-gets-a-spotlight-at-democrats-convention/; Libby A. Nelson, "The Obama Agenda," *Inside Higher Ed* (September 4, 2012), accessed September 10, 2012, http://www.insidehighered.com/news/2012/09/04/higher-education-plays-role-democratic-platform.

11. Republican National Committee, "We Believe in America," 35.

12. Ibid., 37.

13. Nelson, "The Obama Agenda."

14. Stratford, "Democratic Platform Advocates More Higher Education and Attacks Romney on For-Profits."

15. Republican National Committee, "We Believe in America," 37.

16. Ibid.

17. Libby A. Nelson, "Pell Grants in the Spotlight," *Inside Higher Ed* (August 1, 2008), accessed September 9, 2012, http://www.insidehighered.com/news/2012/09/05/higher-ed-first-night-democratic-national-convention.

18. Scott Carlson, "Self-Sufficient, with a Hand from the Government," *Chronicle of Higher Education* (August 29, 2012), accessed September 10, 2012, http://chronicle.com/blogs/decision2012/2012/08/29/self-sufficient-with-a-hand-from-the-government/.

19. Paul Fain, "Pell Spending Levels Off," *Inside Higher Ed* (September 7, 2012), accessed September 10, 2012, http://www.insidehighered.com/news/2012/09/07/pell-spending-declines-despite-growth-grant-recipients.

20. Paul Fain, "Heard but Not Seen," *Inside Higher Ed* (August 30, 2012), accessed September 10, 2012, http://www.insidehighered.com/news/2012/08/30/student-debt-and-profit-issues-largely-absent-tampa.

21. Michael Stratford, "On Republican Convention's Last Night, Fleeting Nods to Student Debt," *Chronicle of Higher Education* (August 31, 2012), accessed September 10, 2012, http://chronicle.com/blogs/decision2012/2012/08/31/on-republican-conventions-last-night-fleeting-nods-to-student-debt/.

22. Republican National Committee, "We Believe in America," 28.

23. "Obama Campaign Emphasizes College Affordability," *Inside Higher Ed* (August 22, 2012), accessed September 10, 2012, http://www.insidehighered.com/quicktakes/2012/08/22/obama-campaign-emphasizes-college-affordability.

24. Republican National Committee, "We Believe in America," 37.

25. Democratic National Committee, "Moving America Forward," 37.

26. Michael Stratford, "Democratic Platform Advocates More Higher Education and Attacks Romney on For-Profits," *Chronicle of Higher Education* (September 4, 2012), accessed September 10, 2012, http://chronicle.com/blogs/decision2012/2012/09/04/democratic-platform-advocates-more-higher-ed-and-attacks-romney-on-for-profits/.

27. Democratic National Committee, "Moving America Forward," 38, 48.

28. Rosalind S. Helderman, "Obama Signs Executive Order to Protect Troops from For-Profit College Deceptive Practices," *Washington Post* (April 27, 2012), accessed September 22, 2012, http://www.washingtonpost.com/blogs/44/post/obama-signs-executive-order-to-protect-troops-from-for-profit-college-deceptive-practices/2012/04/27/.

29. Republican National Committee, "We Believe in America," 37.

30. Ibid., 7.

31. Democratic National Committee, "Moving America Forward," 37.

Section III

SELECTED ISSUES

6

INSTITUTIONAL EFFECTIVENESS

Peter Hernon

Effectiveness, a concept that has been the subject of multiple interpretations and definitions, has often been linked to the accomplishment of the organizational and, by extension, institutional mission statement. Such a definition assumes that the organization or institution has a coherent mission statement, with measurable components, and that those components are linked to a planning process (e.g., a strategic plan). Any such plan is assumed to contain an evaluation component and to require use of any evidence gathered to review the goals set, making adjustments as necessary. Evaluation is not an end in itself. In the case of assessment, one driving force for institutional effectiveness is accreditation organizations, whether they accredit institutions or programs, and another is governments, federal and state.

The Southern Association of Colleges and Schools Commission on Colleges (SACS-COC), in 1985, was one of the earliest higher education accreditation organizations to equate institutional effectiveness with institutional performance. The infusion of statements about institutional effectiveness into the 1998 SACS-COC *Criteria for Accreditation* was intended to ensure that the concept of institutional effectiveness would echo throughout institutional self-management.[1] Other institutional accreditation organizations, as well as a number of program accreditation organizations, have the same expectation, namely, that the assessment of student learning is a major component of institutional effectiveness.

The Middle States Commission characterizes institutional assessment in terms of "a four-step planning-assessment cycle:

1. Defining clearly articulated institutional and unit-level goals;
2. Implementing strategies to achieve those goals;
3. Assessing achievement of those goals; and
4. Using the results of these assessments to improve programs and services and inform planning and resource allocation decisions."[2]

Institutional effectiveness, as the Middle States Commission noted, "rests upon the contribution that each of the institution's programs and services makes toward achieving the goals of the institution as a whole."[3] This view of effectiveness applies to all programs and services offered by the institution, including those provided by the library, and expects those programs and services to help answer the following set of questions:

- "As an institutional community, how well are we collectively doing what we say we are doing?"
- "How do we support student learning, a fundamental aspect of institutional effectiveness?"[4]

Naturally, institutional effectiveness is not judged solely in terms of student learning. Institutional mission statements make other *promises* such as about the contribution of faculty and students to knowledge creation. Faculty productivity, for instance, becomes another component of broad-based effectiveness. However, this chapter focuses exclusively on the promise related to student learning.

For years, economic efficiency has been treated separately from effectiveness but as within the realm of evaluation. However, any discussion of institutional effectiveness must recognize that stakeholders connect effectiveness and efficiency, with efficiency defined in terms of college affordability. Today, institutions examine and report on both effectiveness and efficiency and need to relate them to the planning process. The purpose of this chapter is to provide an overview of both concepts from an assessment perspective.

INSTITUTIONAL EFFECTIVENESS PLAN

The purpose of an institutional effectiveness plan is, in part, to lay out the institutional approach to student learning, identify student learning outcomes, show what evidence will be gathered, and indicate how that evidence improves learning. Such a plan integrates program activities throughout the institution and reflects the commitment of faculty and central administration to improved learning. Different institutions are unlikely to produce exactly the same plan, as they differ in their stated missions. In general terms, the missions might be similar; however, they have different nuisances and emphases. Reviewing a number of such plans shows a focus on student outcomes and a tendency to define learning outcomes partly in terms of satisfaction. The metrics often highlighted are student retention and placement rates, and the level of graduate and employer satisfaction. Still, there might be coverage of student learning outcomes, and Chapter 9 summarizes what institutional self-studies reveal.

The plan may encourage institutions to publish annual placement and retention goals that address the retention and placement rates gathered from past institutional reports and the activities undertaken to meet related goals. The activities demonstrate the institution's commitment to maintaining and improving student retention and placement. Regarding student learning, the Middle States Commission plan recommends the inclusion of some type of "teaching-learning-assessment cycle," which includes "clearly articulated *learning* outcomes;" "courses, programs, and experiences that provide purposeful opportunities for students to achieve those learning outcomes;" assessment of student achievement of those learning goals; and use of the assessment results "to improve teaching and learning and inform planning and resource allocation decisions."[5]

The plan, in effect, addresses a key question that the Middle States Commission raises: "Is the institution fulfilling its mission and achieving its goals" related to student learning? Assessment processes covered in the plan "ensure that:

- Institutional and program-level goals are clear to the public, students, faculty, and staff.
- Institutional programs and resources are organized and coordinated to achieve institutional and program-level goals.
- The institution is indeed achieving its mission and goals.
- The institution is using assessment results to improve student learning and otherwise advance the institution."[6]

Colleges and universities might have an office of institutional effectiveness, or an office of institutional research might fulfill that role. Such an office might be responsible for developing and directing a comprehensive program of institutional effectiveness; providing information and analytic support to administrative decision makers to facilitate strategic planning, resource allocation, and enrollment and retention projections; and ensuring compliance with the expectations of reporting entities such as accreditation organizations.

EFFECTIVENESS

In a classic study that was published in 1978, Kim Cameron examined organizational, instead of institutional, effectiveness and its measurement in higher education. He shows a way to portray organizational effectiveness and notes that critical problems relate to the selection of appropriate criteria and indicators of effectiveness and the sources of those criteria and indicators. His approach to organizational effectiveness has application at the institutional level. In the appendix to his study, he offers a number of outputs that reflect nine dimensions of organizational effectiveness.[7] However, the list lacks the richness that accreditation organizations expect today, and these organizations have shaped how organizational effectiveness, in terms of student learning, is defined. Many of the outputs that Cameron reports (e.g., number of continuing education courses and percentage of students with jobs in the community) do not reflect learning. Still, the outputs reflect the progress in thinking about metrics from the 1970s to the second decade of the 21st century.

ECONOMIC EFFICIENCY

From the point of view of a number of stakeholders, the most important question related to accountability is "Why are higher education costs increasing at rates higher than costs of the U.S. economy as a whole?" It is insufficient to answer the question by ignoring the issue of affordability and focusing instead on the fact that college graduates earn considerably more than those with only high school diplomas, especially in the light of overwhelming student loan debt.[8] Research regarding costs in higher education has shown an association between costs and effectiveness, but they have not linked cost to both effectiveness and efficiency. Brett A. Powell, Diane S. Gilleland, and L. Carolyn Pearson believe that they found that linkage when they focused on degrees awarded. To make the connection, they examined two national datasets: Integrated Postsecondary Education Data System (IPEDS) and the National Study of Postsecondary Faculty (NSOPF). Their model examines institutional characteristics reflected in the Carnegie classification of institutions of higher education and IPEDS data, expenditures from IPEDS data, efficiency from NSOPF faculty variables, and effectiveness from IPEDS retention and graduation rates.[9] However, their model fails to factor in a wide array of student outcomes and any characterization of student learning outcomes. Thus, they advance the knowledge of costs but not the association with effectiveness as framed by accreditation organizations.

The Middle States Commission discusses cost-effective assessment processes that measure "student retention, graduation, transfer, and graduation rates" and factor in the institution's investment in terms of faculty and staff time.[10] Such assessment might also report on value as reflected in terms of tuition dollars that students and their families expend.

The literature on efficiency assessment is summarized in *Viewing Library Metrics from Different Perspectives*,[11] and this chapter does not repeat that discussion. Suffice it to say, the existing literature on the topic from the library perspective contains substantial weaknesses, namely, the writings focus on inputs and exclude outputs, ignore student outcomes and student learning outcomes, and assume that *all* students need and use the library as part of their undergraduate experience. Instead of focusing on library use from the organizational perspective, assessment encourages examination from the student perspective and looking at value, for instance, in terms of tuition monies: what have students received for their monies if they have availed themselves of library services.[12] Another way to calculate return on investment (ROI) is to focus on the following services: students studying in the library; borrowing books, e-books, DVDs, and laptops; students or faculty members asking reference questions or meeting with reference librarians for individual research consultations; students attending library instruction sessions; and students or faculty members using subscription databases when on and off-campus.[13]

As Randy L. Swing and Christopher S. Coogan point out, in their consideration of institutional ROI,

> There are no simple answers or even simple ways to calculate which expenditures should be counted, or not counted, as assessment costs. Certainly there are direct costs that are easy to identify and indirect costs, such as faculty time, that are far more difficult to estimate and that should be counted. Unfortunately, campuses may focus too much on controlling their spending on assessment without equal focus on maximizing the value of the benefits derived from assessment. The true cost of assessment is determined by comparing costs relative to benefits. As such, there are two opportunities for a campus to influence the cost of assessment; prudence in using campus resources (controlling expenditures), and assurance that assessment results produce tangible benefits (increasing the value). The application of basic cost accounting principles . . . and [the] application of cost-saving approaches can inform decisions about resource allocations in support of assessment.[14]

The challenge is to link student learning outcomes and their accomplishment with the ROI. This becomes more difficult to do when assessment focuses on more than the course level. For libraries with a commons (information, learning, or other), it should not be assumed that the mere existence of the commons and a high volume of student traffic translates into ROI from the perspective of the assessment of student learning. Facilitating collaboration among students, faculty, and others, with the aid of technology and library resources, is an important goal for libraries, but, by itself, it is unconnected to assessment—at the course level or higher.

Voluntary System of Accountability

The Voluntary System of Accountability® (VSA), developed in 2007 and sponsored by the Association of Public and Land-grant Universities and the Association of State Colleges and Universities, is an initiative by public four-year universities to provide comparable information on the undergraduate student experience to stakeholders through the College Portrait, http://www.collegeportraits.org/. One of the metrics available through the VSA is the Success and Progress Rate, which monitors student progress toward graduation. "Such a measure is increasingly valuable as the majority of students now attend more than one institution before they graduate."[15] The rate is generated using data from the National Student Clearinghouse for first-time, full-time students and full-time transfer students.[16] Combining financial data, such as the dollar amount of the tuition (both in and out-of-state), with the metric provides a richer view of efficiency.

Effectiveness beyond the course level might look at rubrics and link dollar amounts to student progress from one rubric level to the next. Clearly, there is now the opportunity to benchmark performance among institutions and to combine VSA data with other types of assessment measures such as electronic portfolio data and program review results.[17] However, such assessment must factor in the progressions stated in rubrics and not merely provide an overview of critical thinking, communication skills, or some other learning goal.

The results taken from the VSA and student learning goals measured in terms of progress in moving from the novice to the master level in any rubric can be reported and discussed across campus to determine appropriate strategies to improve learning outcomes in a program. Clearly, the linkage of effectiveness and efficiency with assessment is in its infancy. As research and conceptual thinking progress, two related questions are (1) "What metrics are acceptable to faculty, administrators, and institutional stakeholders?" and (2) "Can libraries contribute meaningfully to those metrics and demonstrate their contribution to student learning?" As librarians formulate their answer to the second question, they need to move beyond course-level assessment and be active in program- and institutional-level assessment.

METRICS FOR EFFECTIVENESS AND EFFICIENCY IN HIGHER EDUCATION

The National Governors Association (NGA), the bipartisan organization of governors, has a Center for Best Practices, pointing out that the nation's

> Governors recognize the need to adapt workforce and education policies to the reality of economic change in their states and communities. Access to postsecondary education, and the completion of degrees and certificates, gives individuals a wider array of basic skills including reading and writing, oral communications, mathematical reasoning, critical thinking and reasoning, problem solving, teamwork, interpersonal skills and an ability to learn continuously.[18]

The NGA recognizes the importance of institutions setting and accomplishing learning goals. Relevant student outcomes might focus on "pass rates in remedial and core courses," "advancement from remedial to credit-bearing courses," "transfer from a two-year institution to a four-year institution," and "credential attainment."[19] Further, the NGA encourages institutions of higher education to focus on the stakeholders listed in Figure 6.1 and the type of questions important to each stakeholder.

When the NGA reviewed the set of effectiveness and efficiency metrics under development from the Lumina Foundation, it was looking at quality assurance for student learning based on cost (affordability) and a nebulous concept of quality. In a paper for the foundation, William F. Massy, professor emeritus and former vice president for Business and Finance, Stanford University, discusses metrics associated with the number of "degrees and certificates awarded, enrollment in remedial education, success beyond remedial education, success in firstyear college courses, credit accumulation, and course completion" as effectiveness metrics. However, he views "graduation rates, transfer rates, time and credits to degree, and retention rates . . . [as] not proper measures of effectiveness, efficiency, or productivity."[20] What he fails to recognize is that viewing effectiveness exclusively in terms of faculty productivity does not address the accreditation perspective.

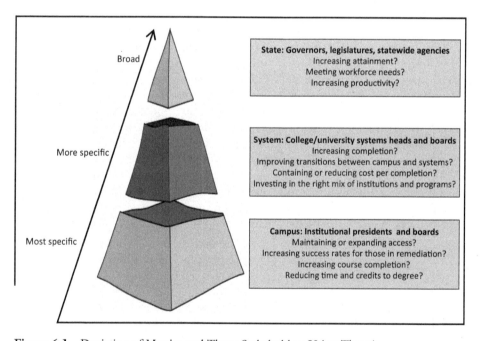

Figure 6.1   Depiction of Metrics and Those Stakeholders Using Them*

The NGA went on to examine metrics that would "help answer four policy questions:

1. To what extent are public higher education institutions meeting the state's need for an educated workforce and supporting progress toward longer term economic goals?
2. How many students at public institutions are graduating relative to total enrollment?
3. What is the return on states' and students' investment in public institutions in terms of completed certificates and degrees?
4. How can public institutions demonstrate that efficiency gains are being achieved without sacrificing student learning?"[21]

With answers to these questions, the nation's governors could use accountability metrics to make decisions regarding

- Budgeting. Governors can use performance metrics to help set parameters for budget requests and determine priorities for campus and higher education system requests.
- Funding. Governors can use performance metrics to allocate a portion of state funding to higher education institutions.
- Regulation. Governors can exempt campuses and educational systems from specific regulations, such as caps on tuition increases, purchasing and procurement rules, or financial or real estate management policies, in exchange for achievement on negotiated performance benchmarks.[22]

In an important report, *Complete to Compete*, the NGA divided metrics into two categories:

- "Progress metrics" such as enrollment and success in remedial education programs, success in first-year college courses (English and mathematics), and credit accumulation, retention rates, and course completion; and
- "Outcome metrics" such as degrees awarded annually, graduation rates, transfer rates, and time and credits toward degree.

Clearly, the focus is no longer on student learning outcomes. With the earlier types of metrics, it becomes easier to make comparisons across institutions and place monies where the governors deem most relevant.[23] As librarians review this report and the metrics provided, the question is "What role, if any, might libraries play directly in contributing to the statistics?" Perhaps librarians might better focus on student learning outcomes and contributing to affordability in that context.

Lumina Foundation for Education

As librarians focus on the question mentioned earlier, they (as well as anyone in academe) should follow the activities of the Lumina Foundation and its reports on higher education productivity, which refocus the discussion of metrics around productivity, which the foundation defines as

<u>educational resources used</u>
degrees produced

According to Social Program Evaluators and Consultants, Inc., which produced a consulting report for the foundation, productivity, as defined this way, "is a measure of how well inputs are utilized to produce output. It combines the concepts of effectiveness, efficiency and quality."[24] This definition therefore avoids any need to consider student learning outcomes or to focus on learning at all, and it calls into question the set of metrics commonly used. Only those metrics that track graduation rate become important, and institutional planning needs to focus on meeting or excelling on this one student outcome.[25] Equally as important, the definition of institutional effectiveness shifts to institutional productivity and does not consider student learning as a major component of institutional effectiveness.

CONCLUDING THOUGHTS

As this chapter has shown, there are two completing perspectives, one on institutional effectiveness and the other on institutional productivity. The former has broad support from accreditation organizations and the federal government, whereas the latter has support at the state level for application to public institutions. Institutional effectiveness emphasizes student outcomes more than it does student learning outcomes. It also concurs with institutional productivity on the importance of graduation rate. However, institutional productivity examines that rate within the context of "educational resources used," a term that returns libraries to the past and, for them, places greater emphases on inputs.

Higher education should represent "a challenging and rigorous experience for all students—for their benefit and society's as well. To do so, we in higher education must constantly monitor the quality of student learning and development, and use the results both to improve achievement and to demonstrate the value of our work to the public. We must not settle for anything else."[26] This conclusion of the Association of American Colleges & Universities and Council for Higher Education is laudable but ignores the pressures on faculty and programs to increase enrollments, contribute to the health of the institution, and aim for high student satisfaction as reflected in course evaluation. Viewing faculty productivity solely, or largely, in terms of how much they do (or in terms of the Lumina Foundation definition) presents a challenge to higher education and the different roles that faculty and librarians play. Student learning outcomes and the effectiveness of the learning process are becoming hostages to student outcomes and the desire to increase enrollments and create student and graduate contentment. Those in any doubt that this is the case should monitor reports coming from the Lumina Foundation.

NOTES

1. Southern Association of Colleges and Schools Commission on Colleges, *Criteria for Accreditation* (Decatur, GA: Southern Association of Colleges and Schools Commission on Colleges, 1998).

2. Middle States Commission on Higher Education, *Assessing Student Learning and Institutional Effectiveness: Understanding Middle States Expectations* (Philadelphia: Middle States Commission on Higher Education, 2005), 3. An assessment plan is part of planning

related to institutional effectiveness. For a relevant discussion, see Peggy L. Maki, who elaborates on the assessment cycle in *Assessing for Learning: Building a Sustainable Commitment across the Institution*, 2nd ed. (Sterling, VA: Stylus Publishing, 2010). For additional context to this chapter, see Michael F. Middaugh, *Planning and Assessment in Higher Education: Demonstrating Institutional Effectiveness* (San Francisco: Jossey-Bass 2010).

3. Middle States Commission on Higher Education, *Assessing Student Learning and Institutional Effectiveness.*

4. Ibid., 3.

5. Ibid., 3–4.

6. Ibid., 4.

7. Kim Cameron, "Measuring Organizational Effectiveness in Institutions of Higher Education," *Administrative Science Quarterly* 23, no. 4 (December 1978): 624–32.

8. Robert Longley, "College Degree Nearly Doubles Annual Earnings," *About.com US Government Info*, accessed June 21, 2012, http://usgovinfo.about.com/od/censusandstatistics/a/collegepays.htm.

9. Brett A. Powell, Diane S. Gilleland, and L. Carolyn Pearson, "Expenditures, Efficiency, and Effectiveness in U.S. Undergraduate Higher Education: A National Benchmark Model," *Journal of Higher Education* 83, no. 1 (January/February 2012): 103–27.

10. Middle States Commission on Higher Education, *Assessing Student Learning and Institutional Effectiveness*, 4.

11. Robert E. Dugan, Peter Hernon, and Danuta A. Nitecki, *Viewing Library Metrics from Different Perspectives* (Santa Barbara: Libraries Unlimited, 2009), 35–36.

12. University of West Florida Libraries, Office of the Dean of Libraries, "Student Return on Investment" (2012), accessed June 21, 2012, http://libguides.uwf.edu/content.php?pid=188487&sid=2183215.

13. University of West Florida Libraries, Office of the Dean of Libraries, "Institutional Return on Investment" (2012), accessed June 21, 2012, http://libguides.uwf.edu/content.php?pid=188487&sid=2184200.

14. Randy L. Swing, and Christopher S. Coogan, *Valuing Assessment: Cost-benefit Considerations*, NILOA Occasional Paper no. 5 (Urbana, IL: University of Illinois and Indiana University, National Institute for Learning Outcomes Assessment, 2010), accessed June 21, 2012, http://www.learningoutcomeassessment.org/occasionalpaperfive.htm.

15. Voluntary System of Accountability®, "About the College Portrait," accessed June 21, 2012, http://www.voluntarysystem.org/index.cfm?page=about_cp.

16. Voluntary System of Accountability®, "Methodology for Calculating the Success and Progress Rate," accessed June 21, 2012, http://www.voluntarysystem.org/docs/cp/SP_Methodology.pdf.

17. The ETS® Proficiency Profile is "one of three VSA-approved instruments for measuring student learning outcomes." It covers critical thinking and written communication for both freshmen and seniors. See "ETS® Proficiency Profile and the Voluntary System of Accountability (VSA)," accessed June 21, 2012, http://www.ets.org/proficiencyprofile/about/vsa; John W. Young, "Validity of the Measure of Academic Proficiency and Progress (MAPP)" (2007), accessed June 21, 2012, http://www.ets.org/s/mapp/pdf/5018.pdf.

18. National Governors Association, Center for Best Practices, "Access and Compliance" (2010), accessed June 21, 2012, http://www.nga.org/cms/home/nga-center-for-best-practices/center-issues/page-edu-issues/col2-content/main-content-list/access-and-completion.html.

19. National Governors Association, Center for Best Practices, "Issue Brief: Measuring Student Achievement at Postsecondary Institutions" (2009), accessed June 21, 2012, http://www.nga.org/files/live/sites/NGA/files/pdf/0911MEASURINGACHIEVEMENT.PDF.

20. William F. Massy, "Metrics for Efficiency and Effectiveness in Higher Education: Completing the Completion Agenda," paper produced with support from the Lumina

Foundation (n.d.), accessed June 22, 2012, http://www.sheeo.org/annualmeeting/Metrics%20for%20Efficiency%20and%20Effectiveness%20in%20Higher%20Education.pdf.

21. National Governors Association, Center for Best Practices, *Complete to Compete: From Information to Action: Revamping Higher Education Accountability Systems* (2011): 3, accessed June 22, 2012, http://www.nga.org/files/live/sites/NGA/files/pdf/1107C2CACTIONGUIDE.PDF.

22. Ibid.

23. Ibid., 6.

24. Social Program Evaluators and Consultants, Inc., *Year One Evaluation of Lumina Foundation's Higher Education Productivity Work in Seven States* (Detroit: Social Program Evaluators and Consultants, Inc, 2011), 1–2, accessed June 22, 2012, http://www.specassociates.org/docs/Year%20One%20Evaluation%20of%20Lumina%20Foundation's%20HE%20Productivity%20Work%20in%20Seven%20States.pdf.

25. Ibid., 22–24. See also Lumina Foundation for Education, *College Productivity: Four Steps to Finishing First* (Indianapolis: Lumina Foundation, n.d.), accessed June 22, 2012, http://www.luminafoundation.org/publications/Four_Steps_to_Finishing_First_in_Higher_Education.pdf.

26. Association of American Colleges & Universities and Council for Higher Education, "A Statement of Principles, Commitments to Action" (Washington, DC: Association of American Colleges & Universities and Council for Higher Education, 2009), 1.

APPENDIX

APPENDIX
Efficiency and Effectiveness Metrics

The recommended metrics in this guide focus on public postsecondary institutions. This is for three reasons:

1. States have primary responsibility for public colleges and universities (funding and regulation);
2. The vast majority of students attend public institutions; and
3. Performance data for non-public institutions (not-for-profit and for-profit) are not available to most states.

States should include data for non-public institutions on these metrics as available and appropriate.

The purpose of this appendix is to increase consistency and commonality across states in reporting benchmark data and measuring future progress in improving the collection and use of efficiency and effectiveness metrics for higher education accountability. NGA Center staff are available to assist states in the collection and analysis of the recommended metrics.

The most general data source for each metric is provided; however, states with unit record systems should use their system- or state-level data to construct the metrics for reporting purposes. States without unit record systems should request that colleges and universities provide data in a way that allows for aggregation at the state level and can be used to construct the metrics. These states should begin the process of adding the additional data elements to their unit record systems as soon as possible.

For policy questions 1–3, the proposed calculations are based on change over five years. Although this time span is not required, NGA Center recommends that states collect and report trend data for at least a three-year period, but preferably for five years or longer.

The National Center for Higher Education Management Systems (NCHEMS) has collected data for all 50 states on each of the efficiency and effectiveness metrics, as well as state-specific weights based on median earnings for the metrics found in policy question 3. Governors' staff should contact NGA Center to obtain their data and weights.

POLICY QUESTION 1:
To what extent are public institutions meeting the state's need for an educated workforce and supporting progress toward longer term policy goals?

Metric: **Certificates and Degrees Awarded Relative to the Number of Jobs Requiring a Postsecondary Degree**

Definition: Ratio of undergraduate degrees and certificates (of at least one year in expected length) awarded per 1,000 employed individuals with postsecondary degrees.

$$\left\{ \frac{\text{Number of undergraduate degrees and certificates awarded}}{\text{Number of employed individuals with a postsecondary degree}} \right\} * 1,000$$

Source: National Center for Education Statistics in the Integrated Postsecondary Education Data System (IPEDS) Completions and Enrollment Surveys and U.S. Census Bureau in the American Community Survey (Public Use Microdata Samples).

Metric: **Certificates and Degrees Awarded Relative to the Number of Adults in the State with No College Credential**

Definition: Ratio of undergraduate degrees and certificates (of at least one year in expected length) awarded per 1,000 18–44 year-olds with no postsecondary degree.

$$\left\{ \frac{\text{Number of undergraduate degrees and certificates awarded}}{\text{Number of adults in state with no postsecondary degree or certificate}} \right\} \begin{array}{c} * \\ 1,000 \end{array}$$

Source: National Center for Education Statistics in the Integrated Postsecondary Education Data System (IPEDS) Completions and Enrollment Surveys and U.S. Census Bureau in the American Community Survey (Public Use Microdata Samples).

POLICY QUESTION 2:

How many students at public institutions are graduating relative to the overall student population?

Metric: **Certificate and Degree Completions per 100 Students Enrolled**

Definition: Ratio of undergraduate degrees and certificates (of at least one year in expected length) awarded per 100 full-time-equivalent (FTE) undergraduate students.

$$\left\{ \frac{\text{Number of undergraduate degrees and certificates awarded}}{\text{Number of full-time-equivalent undergraduate students}} \right\} \begin{array}{c} * \\ 100 \end{array}$$

Source: National Center for Education Statistics in the Integrated Postsecondary Education Data System (IPEDS) Completions and Enrollment Surveys. Individual year data for this metric is also available on the NCHEMS data dashboard website, www.higheredinfo.org.

POLICY QUESTION 3:

What is the return on the state and student investment in public institutions in terms of certificate and degree completion?

Metric: **Certificate and Degree Completions (Weighted by Field) per $100,000 of State Appropriations and Net Tuition Revenues**

Definition: Ratio of undergraduate degrees and certificates (of at least one year in expected length) awarded per $100,000 of state and local appropriations and tuition and fee revenue, weighted according to median earnings of graduates by degree level (e.g., certificate, associate's, and bachelor's) and field (e.g., science, technology, engineering, math [STEM]; health; and other).

$$\left\{ \frac{\text{Number of degrees and certificates awarded}}{\text{State/local appropriations and net tuition revenue}} \right\} \begin{array}{c} * \\ 100,000 \end{array}$$

Source: National Center for Education Statistics in the Integrated Postsecondary Education Data System (IPEDS) Completions and Finance Surveys and U.S. Census Bureau in the American Community Survey (Public Use Microdata Samples). States may find single year data for the revenue metric on the NCHEMS data dashboard website, www.higheredinfo.org.

Metric: **Certificate and Degree Completions (Weighted by Field) per $100,000 of Education and Related Spending by Institutions**

Definition: Ratio of undergraduate degrees and certificates (of at least one year in expected length) awarded per $100,000 of education and related spending (see below for definition), weighted according to median earnings of graduates by degree level (e.g., certificate, associate's, and bachelor's) and field (e.g., science, technology, engineering, and math [STEM]; health; and other).

$$\left\{ \frac{\text{Number of degrees and certificates awarded}}{\text{Education and related spending}} \right\} \quad {}^{*}_{100,000}$$

Source: National Center for Education Statistics in the Integrated Postsecondary Education Data System (IPEDS) Completions and Finance Surveys and U.S. Census Bureau in the American Community Survey (Public Use Microdata Samples).

Notes on collection and reporting:

Education and related (E&R) spending is defined as the full cost of instruction and student services, plus the portion of institutional support and maintenance assigned to instruction.

The denominator for each metric should be adjusted using an appropriate deflator and weighted according to the median earnings in the state employment market by degree level (e.g., certificate of at least one year in length, associate's, and bachelor's) and field (e.g., STEM, health, and other). Each weight is indexed to the bachelor's degree median earnings in the state and is multiplied by the number of awards in the corresponding degree level and field. For example:

Degree Level	Median Earnings	Indexed to Bachelor's Degrees	Awards	Weighted Awards
Certificates	$20,589	0.56	0	0
Certificate STEM	$45,554	1.24	0	0
Certificate Health	$26,396	0.72	0	0
Associate's	$30,552	0.83	121	101
Associate's STEM	$51,737	1.41	11	16
Associate's Health	$42,234	1.15	0	0
Bachelor's	$36,662	1.00	1,085	1,085
Bachelor's STEM	$63,351	1.73	200	346
Bachelor's Health	$52,793	1.44	145	209
TOTAL			1,562	1,757

Finally, it should be noted that the metrics for policy question 3 cover graduate and professional credentials, but the metrics for policy questions 1 and 2 do not. This has been done for the following reasons:

- Recent workforce projections indicate that states' most acute needs for additional post–high school credentials are at the undergraduate level. This does not preclude states from including graduate and professional credentials in their calculations for metrics related to policy questions 1 and 2.

- Collection and reporting methods for revenues and expenditures do not allow for the separation of undergraduate, graduate, and professional programs, necessitating their inclusion in the completion component calculation for the policy question 3 metrics.

POLICY QUESTION 4:

How can public institutions demonstrate that gains in efficiency are not achieved at the expense of student learning?

Direct Measures of Learning

Skill Assessments

Purpose: Measure an institution's value-added contribution to student knowledge.

Source: Collegiate Assessment of Academic Proficiency (CAAP), Collegiate Learning Assessment (CLA), or Measure of Academic Proficiency and Progress (MAPP). All three instruments are approved learning outcomes measures for the Voluntary System of Accountability.

Licensure Exams

Purpose: Determine whether students graduating from particular fields, institutions, or sectors pass licensure exams required to practice in a specified field (i.e., nursing).

Source: States require different exams based on the specified profession. Data are available from the respective professional associations that require certification.

Degree Qualifications Framework

Purpose: Provide a framework within which states can monitor the expectations for degrees in various fields of study.

Source: Lumina Foundation for Education, available at: www.luminafoundation.org/publications/The_Degree_Qualifications_Profile.pdf.

Indirect Measures of Learning

Acceptance Rates for Graduate Education

Purpose: Determine whether students graduating from particular fields, institutions, or sectors are accepted in graduate programs.

Source: Institutions.

Employer and Alumni Surveys

Purpose: Determine the satisfaction of alumni with respect to education received at their respective institutions and the employer satisfaction regarding the skill levels of students who graduated from particular institutions.

Source: Employer and alumni surveys conducted by colleges and universities.

Placement Rates for Recent Graduates

Purpose: Determine whether students graduating from particular fields, institutions, or sectors are employed within a certain timeframe.

Source: State workforce data, such as unemployment insurance wage records, matched against postsecondary completion records.

Measures of the Learning Environment

Student Surveys

Purpose: Gauge presence of institutional practices and student behaviors that are associated with student learning and retention.

Source: National Survey of Student Engagement (NSSE) for four-year institutions or Community College Survey of Student Engagement (CCSSE) for two-year institutions.

Academic Audits

Purpose: Evaluate how institutions ensure and improve educational quality, particularly at the undergraduate level. The process includes an institutional self-study, followed several months later by a visit from an external audit team. The process is currently in place at institutions in Australia, Hong Kong, and **Tennessee**.

Source: For additional information on the audit process and rationale, please consult William Massy's paper Metrics for Efficiency and Effectiveness in Higher Education: Completing the Completion Agenda, available at **web1.millercenter.org/ conferences/papers/conf_2010_1206_massy.pdf**.

Other Metrics to Consult

Workforce Projections

Definition: Education requirements relative to forecasted job growth.

Source: Georgetown University's Center on Education and the Workforce produced projections for all 50 states. They can be found at **cew.georgetown.edu/jobs2018/states**. Data also can be obtained from the U.S. Department of Labor, Bureau of Labor Statistics, Employment Projections Program.

Credentials Awarded

Definition: Annual number of certificates of one year or greater in length, associate's degrees, and bachelor's degrees awarded, disaggregated by age group, gender, race/ethnicity, Pell Grant status (at any time), remedial status, and discipline.

Source: State longitudinal data systems.

Educational Attainment

Definition: The percentage of the population that has attained different educational levels (e.g., less than a high school graduate, high school graduate, some college, associate's degree or higher), disaggregated by racial/ethnic subgroups.

Source: U.S. Census Bureau in the American Community Survey (Public Use Microdata Samples).Additional data are available from the National Center on Higher Education Management Systems (NCHEMS) data dashboard website, **www.higheredinfo.org**.

Student Migration

Definition: Change over time in the ratio of high school students enrolling in institutions of higher education in state versus out of state.

Source: National Student Clearinghouse.

Time and Credits to Credential

Definitions: *Time to credential.* Average length of time in years a student takes to earn an associate's degree, bachelor's degree, or a certificate of one year or greater compared with normal program time. Start with the degrees/certificates awarded in a specified year and determine how many total years and months elapsed from the first date of entry to the date of completion. Partial years should be expressed as a decimal. Average the number of years across students and report by degree type.

Credits to credential. Average number of credits students have accumulated when they earn an associate's degree, a bachelor's degree, or a certificate of one year or greater. Start with the degrees/certificates awarded in a specified year and determine the total number of credit hours each student completed since first enrolling. Average the number of credit hours across students and report by degree type.

Source: State longitudinal data systems, if available; otherwise, from institutions directly.

Enrollment

Definition: Annual, unduplicated number of students enrolled over a 12-month period at public institutions of higher education, disaggregated by attendance status at entry (full- time or part-time), race/ethnicity, gender, age, and Pell recipient status at entry. Enrollment should be reported for each public institution, and aggregated by sector and by certificate-seeking, associate degree-seeking, bachelor's degree-seeking, status undetermined, or courses only.

Source: State longitudinal data systems.

Enrollment in Remedial Education

Definition: Annual number and percentage of entering first-time undergraduate students who enroll in remedial math, English/reading, or both math and English/reading courses, disaggregated by race/ethnicity, gender, age groups, and Pell status at time of entry.

Source: State longitudinal data systems, if available; otherwise, from institutions directly.

Success in Remedial Education

Definition: Annual number and percentage of entering first-time undergraduate students who complete* remedial education courses in math, English/reading, or both and who complete a college-level course in the same subject, disaggregated by race/ethnicity, gender, age groups, and Pell status at time of entry.

Source: State longitudinal data systems, if available; otherwise, from institutions directly.

Transfer Rates

Definition: Annual number and percentage of students who transfer from a two-year campus to a four-year campus or from a four-year campus to another four-year campus, disaggregated by race/ethnicity, gender, age group, Pell status at time of entry, and remedial status at time of entry.

Numerator: Number of students from the cohort (denominator) who enroll at a four-year public institution of higher education.

Denominator: Number of entering students in two-year public institutions of higher education in the fall semester of a specified year.

Source: State longitudinal data systems, if available; otherwise, from institutions directly.

State Appropriations

Definition: Change over time in the amount of state dollars invested in institutions of higher education per full-time equivalent student.

Source: State Higher Education Executive Officers (State Higher Education Finance [SHEF] Survey).

Tuition Revenue

Definition: Change over time in the amount of student tuition revenue captured by institutions of higher education per full-time equivalent student.

Source: State Higher Education Executive Officers (SHEF Survey).

Graduation Rates

Definition: Number and percentage of entering undergraduate students who graduate from a degree or certificate program within 100 percent, 150 percent, and 200 percent of program time. Disaggregate information by degree/credential type and by race/ethnicity, gender, age group, Pell status at time of entry, and remedial status at time of entry.

Source: State longitudinal data systems, if available; otherwise, from institutions directly.

---

* In this scenario, "complete" means passing or earning a credit for the course. Institutions should determine what counts as the successful completion of a course (e.g., a mark of "pass" for a pass/fail course or a grade of "C" or better).

7

INFORMATION LITERACY AS A STUDENT LEARNING OUTCOME: INSTITUTIONAL ACCREDITATION

Laura Saunders

Higher education is under close scrutiny, driven in part by the ever-increasing cost of tuition coupled with a tough labor market and questions about the quality of education. Stakeholders, ranging from federal and state governments to employers, parents and students, research organizations, and even the press, demand that institutions hold themselves accountable for student outcomes and student learning outcomes. While student outcomes such as retention and graduation rates, employment rates, and acceptance rates to graduate study provide some information on student performance, they do not measure student learning. In order to demonstrate such learning, institutions of higher education must define measurable learning outcomes, assess progress toward those learning outcomes, and make the results of those assessments accessible to stakeholders so that they can review them and make comparisons across different institutions.

Academic libraries are not immune to the increased scrutiny and demands. Once portrayed as the heart of the university, and an unquestioned necessity for educational institutions, libraries now find themselves competing with other academic and student services departments for limited budget money. One way for academic libraries to demonstrate their value to their institutions is to align their activities with the mission and goals of the larger institution and to provide evidence of the contributions of the library to teaching and learning. Many of the competencies associated with information literacy have historical roots in traditional library instruction; information literacy provides academic librarians an opportunity to become more directly involved with their institutions' curricula and provide evidence of their value to the institution.

HIGHER EDUCATION: ACCREDITATION, ACCOUNTABILITY, AND STUDENT LEARNING OUTCOMES

The perceived value of postsecondary education is correlated with higher salaries over a person's career,[1] and predictions from the Bureau of Labor Statistics and

research centers indicate that the proportion of jobs requiring at least some college work will increase at a much higher rate than other jobs in the coming years.[2]
These factors suggest that, while not everyone will need a bachelor degree, "everyone needs a postsecondary education,"[3] to compete in the new economy.

Even while acknowledging the importance of postsecondary education, however, many stakeholders have also been critical of the current system of higher education. There are a number of direct and indirect stakeholders who are interested
in higher education. They range from the students and parents paying for college,
to the institutions and their faculty who are responsible for the curricula, to federal
and state governments that provide financial aid and tax breaks to not-for-profit
institutions and the general public who ultimately funds these tax-based programs.
While the concerns vary, many stakeholders are critical of the cost of postsecondary
education and want to see some return on their various investments. In general,
the return on investment could take the form of employment, acceptance rates
to graduate schools, or passage rates on licensure examinations. However, more
stakeholders demand evidence of the quality of education in terms of the attainment of student learning outcomes. In other words, these stakeholders want institutions to demonstrate that students are learning and even mastering the skills and
competencies necessary to succeed in the 21st-century workplace.

One of the first direct challenges to higher education came from the administration of President George W. Bush and the then-secretary of education Margaret
Spelling. In a report entitled *A Test of Leadership: Charting the Future of U.S.
Higher Education*, a commission appointed by Spelling noted that while there was
much in higher education of which to be proud, there were also areas in urgent
need of reform.[4] When President Barack Obama first took office, his emphasis on
increasing access to and enrollment in higher education made it appear that his
focus would be more on the quantity of people enrolling in higher education,
rather than the quality of that education.[5] More recently, however, the president
has echoed the more critical perspectives of the previous administration, telling
colleges during the 2012 State of the Union address that they are "on notice." He
proposed basing federal aid to institutions in part on whether those institutions
provide value to their students.[6]

One major area of concern is the high, and ever-increasing, cost of tuition. The
Spellings Commission notes the "seemingly inexorable increase in college costs,
which have outpaced inflation for the past two decades and have made affordability an ever-growing worry."[7] Six years after the Spellings Commission paper, the
Higher Education Strategy Associates reported substantial increases in tuition in
the United States, with in-state tuition at four-year colleges averaging 8.3 percent
higher in 2011–2012 compared with the previous fiscal year, although student aid
generally increased as well.[8] These high costs result in many students accumulating
burdensome debt and some populations, particularly low-income and minorities,
being discouraged from entering college at all. Indeed, the United States is currently ranked 14 among industrialized nations for postsecondary education attainment, down from 12 at the time of the Spellings Commission report.[9]

In addition to concerns over cost, critics also call into question the overall quality of the education provided, noting "disturbing signs that many who do earn
degrees have not actually mastered the reading, writing, and thinking skills we expect of college graduates."[10] Similarly, in *Academically Adrift*, Richard Arum and
Josipa Roska decry the state of education in colleges and universities, contending

that gains in student learning at the undergraduate level are modest at best, with more than one-third of students not making significant gains in learning over the four years.[11] These criticisms appear to be borne out by the National Assessment of Adult Literacy, which reports declines in both prose and document literacy of college graduates from 1992 to 2003.[12] In the face of these dismal reports, stakeholders are demanding greater accountability from institutions of higher education. In essence, those who invest directly or indirectly in higher education want to see evidence of a return on that investment. In addition to scrutinizing the institutions themselves, stakeholders criticize the accreditation organizations whose job it is to ensure quality and facilitate continuous improvement in colleges and universities. Higher education in the United States is unique in that it is not overseen directly by the government, but rather by nongovernmental agencies called accreditation organizations. Under the current system, regional accreditation organizations accredit colleges and universities in specific geographic areas of the country at the institutional level, while special and professional accreditation organizations accredit individual programs within an institution. The purpose of accreditation organizations is to set baseline standards against which institutions are expected to develop their own outcomes and goals in light of their individual missions. Institutions are then expected to gather and analyze data to measure progress toward their goals. Approximately every 10 years, the institutions submit self-study reports to the accreditation organizations in order to maintain their accredited status.

In theory, the system of accreditation is voluntary, but since accredited status is required in order for students of an institution to receive federal financial aid, it has become "a nearly universal obligatory review."[13] As a result, some critics contend that accreditation organizations are not rigorous enough in their reviews and are not fulfilling their obligation to maintain and improve quality in higher education. The Spellings Commission accused accreditation organizations of "significant shortcomings" and lamented the fact that they do not make most of their findings available to the public.[14] Since then, the federal government has continued to increase its scrutiny of the accreditation system, with President Obama asking for ideas to improve quality and consumer protection.[15] A recent report from the National Advisory Committee for Institutional Quality and Integrity, while it recommended retaining the link between accreditation and financial aid, also contended that the accreditation model had to be reviewed and restructured to be more flexible and innovative.[16] Traditionally, educational institutions have focused attention on inputs, outputs, and outcomes, which include areas such as retention and persistence, graduation rates, employment, and acceptance to graduate school. The problem with such metrics is that they do not indicate whether and how much students have learned during their college education. Even metrics such as high school grade point average, class ranking, and scores on entrance examinations, which are often made public and factor into college rankings such as the *U.S. News and World Report* rankings, only indicate how smart students are when they enter the institution. What is currently missing are data about how much students learn at college. Such student learning outcomes can be defined as "not only knowledge leading to understanding, but also abilities, habits of mind, ways of knowing, attitudes, values and other dispositions that an institution and its services and programs asserts they develop."[17] In order to be accountable for student learning, institutions of higher education must first define a set of learning goals expected of students and then must assess progress toward those learning goals. Stakeholders also want these measures to be transparent; that is, they want institutions to make more assessment data about student learning outcomes available for public consumption.

INFORMATION LITERACY AS A STUDENT LEARNING OUTCOME

As college curricula have developed over time from the classics model with its focus on recitation through a more empirical model to the current emphasis on active learning, certain abilities have been identified as central to all students regardless of major or program concentration. Information literacy, or the ability to locate, access, evaluate, and use information efficiently and effectively, has long been a popular topic in the library and information science literature. The competencies associated with information literacy are often linked to critical thinking and lifelong learning, and within recent years, these competencies have gained acceptance in the broader field of higher education as essential for college students' success at school, at work, and in their personal lives.

The Association of American Colleges and Universities lists information literacy as one of its essential learning outcomes for college graduates.[18] More recently, the Lumina Foundation included the use of information sources as a key intellectual skill for students from the associate through the master degree levels.[19] Other stakeholders note the importance of information literacy after college, for success in the workplace and in personal life. In fact, 68 percent of employers indicate that they would like colleges to put more emphasis on information literacy, even more than quantitative literacy.[20] The American Library Association (ALA) underscores information literacy as not only essential for employment in a knowledge economy, but also a social equalizer that might help diminish some socioeconomic differences,[21] a sentiment that was echoed by President Obama when he declared October 2009 National Information Literacy Awareness Month.[22] Successive reviews of regional accreditation standards have found that all six organizations include information literacy either explicitly or implicitly in their standards.[23] The Middle States Commission evinces the greatest support for information literacy as a student learning outcome, calling it a meta-cognitive skill that "applies to anyone learning anything, anywhere at any time."[24] In order to guide their constituents in achieving these outcomes, the Middle States Commission publishes a number of guides, including the handbook *Developing Research and Communication Skills*. This text contends that information literacy must go beyond one-shot instruction session and general education courses, and should be addressed throughout a student's program of study, including within the disciplines. It notes that students continue to develop their critical thinking abilities and deepen their understanding throughout their course of study, and as such, they cannot necessarily develop information literacy competencies fully unless the instruction is integrated throughout the curriculum. To this end, the Middle States Commission suggests that "information literacy might be taught through the general education program, reinforced in specific courses designated as information literacy courses . . . or embedded either seamlessly or explicitly within all courses in the major fields of study."[25] Institutions are also expected to assess student learning in this area, and faculty and librarians are encouraged to collaborate on both instruction and assessment.

In 1989, ALA issued a report that identified information literacy as central to a participatory democracy and called on schools and institutions of higher education, as well as libraries, to facilitate the development of information literacy

Middle States Commission Framework for Information Literacy*

Potential Objectives for an Assessment Plan	Lead Instructional Responsibility	Critical Loci of Instruction (Potential Sources for Data)
Determining nature and extent of an information need	Faculty lead; Librarians support	Classroom discussions; Individual consultations; Online tutorials; Peer-group discussions; Other mentors
Accessing information effectively and efficiently	Librarians lead; Faculty support	Classroom discussions; Individual consultations; Online tutorials; Peer-group discussions; Other mentors
Evaluating critically sources and content of information	Librarians lead on critique of sources; Faculty lead on critique of content	Classroom discussions; Individual consultations; Online tutorials; Peer-group discussions; Other mentors
Incorporating information in learner's knowledge base and value system	Faculty lead; Librarian may be asked to support	Classroom discussions; Individual consultations; Online tutorials; Peer-group discussions; Other mentors
Using information to effectively accomplish a specific purpose	Faculty lead; Librarians may be asked to support	Artistic performance; Project demonstration; Classroom discussions; Individual consultations; Online tutorials; Peer-group discussions; Other mentors
Understanding economic, legal, and social issues in the use of information and technology	Faculty and librarians (individually, jointly, and continuously)	Plans or rehearsals for projects/performances; Classroom discussions; Individual consultations; Online tutorials; Peer-group discussions; Other mentors

Figure 7.1   Middle States Commission Framework for Information Literacy*

*Reprinted from *Journal of Academic Librarianship*, 28(6), Oswald M. T. Ratteray, "Information Literacy in Self-Study and Accreditation," p. 371 (2002), with permission from Elsevier.

competencies in students and patrons. Through the years, a number of different conceptualizations of information literacy have been developed, but the most widely used are the Association of College and Research Libraries' (ACRL)

Information Literacy Competency Standards for Higher Education. According to ACRL, an information literate person can

- determine the extent of information needed;
- access the needed information efficiently and effectively;
- evaluate information and its sources critically;
- incorporate selected information into one's knowledge base;
- use information effectively to accomplish a specific purpose; and,
- understand the economic, legal, and social issues surrounding the use of information, and access and use information ethically and legally.[26]

These standards form the basis for the Middle States Commission standards and guidelines for information literacy and have been endorsed by the American Association of Higher Education and the Council of Independent Colleges.[27] Writing for the Middle States Commission, Oswald Ratteray offers institutions a framework for implementing an information literacy program, with suggested lead and support roles for teaching faculty and librarians aligned with the ACRL competencies (see Figure 7.1).[28]

The area of information literacy represents a major opportunity for academic libraries. Like their parent institutions, academic libraries are being called on to collect and present data that measure their contributions to institutional missions and goals. As Megan Oakleaf points out, "to be successful contributors to their overarching institutions, academic libraries must maximize their contributions to student learning."[29] With accreditation organizations and other stakeholders emphasizing including information literacy in their standards and expectations for college graduates, academic librarians have an opportunity to contribute directly to the educational mission of the institution and to adopt a culture of assessment to provide evidence of that contribution.

INSTITUTIONAL RESPONSES TO ACCREDITATION STANDARDS FOR INFORMATION LITERACY

Despite widespread support for information literacy as a student learning outcome, it is unclear the extent to which academic libraries and the institutions they serve are responding to standards for information literacy as a student learning outcome. The regional accreditation organizations, especially the Middle States Commission, are clear in their expectations that college graduates should demonstrate the abilities outlined by ACRL and that librarians and teaching faculty should partner to teach and assess those competencies. As is the case with many student learning outcomes, there is no systematic collection and dissemination of data related to information literacy. However, the decennial self-studies compiled by institutions applying for reaffirmation of accreditation could serve as a source of information, as part of the requirement is for institutions to provide evidence of progress toward achieving the accreditation standards. The remainder of this chapter reports on a nationwide study of such accreditation documents, which was undertaken to explore whether and how institutions of higher education are responding to accreditation standards for information literacy as a student learning outcome.

The research for this study was undertaken in four phases, with the bulk of the research centered on content analysis of self-study documents that institutions submit to accreditation organizations.[30] Phase one consisted of a pilot study of decennial self-studies of American institutions outside of the continental United States that had been accredited by the Middle States Commission. These documents were analyzed for use of the term *information literacy* or equivalent language referencing the access, evaluation, analysis, and use of information, and a codebook was developed based on these documents. In phase two, the codebook was used to analyze self-study documents for not-for-profit four-year and above institutions of higher education accredited by the Middle States Commission. To collect documents for the analysis, the researcher first reviewed institutional websites to find any decennial studies that were publicly posted. In phase three, letters were sent to the remaining institutions to request access to the self-studies that were not publicly posted online. Based on the analysis of this set of self-studies, four institutions from the Middle States region were selected to serve as case studies, consisting of campus visits and interviews with librarians, faculty, deans, and provosts. In the last phase, the research was extended to include the five remaining accreditation regions. For this phase of the study, the researcher relied solely on publicly posted self-studies available on institutional websites.

The different phases of the study addressed separate questions. Specifically, phases two and four, which centered on the self-studies, examined the following questions:

- Coverage of information literacy in accreditation documents:
  - Is information literacy mentioned? If not, is equivalent language used?
  - Are ACRL or Middle States Commission documents referenced?
  - Is information literacy identified as an outcome?
    - If so, in what context (i.e., general education, library, other)? Is information literacy listed as a separate learning outcome, or as a subset of critical thinking?
  - Are information literacy learning outcomes being assessed?
    - If so, how and at what level?
  - Who takes responsibility for instruction and assessment?
    - Is there evidence of collaboration?
  - Are there any individuals or departments taking a leadership role for information literacy on campus?

The case study phase offered further depth and context to the content analysis of the self-studies. This phase addressed the following questions:

- Is there acknowledgment and agreement about who leads information literacy efforts on campus?
- Is there evidence of collaboration?
  - If so, who is involved?
  - How are responsibilities divided (e.g., as in Figure 7.1)?
  - At what level are programming/planning decisions made (institutional/program/course)?

- Who is involved in planning the curriculum?
- What characteristics from pretest or phase one categories might account for the successful implementation of information literacy programs?

The findings of this study reveal some interesting patterns that generally cluster around five main themes of collaboration, assessment, accountability and transparency, institutional culture, and leadership.

GENERAL FINDINGS

In total, 326 self-studies from across the country were reviewed and analyzed. Figure 7.2 shows the number of documents from each of the six accreditation regions (keep in mind that the self-studies from the Middle States region include both publicly posted documents and documents received upon request, while other regions include publicly posted only). As illustrated in the figure, the Middle States region offered the largest proportion of documents. In total, 97 self-studies were retrieved from 264 institutions in the Middle States region, equaling an overall participation rate of 36.7 percent. Of those 97 documents, 63 (18.2 percent) were publicly available online. Institutions under the aegis of the Western Association of Schools and Colleges had the highest proportion of publicly available documents, with 24 institutions out of 76 (34.3 percent) online, closely followed by the Northwest Commission on Colleges and Universities also with 24 institutions offering documents online out of a total of 76 (31.6 percent). Thirty-six institutions out of 158 (22.8 percent) under the New England Association of Schools and Colleges posted their self-studies publicly online, as did 107 institutions out of 538 (19.9 percent) from the North Central Association of Colleges and Schools. The lowest proportion of documents came from the region accredited by the Southern Association of Colleges and Schools (SACS), where 38 out of 414 (9.2 percent) institutions made their documents available.

Content analysis of these documents reveals that the majority of institutions across the nation are addressing information literacy in their self-studies. Of the 326 total documents reviewed, 228 (69.9 percent) include the term *information*

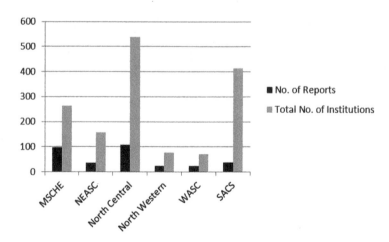

Figure 7.2   Number of Reports by Region

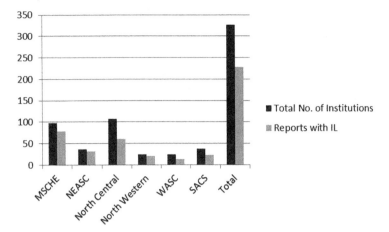

Figure 7.3   Number of Reports and Number of Reports with Information Literacy by Region

literacy at least once. A breakdown by region reveals that, although inclusion of the term varies somewhat, more than half of the documents in each region include the term (see Figure 7.3). However, the level of attention information literacy receives, as well as how it is addressed and who is involved, varies from campus to campus and region to region.

In addition to simple appearance of the term *information literacy*, the content analysis sought to uncover the uses and context of the term within the documents. Placement of the term within the documents gives some clue as to the level of attention and importance afforded to the concept, as well as how the concept is addressed on campus. For instance, across all six regions, only two institutions include information literacy within their mission statements, while one other uses equivalent language indicating the intention to "teach our students how to obtain, evaluate, and use information." In addition to these two examples of a high level of emphasis on information literacy, several other institutions underscored their commitment to the concept by making it a focus of their self-study. Two institutions accredited by the Middle States Commission undertook thematic self-studies focused specifically on information literacy. Similarly, two institutions in the SACS region created quality enhancement plans, a supplement to the decennial self-study, for information literacy.

These examples are exceptions however. By far, the majority of institutions address information literacy within the undergraduate curriculum and at the course level. Across regions, institutions tend to place information literacy within the sections of their self-studies devoted to undergraduate education and/or general education. Putting information literacy into this context indicates that these institutions recognize that the concept is neither limited to library skills, nor solely the responsibility of the library to address information literacy. However, most of these institutions also indicate that they address information literacy solely or mostly in the general education program and even then often through one-shot sessions or stand-alone courses. Most institutions provide little evidence that information literacy is integrated into the disciplines or that it is being addressed through a systematic program that builds competencies sequentially and developmentally as students progress through their education. Only nine institutions (2.8 percent) provided examples of information literacy at the program level. For example, one self-study described a tiered approach in which students received three information literacy sessions throughout their education, two within the general education program and one that was subject specific within their major program. As the Middle States Commission notes, "it is unlikely that a single course can satisfy all of an institution's information literacy goals,"[31] and an approach that relegates information literacy to the general education curriculum "provides only a baseline of skills."[32] In other words, such approaches do not fully satisfy accreditation expectations with regard to student learning outcomes related to information literacy. The five themes of collaboration, assessment, accountability and transparency, institutional culture, and leadership affect these various campus approaches to information literacy.

Collaboration

Collaboration is an essential element of learning outcomes for information literacy. The term *information literacy* and its related competencies are often associated with the library, and as a result, some faculty member and high-level administrators assume that instruction and assessment of information literacy can be accomplished by academic librarians through workshops or ad hoc instruction sessions. However, the Middle States Commission and other regional accreditation organizations assert that such cocurricular approaches to information literacy are not sufficient, and rather information literacy learning outcomes should be integrated into the curriculum both within the general education programs and in the disciplines. In order to achieve such integration, teaching faculty and librarians should collaborate in information literacy instruction and assessment.

Teaching faculty usually are in control of the curriculum. They also have direct and ongoing access to the students in their courses, and as the people who develop assignments and assign grades, they tend to have the most direct motivating influence on students. It follows, then, that faculty buy-in is crucial to the integration of information literacy in the curriculum. On the other hand, librarians can offer support either through direct instruction to students or by working with faculty to develop and even assess assignments that specifically address learning outcomes for information literacy.

Self-studies reveal that the levels and types of collaboration that occur between teaching faculty and librarians vary across campuses. Many institutions across the country (110, 33.7 percent) indicated that they offer course-integrated instruction for information literacy. The term *course integrated* was rarely defined within these self-studies and could be used to describe many different models of instruction from a link to the library website and/or the coordinating librarian on a course homepage to instances of librarians and faculty co-teaching a course. In general, it was unclear from these descriptions the extent to which the librarians and faculty in these course-integrated sessions are working together. Fewer documents offered clear examples of high levels of collaboration, and those that did were still largely at the course level. Still, some institutions described instances of faculty and librarians working together to design or revise assignments to include information literacy outcomes or courses that included two or more library instruction sessions. Finally, many documents, including the two quality enhancement plans (QEP) plans from the SACS region, indicated plans for further integrating learning outcomes for information literacy on their campuses. However, these projects were still in the planning stages at the time of writing, and further research would be necessary to determine if the plans were carried out and how successful they are.

Assessment

Assessment, or the methods by which institutions measure their progress toward learning outcomes, is essential in understanding and improving teaching and learning. Data gathered during assessment provide institutions with baseline information of how well they are performing and can inform their decision making for how to improve. In addition, assessment data can provide stakeholders with the evidence of the standards of quality and performance that they demand. According to the self-studies, assessment for learning outcomes for information literacy, similar to instruction, takes place almost exclusively at the course level, with far fewer examples of institutional or program-level assessment.

Of the 326 institutions reviewed, 116 (35.6 percent) indicated that they assess for learning outcomes related to information literacy. Most institutions rely heavily on indirect methods of assessment, such as surveys, focus groups, or debriefings with faculty. Fewer institutions use direct measures such as tests or quizzes, or assignments including senior capstone projects and portfolios. In some cases, the assessment of these measures is tied to scoring rubrics. However, there was widespread confusion between assessment and evaluation on campuses across the regions. Many institutions reported relying on course evaluations, service quality tests such as LibQUAL+™, or other methods not related to student learning. It is not clear from the self-studies whether these institutions did not understand the difference between assessment and evaluation, but the accreditation organizations appeared to be accepting these measures even though they are not truly assessments of learning. These findings suggest that institutions may need more training and guidance on how to implement assessment measures.

Accountability and Transparency

Related to assessment are issues of accountability and transparency. Accountability derives from the data that institutions gather and the evidence those data provide related to the achievement of learning outcomes. Transparency describes the extent to which institutions are willing to make such information available to the public so that stakeholders can make comparisons across institutions. In order for institutions to meet stakeholder demands for accountability and transparency, they must set learning outcomes, assess learning in those outcome areas, and make information related to that assessment available to the public. Analysis of the self-studies gave some insight into the levels of accountability and transparency.

An institution's willingness to share self-study documents and the information those documents contain about assessment and learning is one measure of transparency. While accreditation organizations encourage institutions to share self-study information, they do not require it. Two hundred and ninety-two of the documents reviewed for this study were publicly available on the college or university's website. These institutions exhibited a high level of transparency in their willingness to share information without restriction. In addition, another 46 institutions from the Middle States region agreed to share documents upon request, also demonstrating a certain level of transparency. At the opposite end of the spectrum, 67 institutions declined to share self-study documents, even when assured of privacy and confidentiality. While some of these institutions offered to provide other materials in lieu of self-studies, their reluctance to provide the requested materials shows a much lower level of transparency. Finally, because accountability depends on assessment, the overall lack of assessment being carried out, as well as the focus on course as opposed to program-level assessment, suggests that these institutions are not fully meeting accreditation or other stakeholder expectations for accountability.

Institutional Culture

A college or university's institutional culture describes the set of values, behaviors, priorities, and attitudes that define the community and guide its behavior. Each of the theme areas of this study, including whether and how members of the institutions collaborate, whether and how they assess student learning outcomes, as well as their levels of accountability and transparency, speaks to the overall culture of that institution. Institutions that post their self-studies publicly on their websites, for instance, could be said to exhibit a culture of transparency. Likewise, information literacy can be related to the institutional culture. Several of the self-studies offer examples that illustrate a culture of information literacy. Certainly, those institutions that chose to focus their self-studies on information literacy, and those that include information literacy in their mission statement, exhibit a high level of commitment to the concept. Similarly, as noted earlier, there are several institutions that are moving toward program-level integration, in which students receive several planned instruction sessions both at the general education level and within their disciplines, rather than relying on ad hoc and one-shot sessions.

For these institutions to integrate information literacy as they do requires support and buy-in from faculty, including department heads, as well as high-level administrators. Because faculty and administrators typically oversee the curriculum and set the mission and vision for the institution, they would have to agree on the relevance and importance of information literacy for it to be addressed at those levels. This implies that information literacy is permeating the culture at these institutions. A future study might examine which factors contribute to cultivating and developing such a culture.

Leadership

Leadership, or the ability to help create a vision and inspire people to work toward that vision, underpins success in other areas. Campus leaders help to set the institutional culture, which in turn influences how the community responds to and participates in activities such as collaboration and assessment. Evidence from the self-studies indicates that institutions are talking about information literacy. However, the focus on undergraduate and general education, as well as reliance on one-shot sessions, and the low levels of collaboration and assessment suggests that overall most institutions lack strong leadership for information literacy. Librarians might champion the cause, but in general, the front-line librarians who are responsible for reaching out to faculty and implementing the in-class instruction seem to lack the authority or influence to move information literacy from the course to the program level.

Front-line librarians might initiate conversations about information literacy, but integration into the curriculum will require the support of faculty and high-level administrators. If people at that level believe that information literacy is important, they can take action to make the concept a priority. Faculty members might establish learning outcomes and identify courses and areas of the curriculum to address information literacy. High-level administrators can establish infrastructures and reward systems that support and encourage collaboration between librarians and faculty, as well as instruction and assessment of learning outcomes for information literacy. Without that level of buy-in, however, it seems that most campus efforts for information literacy will remain stalled at the course level.

CONCLUDING THOUGHTS

Information literacy, with its links to critical thinking and life-long learning, has wide support among stakeholders in higher education, in addition to a well-established and widely accepted set of standards that could guide instruction and assessment. Librarians have long championed information literacy competencies as essential for student success, not only in school but for work and personal life as well. Nevertheless, librarians do not seem to have the level of campus influence that would be needed to integrate information literacy fully into the curriculum beyond the course level. Further, overidentification of information literacy with library skills means that some faculties assume that they do not need to address information literacy competencies within their courses. Even on campuses with higher levels of collaboration between faculty and librarians, there is little evidence of information literacy being integrated or assessed at the program level, and there is widespread confusion between evaluation and assessment measures. In order for information literacy to become part of the institutional culture, there must be leadership and high-level support not only among librarians, but also from faculty, department heads, and high-level administrators who can set priorities and put in place systems that will support such integration.

While the kind of cultural change needed to achieve full integration of information literacy must arise organically from within the campus community, external expectations and pressures could help to motivate change. Accreditation organizations, themselves under greater scrutiny from the government, are tasked with ensuring quality and improvement for institutions under their aegis. These organizations might promote change by being more clear and explicit in their expectations with regard to information literacy and also assessment and evaluation. Perhaps accreditation organizations could offer workshops for institutions on the differences between evaluation and assessment and best practices for implementing assessment programs. Further, they could include training on recognizing assessment for their visiting team members, so the teams would be better able to identify concerns during accreditation visits and make recommendations to institutions for improvement. Ultimately, however, campus leaders must emerge who can create a vision and bring together followers to work toward a culture of information literacy and assessment.

NOTES

1. Aud, W. Hussar, G. Kena, K. Bianco, L. Frohlich, J. Kemp, and L. Tahar, *The Condition of Education 2011* (Washington, DC: U.S. Department of Education, 2011), accessed June 7, 2012, http://nces.ed.gov/programs/coe/pdf/coe_er2.pdf.

2. Anthony P. Carnevale, Nicole Smith, and Jeff Strohl, *Help Wanted: Projections of Jobs and Education Requirements through 2018* (Washington, DC: Georgetown University: Center on Education and the Workforce, n.d.), accessed June 7, 2012, http://www9.georgetown.edu/grad/gppi/hpi/cew/pdfs/FullReport.pdf.

3. U.S. Department of Education, *A Test of Leadership: Charting the Future of U.S. Higher Education* (Washington, DC: Department of Education, 2006): x, accessed June 7, 2012, http://www2.ed.gov/about/bdscomm/list/hiedfuture/reports/pre-pub-report.pdf.

4. Ibid.

5. Doug Lederman, "Dissecting Obama's Message," *Inside Higher Ed* (February 26, 2009), accessed May 9, 2012, http://www.insidehighered.com/news/2009/02/26/oneyear.

6. Libby A. Nelson, "'Gainful Comes to the Nonprofits,'" *Inside Higher Ed* (January 30, 2012), accessed May 9, 2012, http://www.insidehighered.com/news/2012/01/30/obama-higher-education-plan-signals-policy-shift.

7. U.S. Department of Education, *A Test of Leadership*, 2.

8. Pamela Marcucci, and Alex Usher, *2011 in Review: Global Changes in Tuition Fee Policies and Student Assistance* (Toronto: Higher Education Strategy Associates, 2012), accessed June 7, 2012, http://higheredstrategy.com/wp-content/uploads/2012/03/YIR2012.pdf.

9. Organization for Economic Cooperation and Development, *Education at a Glance: Summary of Key Findings* (2009), accessed June 7, 2012, http://www.oecd.org/dataoecd/40/60/43634212.pdf.

10. Department of Education, *A Test of Leadership*, x.

11. Richard Arum and Josipa Roska, *Academically Adrift: Limited Learning on College Campuses* (Chicago: University of Chicago Press, 2010).

12. U.S. Department of Education, National Center for Education Statistics, "National Assessment of Adult Literacy," accessed May 9, 2012, http://nces.ed.gov/naal/kf_dem_edu.asp.

13. The American Council of Trustees and Alumni, *Why Accreditation Doesn't Work and What Policymakers Can Do about It* (Washington, DC: American Council of Trustees and Alumni, 2007), 12.

14. Department of Education, *A Test of Leadership*, 14.

15. Doug Lederman, "Fixing Accreditation, from the Inside," *Inside Higher Ed* (May 13, 2011), accessed May 9, 2012, http://www.insidehighered.com/news/2011/05/13/higher_ed_group_creates_panel_to_weigh_new_future_for_accreditation.

16. National Advisory Committee on Institutional Quality and Integrity, *NACIQI Draft Report: Higher Education Accreditation Reauthorization Policy Recommendations* (February 8, 2012), accessed May 10, 2012, http://www2.ed.gov/about/bdscomm/list/naciqi-dir/naciqi_draft_final_report.pdf.

17. Peggy L. Maki, *Assessing for Learning: Building a Sustainable Commitment across the Institution* (Sterling, VA: Stylus Publishing, 2004), 3.

18. Association of American Colleges and Universities, *College Learning for the New Global Century* (Washington, DC: Association of American Colleges & Universities, 2007), accessed June 7, 2012, http://www.aacu.org/leap/documents/GlobalCentury_final.pdf.

19. Lumina Foundation, *Degree Qualifications Profile* (Washington, DC: Lumina Foundation, 2011), 12, accessed June 7, 2012, http://www.luminafoundation.org/publications/ The_Degree_Qualifications_Profile.pdf.

20. Association of American Colleges and Universities, *The LEAP Vision for Learning: Outcomes, Practices, Impact, and Employers' Views* (Washington, DC: Association of American Colleges & Universities, 2011), accessed June 7, 2012, http://www.aacu.org/leap/ documents/leap_vision_summary.pdf.

21. American Library Association, "Presidential Committee on Information Literacy: Final Report" (1989), accessed May 10, 2012, http://www.ala.org/acrl/publications/ whitepapers/presidential.

22. President Barack Obama, "National Information Literacy Awareness Month" (2009), accessed May 10, 2012, http://www.whitehouse.gov/the_press_office/Presidential-Proclamation-National-Information-Literacy-Awareness-Month.

23. Bonnie Gratch-Lindauer, "Comparing the Regional Accreditation Standards: Outcomes Assessment and Other Trends," *Journal of Academic Librarianship*, 28, no. 1/2, (2002): 14–26; Laura Saunders, "Regional Accreditation Organizations' Treatment of Information Literacy: Definitions, Collaboration, and Assessment," *Journal of Academic Librarianship*, 33, no. 3, (2007): 317–26.

24. Middles States Commission on Higher Education, *Developing Research and Communication Skills: Guidelines for Information Literacy in the Curriculum* (Philadelphia: Middle States Commission on Higher Education, 2003): 2, accessed June 7, 2012, http://www .msche.org/publications/Developing-Skills080111151714.pdf.

25. Ibid., 10.

26. American Library Association, Association of College and Research Libraries, "Information Literacy Competency Standards for Higher Education" (2000), accessed May 10, 2012, http://www.ala.org/acrl/standards/informationliteracycompetency.

27. Patricia S. Breivik, "Information Literacy and the Engaged Campus," *AAHE Bulletin* 53 (2000): 3–6, accessed June 7, 2012, http://www.aahea.org/articles/nov2000_1 .htm; Council of Independent Colleges, "CIC Endorses ACRL Information Literacy Competency Standards," *Independent Online Newsletter*, accessed June 7, 2012, http://www.cic .edu/publications.

28. Oswald M. T. Ratteray, "Information Literacy in Self-Study and Accreditation," *Journal of Academic Librarianship* 28, no. 6 (2002): 368–76.

29. Megan Oakleaf, *The Value of Academic Libraries* (Chicago: Association of College and Research Libraries, 2010), 37, accessed June 7, 2012, http://www.ala.org/acrl/sites/ ala.org.acrl/files/content/issues/value/val_report.pdf.

30. Laura Saunders, *Information Literacy as a Student Learning Outcome: The Perspective of Institutional Accreditation* (Santa Barbara, CA: Libraries Unlimited, 2011).

31. Middle States Commission, *Developing Research and Communication Skills*, 16.

32. Ibid., 15.

8

CRITICAL THINKING AND
INFORMATION LITERACY:
ACCREDITATION AND
OUTCOMES ASSESSMENT

Laura Saunders

The system of accreditation in the United States is intended to ensure quality and facilitate continuous improvement in student learning among institutions of higher education. In order to receive or maintain accredited status, colleges and universities are expected to engage in a process of goal-setting, data gathering, and analysis to inform decisions for improvement. Accreditation organizations guide institutions in this process by providing standards that outline expectations with regard to not only such areas as financial status, human resources, and library and technology resources, but also such curricular issues as student learning.

While accreditation organizations lay out general expectations for student learning, these are considered baseline standards. Institutions are expected to interpret these standards within the context of their individual missions and goals, and then develop their own learning outcomes for students in their programs. Once institutions establish these student learning outcomes, they have to be accountable for them. Part of the accreditation process requires institutions to reflect on their progress toward achieving them through engaging in a cycle of assessment, which includes gathering and analyzing data to track progress, and then using the data to inform decision making to improve teaching and learning.

One of the hallmarks of the American system of education and accreditation is respect for the individual mission. Institutions can be very different from one another. There are specialized institutions that focus on a specific field or discipline such as medicine, law, or technology, while some have a religious affiliation. Institutions also vary in the levels of degree they offer (from associate to doctorate), the number and size of their programs, and whether they have a research focus. Each of these differences affects the focus of the curriculum to some extent, which is why accreditation standards are considered baselines and expected to be interpreted within this diversity of missions and focus. While respecting individual missions, however, stakeholders in higher education, from parents and students to the government to research and policy organizations, identify certain competencies and abilities as important to all students regardless of the institution they attend or their field of study.

STUDENT LEARNING OUTCOMES

The Project on Accreditation and Assessment's national survey of higher education administrators, educators, and business leaders found that there is some consensus regarding the skills and competencies college graduates should attain.[1] In general, these stakeholders agree on the importance of a broad, liberal education that emphasizes the higher-order thinking skills of evaluation, synthesis, and integration of knowledge as defined by Bloom's taxonomy.[2] The Association of American Colleges and Universities (AAC&U) developed an initiative entitled Liberal Education and America's Promise (LEAP), to promote liberal education comprising "substantial content, rigorous methodology, and an active engagement with the societal, ethical, and practical implications of our learning."[3] Similarly, the American Council of Trustees and Alumni has issued several reports in strong support of a core curriculum, which it defines as "a required sequence of study that ensures that every student graduates with a solid understanding of such basic subjects as English and history, mathematics and science, foreign and language arts."[4] Further, the council has launched the website "What Will They Learn," which offers a searchable database of more than 1,000 schools nationwide and reports on which of the core curricular areas these institutions require of their students.[5] In a report on undergraduate education in research universities, the Boyer Commission contends that "[m]any students graduate having accumulated whatever number of courses is required, but still lacking a coherent body of knowledge . . . [and] without knowing how to think logically, write clearly, or speak coherently," and goes on to advise institutions to emphasize analysis, evaluation, and synthesis.[6]

Among those learning outcomes commonly identified by these stakeholders are critical thinking, lifelong learning, written and oral communication skills, quantitative literacy, and problem solving. Information literacy, generally defined as the ability to locate, access, evaluate, and use information effectively and ethically, is often included either explicitly or implicitly in these frameworks as well. The following section outlines the development of information literacy as a student learning outcome, placing it within the context of other important learning outcomes and literacies.

INFORMATION LITERACY AS A STUDENT LEARNING OUTCOME

The term *information literacy* has been in use since 1974, when Paul Zurkowski[7] coined to describe the skills and abilities needed to deal successfully with the rapid increase in information, but the concept has roots in traditional library instruction. In fact, the Association of College and Research Libraries (ACRL) developed the most widely accepted definition of information literacy. According to ACRL, an information literate person is able to

• determine the extent of information needed;
• access the needed information effectively and efficiently;

- evaluate information and its sources critically;
- incorporate selected information into one's knowledge base;
- use information effectively to accomplish a specific purpose; and
- understand the economic, legal, and social issues surrounding the use of information, and access and use information ethically and legally.[8]

While librarians have been championing the importance of information literacy for decades, it has recently begun to be recognized by other stakeholders in higher education.

Both LEAP and the Project on Accreditation and Assessment include information literacy as one of the essential learning outcomes for a liberal education. The recently released Degree Qualifications Profile from the Lumina Foundation offers a framework of learning outcomes broken down developmentally from associate to master's degree. While the profile does not use the term *information literacy*, it does include use of information resources—including location, access, evaluation, and use of information—as part of the necessary intellectual skills for college students through the master's level.[9] Successive analyses of regional accreditation standards reveal that all six organizations include learning outcomes for information literacy either explicitly or implicitly within their standards.[10] Similar support for information literacy comes from government and employers. The U.S. Department of Labor states that the ability to negotiate information sources and use them effectively is essential for today's workforce,[11] while the National Center for Education Statistics highlights evaluation and use of information among critical skills for college students.[12] Many of these same stakeholders highlight the relevance of information literacy across disciplines and make connections between information literacy and other essential learning outcomes such as critical thinking and lifelong learning. The Middle States Commission, the regional accreditation organization with the most explicit standards for information literacy, underscores what it calls higher-order information literacy skills "such as thinking more critically about content, pursuing even deeper lines of inquiry with more sophisticated methods, and becoming facile with the tools that enable students to grapple philosophically with the nature of inquiry itself."[13] Further, the Middle States Commission states that by requiring reflection on information and evaluation of content and sources, information literacy encourages critical thinking.

Other authors likewise emphasize the similarities between information literacy and critical thinking. Comparing definitions of information literacy and critical thinking across library and information science education and health literatures reveals areas of overlap in the competencies that each describes.[14] Both critical thinking and information literacy entail reflection and evaluation of the reliability, credibility, and relevance of content and sources, evaluating both evidence and authority.[15] Information literacy can be seen as a particular kind of critical thinking used to negotiate abundant types and forms of information. Indeed, Breivik contends that one can practice critical thinking without information literacy, for instance, by thinking critically through a problem, but then relying on whatever information is available to solve that problem.[16] More than 20 years ago, Sonia Bodi argued that library instruction, and the development of appropriate assignments that encourage the use of library resources, could enhance the teaching of critical thinking in college classrooms.[17] These parallels between critical thinking and information literacy have spurred some authors to adopt the term *critical information literacy*, drawing on the works of educational theorists such as Paolo Freire and Henry Giroux to describe an approach to information literacy that emphasizes the sociopolitical and contextual aspects of information, rather than an information transfer approach.[18] Both critical thinking and information literacy abilities underpin the development of habits of lifelong learning. Lifelong learners are not dependent on formal educational structures or organizations, but "must have learned the skill of independent study and be willing to use them."[19] A crucial aspect of lifelong learning is the ability to use information to learn,[20] and Patricia S. Breivik contends that college students who have learned to access, evaluate, and use information will be able to engage in and direct their own learning after graduation.[21] Rapid and ongoing changes, especially in technology and information, mean that virtually everyone will have to continue to learn in order to keep up with these changes. In other words, to be successful on the job and in their personal lives in an information society, individuals must be "confident, independent, self-regulated learners."[22]

Information Literacy in Context

Despite the strong connections drawn between information literacy, critical thinking, and lifelong learning, and the general support for information literacy as a student learning outcome, the integration of these different concepts is not unchallenged. Researchers and practitioners continue to debate the general definition of information literacy.[23] One area of focus is the extent to which information literacy constitutes a set of competencies applicable to everyone, and the extent to which the competencies might vary across different disciplines. John M. Weiner suggests a merger that "would involve [information literacy] providing tools and techniques in the processing and utilisation of knowledge, and [critical thinking] supplying the particulars and interpretations associated with a specific discipline."[24] ACRL has adapted its general standards of information literacy to reflect a series of disciplines including Journalism,[25] Anthropology and Sociology,[26] Science and Technology,[27] Teacher Education,[28] Political Science,[29] Psychology,[30] and English Literature.[31] Each of these frameworks takes the standards, performance indicators, and outcomes of the general standards and offers specific examples of their applications within these disciplines.

In addition to these discipline-specific standards, information literacy must be viewed within the context of other "new" literacies, which include digital literacy, visual literacy, and media literacy, among others. In general, these literacy types center on a person's ability to interpret, evaluate, and use media and formats other than text. For instance, ACRL defines visual literacy as "a set of abilities that enables an individual to effectively find, interpret, evaluate, use, and create images and visual media."[32] Likewise, digital literacy expands on basic technology literacy to go beyond using computers to being able to find, evaluate, use, and create information.[33] The importance of digital literacy has recently been highlighted by a proposal under consideration by the Federal Communications Commission to provide $200 million of funding to create a digital literacy corps that would train students, teachers, and librarians.[34] A close look at the definitions and standards of these various literacies reveals that the competencies themselves are largely the same—it is the application to non-text media that separates them. Some writers argue that information literacy should be regarded as an umbrella term or metaliteracy of which these other literacies form a subset.[35] However the relationships are defined, the important point is that students will need a set of high-order thinking skills enabling them to interact with text and non-text materials in sophisticated and complex ways in order to not only understand information but also evaluate and use it to create new knowledge in a range of formats.

CRITICAL THINKING, LIFELONG LEARNING, AND INFORMATION LITERACY IN ACCREDITATION SELF-STUDIES

Chapter 7 describes a research study that examined the extent to which institutions of higher education are responding to accreditation standards for learning outcomes related to information literacy. A total of 326 decennial self-studies taken from each of the six accreditation regions across the country were reviewed and analyzed for use of information literacy. Part of that study also considered the use and context of critical thinking and lifelong learning within the accreditation self-studies. This chapter highlights institutional attention to critical thinking and information literacy learning outcomes.

GENERAL FINDINGS

The findings of this study show that institutions nationwide are using all three terms—*critical thinking, lifelong learning*, and *information literacy*—fairly regularly within their accreditation documents. In fact, use of these three terms is relatively consistent, with critical thinking being the most frequent. As noted in Chapter 7, 228 institutions (69.6 percent) of the 326 reviewed include information literacy in their self-studies. Critical thinking was included only slightly more often, in 229 (70.0 percent) of the documents, while lifelong learning appeared in 177 (54.6 percent) of the self-studies. A regional breakdown, however, shows greater variance in the use of the three terms. More than half of institutions in each of the accreditation regions include the term *information literacy*, with 88.9 percent of those institutions accredited by the New England Association of Schools and Colleges (NEASC) using the term, as opposed to 56.1 percent of institutions accredited by the North Central Association of Colleges and Schools. On the other hand, NEASC has the lowest proportional use of the term *critical thinking*, with only 33.3 percent of the institutions using it, as opposed to institutions accredited by the Southern Association of Colleges and Schools where the term appeared in 81.6 percent of documents.

While helpful for providing an overview, frequency counts only indicate that institutions are talking about a particular concept and do not reveal how that concept is being addressed. Further examination of the context in which these terms were used offers more insight. For instance, all three terms were used regularly within the context of the undergraduate and/or general education curriculum, suggesting that institutions tend to see these concepts as desirable learning outcomes for their students, especially at the undergraduate level. In addition, the inclusion of these terms within this context indicates that institutions expect their faculty to incorporate these learning outcomes into the curriculum, although it was not always clear whether they were expected to address the learning outcomes at the course or program level or both.

The numbers and contexts presented so far suggest that the three learning outcomes of critical thinking, lifelong learning, and information literacy receive nearly equivalent treatment within the self studies, but further examination shows greater differences. For instance, critical thinking and lifelong learning are much more likely to be included in an institutional mission statement than information literacy. In fact, of 326 institutions, only three institutions (less than 1 percent) included information literacy in their mission statements, and of those, one did not actually use the term *information literacy* but used equivalent language regarding access, evaluation, and use of information. This contrasts sharply with critical thinking, which appears in 44 (13.5 percent) of mission statements across the country. *Lifelong learning* is actually the most frequently used term, with 63 (19.3 percent) institutions including it in their mission statements.

Including specific learning outcomes such as these in an institutional mission statement demonstrates a high level of commitment to the achievement of that learning outcome. Whereas very few people are likely to read an institution's self-study, or even a detailed statement on a general education program, mission statements state what the institutions are about and, in part, are meant to be marketing devices; they are usually prominently posted on websites, brochures, and other institutional documentation. What is more, accreditation organizations and visiting team members are expected to take mission statements into consideration when reviewing all other aspects of an institution for accreditation. Therefore, it is reasonable to assume that learning outcomes included within a mission statement are among the most important to that institution.

Nonetheless, including a learning outcome in a mission statement, or even stating that a concept is an intended learning outcome of the curriculum, does not mean that the concept is actually being addressed or, if it is, that instructors are assessing students for achievement. The self-studies show that, regardless of which learning outcome is considered, institutions are uneven in their approaches to assessment. To begin with, many institutions appear to confuse evaluation and assessment. Evaluation, which is product-oriented, involves using data to determine whether goals were met and to judge the value or worth of a program. Assessment, on the other hand, is process-oriented and involves the gathering, analyzing, and interpreting of data to gauge progress toward measurable goals. Assessment is crucial to understanding and improving teaching and learning. Only by measuring progress toward learning outcomes can institutions hold themselves accountable to their stakeholders and make informed decisions to continuously improve quality in teaching and learning.

Nevertheless, many of the institutions involved in this study employ evaluation methods when measuring student learning. Course evaluations and surveys are among the most popular methods mentioned as assessment tools, but in reality, these are evaluation measures that rely on self-reporting and do not actually measure learning. Naturally, most course instructors rely on assignments and tests. When scored by rubric, these would count as assessment measures, but the self-studies did not always indicate whether rubrics were used. Similarly, self-studies did not always include clear evidence of program-level assessment, although a number of institutions mentioned the use of capstone projects, portfolios, and internships as a way for students to synthesize their learning and for institutions to measure learning at the program level. Critical thinking was almost always mentioned in the context of capstone projects, whereas information literacy was involved much less often. Only 10 institutions specifically mentioned assessing information literacy as part of the capstone project, and only about half of these indicated that they used a rubric to do so.

CONCLUDING THOUGHTS

The terms *information literacy*, *critical thinking*, and *lifelong learning* are used with similar levels of frequency in self-studies across the country, but the context and usage vary somewhat. All three concepts receive virtually equal treatment within the contexts of undergraduate and general education. It would appear that most institutions view information literacy to be as important for college students as critical thinking and lifelong learning, and they expect instructors to address the concept within their courses and programs. However, critical thinking and lifelong learning are included much more frequently in mission statements than information literacy, suggesting that these learning outcomes might be considered more important. Further, while the three concepts are addressed equitably in general education, critical thinking seems to be included much more frequently in capstone and other program-level projects and assessments.

From a certain perspective, the fact that critical thinking would be included so much more frequently in capstone projects and program level assessments, and that rubrics would be used so seldom in relation to information literacy, seems ironic. While it is true that the concept of critical thinking has been embedded in higher education for much longer than information literacy, in many ways, it is a more abstract and less well-defined term. John M. Weiner argues that critical thinking is inherently private, taking place within the individual, and as such it is difficult to assess or measure.[36] As noted earlier, information literacy has a well-developed set of frameworks and definitions, which have been developed with specific attention to assessment. For instance, for each of the six information literacy standards, ACRL provides a supplementary set of objectives and performance indicators that lay out the specific observable actions or behaviors an instructor could use to assess students for achievement of each standard. Further, the Rubric Assessment of Information Literacy Skills (http://railsontrack.info/) project offers a clearinghouse of rubrics that can be freely accessed, used, and adapted for specific courses and assignments, with the aim of facilitating rubric-based assessments for information literacy. Unfortunately, this extensive support for information literacy assessment does not seem to have led to much in the way of actual implementation.

There are a couple of possible interpretations of these patterns of inclusion and assessment of information literacy and critical thinking. General education programs, where information literacy and critical thinking get equal attention, are usually introductory. Students are generally expected to complete general education courses within the first two years of study, and the program is intended to help students develop a baseline set of competencies that will be refined within their major. Capstone projects, where critical thinking is more likely to be emphasized, are a culmination of the student's learning and tend to focus on program-level learning outcomes. It could be that institutions view information literacy as more of a baseline set of competencies that can be fully addressed within the core courses, rather than higher-order thinking skills with discipline-specific applications. On the other hand, however, the parallels and overlaps between definitions of the concepts might mean that institutions are folding information literacy into the broader term of *critical thinking*. In other words, some institutions might consider competencies such as evaluation or synthesis of information to be a part of critical thinking and might not separate them out as discrete learning outcomes. A future study could examine the extent to which critical thinking is used as an umbrella term to encompass information literacy and perhaps other learning outcomes as well.

Whatever terminology is used, it is obvious that stakeholders believe these competencies of location, evaluation, and use of information—whether text-based, images, digital, or otherwise—and creation of new knowledge with that information are crucial for college students. However, these concepts must be clearly operationalized so that institutions can develop specific learning outcomes and goals based on the concepts, which is a first step toward authentic assessment of learning. In order to be accountable for student learning in the areas of critical thinking, information literacy, or any other learning outcome, institutions must gather and analyze data that measure progress toward those outcomes. Detailed standards and rubrics exist to facilitate such assessment for information literacy. That being the case, information literacy might represent an opportunity for academic librarians to take a lead role in the assessment for information literacy outcomes on their campuses, thereby not only promoting a culture of assessment and of information literacy, but also documenting library contributions to teaching and learning in alignment with institutional goals.

NOTES

1. Project on Accreditation and Assessment, *Taking Responsibility for the Quality of the Baccalaureate Degree* (Washington, DC: Association of American Colleges and Universities, 2004).

2. Benjamin Samuel Bloom, *The Taxonomy of Educational Objectives: The Classification of Educational Goals* (New York: D. McKay Co., 1956).

3. Association of American Colleges and Universities, "Statement on Liberal Learning" (1998), accessed June 10, 2012, http://www.aacu.org/About/statements/liberal_learning.cfm;

Association of American Colleges and Universities, *An Introduction to LEAP* (Washington, DC: AACU, n.d.), accessed June 10, 2012, http://www.aacu.org/leap/documents/Introduction_to_LEAP.pdf.

4. American Council of Trustees and Alumni, *Becoming an Educated Person: Toward a Core Curriculum for College Students* (Washington, DC: ACTA, 2003), foreword, accessed June 10, 2012, http://www.goacta.org/publications/downloads/BEPFinal.pdf.

5. American Council of Trustees and Alumni, "What Will They Learn" (2012), accessed June 10, 2012, http://www.whatwilltheylearn.com/.

6. The Boyer Commission on Educating Undergraduates in the Research University, *Reinventing Undergraduate Education: A Blueprint for America's Research Universities* (Stony Brook, NY: State University of New York, 1998), 6, accessed June 10, 2012, http://www.niu.edu/engagedlearning/research/pdfs/Boyer_Report.pdf.

7. Paul B. Zurkowski, *The Information Service Environment Relationships and Priorities* (Washington, DC: National Commission on Library and Information Science, 1974).

8. American Library Association, Association of College and Research Libraries, "Information Literacy Competency Standards for Higher Education" (2000), accessed June 11, 2012, http://www.ala.org/acrl/standards/informationliteracycompetency.

9. Lumina Foundation, *Degree Qualifications Profile* (Washington, DC: Lumina Foundation, 2011): 6, accessed June 7, 2012, http://www.luminafoundation.org/publications/The_Degree_Qualifications_Profile.pdf.

10. Bonnie Gratch-Lindauer, "Comparing the Regional Accreditation Standards: Outcomes Assessment and Other Trends," *Journal of Academic Librarianship* 28, nos. 1–2 (2002): 14–26, accessed June 18, 2012, LISTA; Laura Saunders, "Regional Accreditation Organizations' Treatment of Information Literacy: Definitions, Collaboration, and Assessment," *Journal of Academic Librarianship* 33, no. 3 (2007): 317–26.

11. U.S. Department of Labor, *What Work Requires of School* (Washington, DC: Department of Labor, 1991), accessed June 12, 2012, http://wdr.doleta.gov/SCANS/whatwork/whatwork.pdf.

12. Elizabeth A. Jones, *National Assessment of College Student Learning: Identifying College Graduates' Essential in Writing, Speech and Listening, and Critical Thinking* (Washington, DC: National Center for Education Statistics, 1995).

13. Middles States Commission on Higher Education, *Developing Research and Communication Skills: Guidelines for Information Literacy in the Curriculum* (Philadelphia: Middle States Commission on Higher Education, 2003), 3, accessed June 7, 2012, http://www.msche.org/publications/Developing-Skills080111151714.pdf.

14. Rebecca S. Albitz, "The What and Who of Information Literacy and Critical Thinking in Higher Education," *portal: Libraries and the Academy* 7, no. 1 (2007): 97–109, accessed June 12, 2012, Project MUSE; John M. Weiner, "Is There a Difference between Critical Thinking and Information Literacy? A Systematic Review 2000–2009," *Journal of Information Literacy* 5, no. 2 (2011): 81–92, accessed June 14, 2012, EBSCO.

15. Corey M. Johnson, Elizabeth Blakesley Lindsay, and Scott Walter, "Learning More about How They Think: Information Literacy Instruction in a Campus-Wide Critical Thinking Project," *College & Undergraduate Libraries* 15, nos. 1–2 (2008): 231–54, accessed June 14, 2012, EBSCO.

16. Patricia S. Breivik, "21st Century Learning and Information Literacy," *Change* 37, no.2 (2005): 20–27, accessed June 12, 2012, EBSCO.

17. Sonia Bodi, "Critical Thinking and Bibliographic Instruction: The Relationship," *Journal of Academic Librarianship* 14, no. 3 (1988): 150–54.

18. James Elmborg, "Critical Information Literacy: Implications for Instructional Practice," *Journal of Academic Librarianship* 32, no.2 (2006): 192–99, accessed June 13, 2012, Science Direct; Heidi L.M. Jacobs, "Information Literacy and Reflective Pedagogical Practice," *Journal of Academic Librarianship* 34, no. 3 (2008): 256–62, accessed June 14, 2012, Science Direct; Troy Swanson, "Applying a Critical Pedagogical Perspective to Information Literacy Standards," *Community and Junior College Libraries*, 12, no. 4 (2004): 65–78, accessed June 14, 2012, EBSCO.

19. Donald W. Mocker and George E. Spear, *Lifelong Learning: Formal, Informal, and Self-Directed* (Washington, DC: National Institute of Education, 1982), accessed June 14, 2012, http://eric.ed.gov/PDFS/ED220723.pdf.

20. Christine Bruce, Hilary Hughes, and Mary M. Somerville, "Supporting Informed Learners in the Twenty-First Century," *Library Trends* 60, no. 3 (2012): 522–45, accessed June 14, 2012, Project MUSE.

21. Patricia S. Breivik, "Information Literacy and the Engaged Campus," *AAHE Bulletin* 53, no. 3 (2000), retrieved June 18, 2012, http://www.aahea.org/articles/nov2000_1.htm.

22. S. Serap Kurbanoglu, "Self-Efficacy: A Concept Closely Linked to Information Literacy and Lifelong Learning," *Journal of Documentation* 59, no. 6 (2003): 645–56, accessed June 14, 2012, Emerald.

23. Edward K. Owusu-Ansah, "Debating Definitions of Information Literacy: Enough Is Enough," *Library Review* 54, no. 6 (2005): 366–74, accessed June 14, 2012, Emerald.

24. Weiner, "Is There a Difference between Critical Thinking and Information Literacy?," 81.

25. American Library Association, Association of College and Research Libraries, "Information Literacy Competency Standards for Journalism Students and Professionals" (2011),

accessed June 11, 2012, http://www.ala.org/acrl/sites/ala.org.acrl/files/content/standards/il_journalism.pdf.

26. American Library Association, Association of College and Research Libraries, "Information Literacy Competency Standards for Anthropology and Sociology Students" (2008), accessed June 11, 2012, http://www.ala.org/acrl/standards/anthro_soc_standards.

27. American Library Association, Association of College and Research Libraries, "Information Literacy Competency Standards for Science and Technology" (2006), accessed June 11, 2012, http://www.ala.org/acrl/standards/infolitscitech.

28. American Library Association, Association of College and Research Libraries, "Information Literacy Competency Standards for Teacher Education" (2011), accessed June 11, 2012, http://www.ala.org/acrl/sites/ala.org.acrl/files/content/standards/ilstandards_te.pdf.

29. American Library Association, Association of College and Research Libraries, "Political Science Research Competency Guidelines" (2008), accessed June 11, 2012, http://www.ala.org/acrl/sites/ala.org.acrl/files/content/standards/PoliSciGuide.pdf.

30. American Library Association, Association of College and Research Libraries, "Psychology Information Literacy Standards" (2010), accessed June 11, 2012, http://www.ala.org/acrl/standards/psych_info_lit.

31. American Library Association, Association of College and Research Libraries, "Research Competency Guidelines for Literatures in English" (2007), accessed June 11, 2012, http://www.ala.org/acrl/standards/researchcompetenciesles.

32. American Library Association, Association of College and Research Libraries, "ACRL Visual Literacy Competency Standards for Higher Education" (2011), accessed June 11, 2012, http://www.ala.org/acrl/standards/visualliteracy.

33. Larra Clark and Marijke Visser, "Digital Literacy Takes Center Stage," *Library Technology Reports* 47, no. 6 (2011): 38–42, accessed June 14, 2012, EBSCO; Matt Ritchel, "Wasting Time Is the New Divide in Digital Era," *New York Times* (May 29, 2012), accessed June 14, 2012, http://www.nytimes.com/2012/05/30/us/new-digital-divide-seen-in-wasting-time-online.html?pagewanted=all.

34. Patricia S. Breivik, "21st Century Learning and Information Literacy," *Change* 37, no. 2 (2005): 20–27, accessed June 12, 2012, EBSCO;

35. Thomas P. Mackey and Trudi E. Jacobson, "Reframing Information Literacy as a Metaliteracy," *College & Research Libraries* 72, no. 1 (2011): 62–78, accessed June 14, 2012, EBSCO.

36. Weiner, "Is There a Difference between Critical Thinking and Information Literacy?".

9

LIBRARY ENGAGEMENT IN OUTCOMES ASSESSMENT

Peter Hernon

Since the late 19th century, academic librarians have assumed an instructional role through teaching credit or non-credit courses on library instruction or bibliography, offering such instruction in courses on a point-of-need basis, upon request, or providing library tours. This teaching role expanded during the next century, but it was not until Kenneth R. Smith, Eller Distinguished Service Professor of Economics, the University of Arizona, wrote "New Roles and Responsibilities for the University Library," in 2000, that attention shifted to collaboration with teaching faculty in engaging in outcomes assessment, in particular for information literacy. As he explained, "the assessment of student outcomes is a means of focusing our collective attention, examining our assumptions and creating a shared academic culture dedicated to understanding what we are doing and how well we are doing it and to improving the quality of learning that results."[1] Using the parlance of today, he was referring to student learning outcomes as opposed to student outcomes, as he noted the shift of accreditation organizations from input metrics to outcomes, defined in terms of what students actually learn. In his introduction to outcomes, he also emphasized that "the focus of outcomes assessment is on the collective success of the [academic] program in developing the competencies of the students in the program" and that "students will . . . be required to approach learning experience differently. They are being asked to become more actively involved in the learning process."[2]

The early writings that presented library involvement in student learning outcomes drew on Smith's landmark article and endorsed his approach but applied it only to course-level assessment. In essence, it might be argued that his article, in part, led to the set of guidelines that the Association of College and Research Libraries (ACRL) developed over time and that address information literacy and, by extension, visual and other literacies.[3]

OTHER INFLUENCES SHAPING THE UNDERSTANDING OF OUTCOMES ASSESSMENT

In 2002, the *Journal of Academic Librarianship* (*JAL*) devoted two issues to outcomes assessment and offered a cross-disciplinary perspective, with articles from individuals associated with institutional accreditation organizations, consultants in the area of outcomes assessment, and librarians engaged in such assessment.[4] The articles explain student learning outcomes, link them to a planning process, present the use of scenarios to gauge student ability to demonstrate what they learned, and show that such outcomes would not be short-lived; they frame an approach to accountability in higher education. One of the authors, Oswald M. T. Ratteray of the Middle States Commission, encourages a partnership between librarians and faculty on making students information literate. He calls for information literacy and other student learning outcomes to be woven into the culture of higher education and for librarians to participate in the dialogue on information literacy but not to dominate that discussion. Like other proponents of outcomes assessment, he wants the evidence gathered on student progress to be used to improve the learning experience.[5]

Ratteray, an early leader on the library's role in assessment, was a driving force for *Developing Research & Communication Skills*, developed by the Middle States Commission. This work discusses information literacy, connects it to outcomes assessment, and lays out the shared responsibility of teaching faculty and librarians.[6] The same year, the Middle States Commission produced a companion volume, *Student Learning Assessment*, which covered information literacy but viewed outcomes assessment more broadly.[7] Together, these works provide an excellent introduction into a subject new to many librarians, but librarians still confuse evaluation with assessment. During the same time frame, the American Library Association published *An Action Plan for Outcomes Assessment in Your Library*, which introduced assessment as separate from evaluation and provided guidance about how to create an assessment program in which librarians played a leadership role.[8] Similar to Ratteray's approach, this work does not view outcomes assessment as solely the province of academic libraries but encourages public libraries to engage in outcomes assessment, however, for different reasons and with a different focus.

One of the best introductions to the assessment of student learning outcomes is Linda Suskie's *Assessing Student Learning*, which explains that "institutional effectiveness is how well an institution is achieving its mission and major institutional goals. Since student learning is the heart of most institutional missions, the assessment of student learning is a major component of the assessment of institutional effectiveness."[9] In the second edition, she notes that "students learn better when their college experiences are not collections of isolated courses and activities but are purposefully designed as coherent, integrated learning experiences in which courses and out-of-class experiences build on an reinforce one another."[10] Her rationale is an argument for assessment at the program and institutional levels.

In *Assessing for Learning*, Peggy Maki, similarly to Suskie, links outcomes assessment to a planning process that encourages faculty to make a sustainable commitment to assessing student learning and to use the acquired evidence to improve the learning process. She defines assessment as "a process of ascertaining how well students achieve higher education's complex expectations through multiple experiences and avenues inside and outside of the classroom." Most importantly, assessment "brings constituencies together from across a campus or across a program, as well as external constituencies who contribute to our students' education through internships, practica, and community-based projects." The goal therefore is to develop "students' knowledge, understanding, abilities, habits of mind, ways of thinking, knowing, and behaving." She further notes that "student development, at both the undergraduate and graduate student levels, is the collective responsibility of all educators in our higher-education institutions."[11]

In the second edition of *Assessing for Learning*, Maki references the growing "assessment movement" spreading across higher education, the "need to humanize assessment," and the increased interest of the Obama administration in assessment.[12] Like Suskie, she focuses on program and institutional assessment, and reminds readers that assessment involves self-reflection and improvement in, and the strengthening of, student learning.[13]

Integrating Information Literacy into the Higher Education Curriculum shows how information literacy programs and partnerships can transform the higher education teaching and learning environments.[14] Finally, building from the framework of the *JAL* articles, Libraries Unlimited published *Outcomes Assessment in Higher Education* and *Revisiting Outcomes Assessment in Higher Education*, which contain chapters written by librarians and library educators, deans of professional schools, members of institutional accreditation organizations, and consultants active in assessment. The goal was to continue the dialogue across disciplines and to build into the discussion what was occurring in other countries.[15] These works, together with the *JAL* issues, document examples of student learning outcomes developed by libraries but focusing beyond the course level.

STUDENT OUTCOMES

As discussed in Chapter 1, there have been some attempts to interpret library-gathered inputs and outputs as reflecting the extent to which libraries contribute to the accomplishment of institutional outcomes. It seems that those taking this approach believe that input and output metrics can serve as substitutes for outcomes-based data and can provide insights into student outcomes (especially retention and graduation rates). As the national government calls for metrics that address the affordability of (and access to) higher education, library input and output metrics could reflect a return on investment from a stakeholder perspective. However, do such metrics really reflect the library's contribution to retention and graduation rates? After all, not all students profess a need for the library and its resources throughout their program of study. Complicating the situation, the government and other stakeholders focus on the institutional level and do not delve into the contributions of support services. The critical questions become, "How do libraries tell their stories and connect them effectively to institutional accountability?" and "How do input and output data relate to institutional effectiveness" (as viewed in terms of student learning outcomes).

ASSESSMENT ISSUES FOR LIBRARIANS

The ACRL had called attention to assessment issues and to both *assessment* and *evaluation*. Although the distinction offered is artificial, assessment is linked to "understanding and improving student learning" and four "different yet inter-related levels:"

1. Within the library. Librarians are involved not just in teaching but also in assessment of student learning and evaluation of program effectiveness. . . . Assessments can include in-class assignments or activities, print or web-based tutorials, and competency tests or self-assessments administered as pre- or post-tests.

2. In the classroom. Assessment in the classroom focuses on the course syllabus, course assignments and activities, and the process by which students create those products. Assessment includes evaluation of bibliographies, reviews of assignments that underscore the research process, and the use of portfolios or journals.

3. Campuswide. Assessment at the campus level includes a review of academic programs for integration of information literacy components and evaluation of syllabi for core courses for incorporation of assignments that promote information literacy.

4. Beyond the campus. Assessment can extend beyond the campus by looking at our graduates as they join the workforce. Are students prepared to function as professionals in their chosen careers? Have they "learned how to learn" and can they remain informed within the constantly changing information venues of their chosen profession.[16]

The distinction between the first two levels is unclear, and the second level might be extended to cover the program level; here, program faculty will play a much larger role. The final level, "beyond the campus," might represent an attempt to examine lifelong learning, or it might be linked to graduation and some type of exit interview or data collection, presumably one not entirely linked to self-reporting. However, such data must be comparable over time—beyond graduation. Further, the examples discussed in the literature of library and information science suggest a level of comfort at the course level and avoidance of considering how to restructure library instruction to make it applicable at the program or institutional level. Compounding the problem, there seems to be a lack of credible leadership to refocus the library and its services beyond the course level[17] and to change the institutional culture through a mutually beneficial partnership between teaching faculty and librarians, as Smith called for more than a decade ago when he encouraged assessment beyond the course level.

RECONCEPTUALIZING THE DIFFERENT LEVELS

A thread running through each level might be information literacy as forming "the basis for lifelong learning" because "it is common to all disciplines, to all learning environments, and to all levels of education. It enables learners to master content and extend their investigations, become more self-directed, and assume greater control over their own learning."[18] The central questions are "To what extent can the library's contribution to the creation of information literate graduates be measured meaningfully over time past graduation?," "What types of research design—experimental and other—might be applied?," and "Can research methodologies isolate on student experience with information literacy at the course, program, or institutional level and make valid projections beyond graduation?" The answers to these questions require more than self-reporting and the reliance on method-ologies with well-established reliability and validity. Memory about what students learned during information literacy instruction becomes a major validity threat as time increases.

Within the Library

When academic libraries create an information, learning, or academic commons, they envision that service and facility as fostering the concepts of community and collaboration by bringing together distinct service points, students from all disci-plines, and faculty/staff with their individual areas of expertise. This campus place or space provides access to cutting-edge technology, integrated support services (seamless support from the library, technology, writing help, tutoring, and perhaps guidance with research as an inquiry process), and the use of flexible furniture to create personalized workspaces.

When academic librarians view the commons on campus, they might observe usage; probe first-year or other students about their perceptions of the impact of li-brary spaces on their learning experiences; ask students to complete a LibQUAL+™ survey; survey students about their levels of satisfaction with student services and the general quality of life on campus; or conduct a web survey to determine how electronic resources are used to support teaching, coursework, and research. They might also conduct a series of focus groups with library users to learn more about their information-seeking behavior, use of the library web-based services, and de-sired new features and improvements. Instead of (or in addition to) focus groups, there might be usability studies of student navigation of the library website and subsequent redesign. However, as Donald Beagle of Belmont Abby College points out, evaluation cannot be limited to the "design aspects of 'learning spaces' or perceptions of 'library as space.' These features must be balanced by qualitative reviews of service effectiveness and quantitative measures of service delivery."[19] Further, the commons represents strategic alignment, meaning the alignment of library goals with institutional goals, as the purpose is to help the institution re-shape "itself around people using technology in the pursuit of learning."[20] From the examples he discusses for data collection (all of which comprise evaluation), librarians typically create partnerships with faculty at the course level, and therefore when assessment occurs, it is confined to the course level. If librarians envision col-laboration as producing more than "an isolated change in library use and effective-ness" and "to be the driver of a transformation change initiative across campus,"[21] assessment beyond the course level must emerge. Still, how course-level assessment occurs within the commons merits discussion.

Course Level

The information literacy literature of library and information science, whether opinion pieces or research, concentrates on the course level and on the question, "Did student understanding of information literacy and student ability to be more information literate improve throughout the school term?" From the examples discussed at conferences and in the literature, it seems that it is common for librar-ians to measure any improvement through a survey of students (self-reporting their perceptions) or completion of some type of test that measures the extent to which student skills and abilities improved during the course. In addition to pre- and post-testing, assessment activities might involve the use of a minute paper to identify areas confusing to students and meriting attention in the next class session; the application of personal response systems (clickers) for registering student learning; and the administration of LibQUAL+™, an instrument for measuring service quality "as a quantitative assessment tool across different types of institutions" without factoring in learning goals.[22] Amy E. Mark and Polly D. Boruff-Jones view the National Survey of Student Engagement as an excellent diagnostic tool to assess the competencies covered in ACRL's Information Literacy Competency Standards for Higher Education "because learning outcomes can be correlated with student engagement."[23] However, the problem with all of these methods is that the focus tends to be on the entire concept of information literacy and not necessarily a subset of skills and abilities prized by the faculty. Further, instruments such as LibQUAL+™ measure service quality and neither satisfaction nor the meeting of specific learning goals.

Such studies and what they recommend do not conform to Ratteray's vision of information literacy as a true partnership centered in the establishment of learning goals, examining the extent to which they are met, and improving learning experiences based on the evidence gathered. In essence, there is no linkage to a planning process and subset of competencies that teaching faculty and librarians work together to accomplish. The purpose of assessment is to plan, document, relate, and improve. Document appears to be the element most common to library-directed information literacy programs. The question left unanswered is "To what extent have student knowledge, understanding, abilities, habits of mind, ways of thinking, and skills improved across courses?"

Program or Major Level

Shifting attention to this level, as institutional accreditation organizations recommend, leads to the increased involvement of librarians in teaching and learning processes. However, depending on the nature of programs, program-level assessment requires faculty within a department or across departments to collaborate with each other (and librarians as relevant) and set learning goals by which they measure student progress at different stages of the program. When information literacy becomes a major or program-level learning goal, faculty and librarians must concur as to which aspects of that goal will be covered and how student knowledge and skills can be improved. They must also agree on the methodologies to measure student progress and how to use the evidence gathered to improve the learning process. Unlike with course assessment, program-level assessment depends on an agreed-upon set of rubrics, providing scaled levels of achievement for a set of criteria or dimensions of quality for a given type of performance (e.g., a term paper or an oral presentation). Scales in a rubric are indexed to a desired or appropriate standard (e.g., to the performance of an expert or to the highest level of accomplishment evidenced by a particular cohort of students).[24]

Assuming that this level of assessment is not merely equated with general education (Gen Ed) programs, the major challenges for libraries in functioning at the program or major level are

- flattening the organization structure to place increased emphasis on assessment, planning, and improving the learning experience;

- having a workforce knowledgeable in teaching and learning pedagogy and skilled with evaluation and assessment research (especially research design, inferential statistics, and indicators of reliability and validity);
- hiring more instruction librarians;
- making program assessment an organization priority; and
- reassigning more librarians to program instruction.

As library managers examine such issues, they realize that they cannot serve all programs on campus equally and fully. How do they select the programs to receive the highest priority? The answer to this question depends, in large part, on the amount of pressure stakeholders place on institutions to engage in program-level assessment.

Institutional Level

Institutions might set learning goals that they either recommend or expect all programs to accomplish. Naturally, libraries have a vested interest in ensuring that information literacy or other outcomes in which they can play a role are adopted at the institutional level and shape the institutional brand. Central to institutional assessment is an assessment strategy that requires the development of a campus climate for student assessment, building an effective support system, and creating a student assessment culture. Institutional assessment, in summary, is more than the creation of an office of institutional research and compliance and charging it with collecting metrics associated with student outcomes. Such assessment indicates institutional effectiveness in terms of how the mission addresses teaching and learning.

REDIRECTING LIBRARY INVOLVEMENT IN ASSESSMENT

The fundamental questions for libraries to consider are

- At which levels do they see their role and does their decision match the expectations of stakeholders, including the strategic direction set at the institutional level?
- Does a continued focus on course-level assessment really comprise institutional effectiveness, especially as accreditation organizations define the term?
- To participate in demonstrating institutional effectiveness, where should libraries concentrate their resources?

As they answer these questions, they must also ask, "Given limited resources, how do they get the most out of an assessment program?" as well as the following:

- How do they prioritize assessment activities?
- How do they put assessment data to practical use?
- How do they sustain assessment activities?

The easiest answer to these questions is to ignore them and to continue what they are doing—focus on the course level and work with participating faculty whenever opportunities arise. As some colleges and universities redefine how they can best meet the institutional mission, they might select an aspect of scholarly communication as their priority. Under the umbrella of scholarly communication, libraries might engage in digital publishing or emphasize special collections and digitize more of these holdings for widespread use, as well as assist faculty with research grants to preserve their datasets and make them available through their institutional repositories as funders require. As a consequence, libraries might embed staff in departments to work with faculty and graduate students and to engage in data curation. They might also redefine information literacy to include other forms of literacy (e.g., visual literacy) or use a substitute term such as creation literacy, which Barbara I. Dewey explains:

> Creation literacy goes beyond information literacy in that it focuses on research output and its impact beyond the process of finding appropriate resources and solving problems for a given project or task. Research libraries in particular are reprioritizing their primary roles to emphasize strategic support and direct involvement in the creation of new knowledge. The open access movement has further underscored the imperative for vastly greater access to new knowledge from a worldwide perspective. Thus, creation literacy deals also with the knowledge and skills needed to choose a format and a venue for one's scholarship with high impact and access in mind.[25]

Creation literacy, perhaps under a different name, might be an appropriate replacement for the term *information literacy*, which in practice calls for library dominance as do not librarians know best what information literacy is? Creation literacy includes problem solving, which raises research as an inquiry process, and thus fits into the strengths of both librarians and faculty. Since outcomes assessment is based on a cooperative partnership, a new term is beneficial. However, whatever the term, it is past time to move from course to program- and institutional-level assessment and to do so through a strategic planning process. As libraries prepare for this reorientation, they must help the professional staff gain new skills and abilities and gain a thorough understanding of outcomes assessment. The goal of any new initiative should always be to start small (perhaps work with one or two programs) and build from there.

CONCLUDING THOUGHTS

When reflecting on information literacy, regardless of the level at which librarians are engaged, Megan Oakleaf of Syracuse University summarizes the assessment challenges for libraries as thus:

• How committed are librarians to student learning?
• What do they want students to learn?
• How do they document student learning?
• How committed are they to their own learning?
• What do they need to learn?
• How can they document their own learning?[26]

In actuality, the second question should be recast as "What do teaching faculty and librarians want students to learn other than course content?" The question presupposes, incorrectly, that both groups participate on an equal basis in shaping learning. A seventh question seems relevant: What are the changing expectations of stakeholders, and how do librarians participate (and perhaps lead) in forming a response that provides better institutional accountability? Oakleaf concludes, "Today, librarians face a new assessment challenge: to articulate the value of academic libraries within an institutional context."[27] Such articulation is complex and requires new ways of collaboration, evidence gathering, and use within a strategic planning process, and most likely new structures for participating in the learning process, be it formal or informal. Creating new types of partnerships and demonstrating a deep understanding of learning should result in an action plan that excites and attracts stakeholders. At the same time, librarians cannot ignore student outcomes and how their service roles contribute directly to graduation, retention, and affordability of a degree.

Returning to Maki and her expectation that assessment move beyond the course level, an additional challenge is "Will libraries embrace broader assessment and carve out a role, or will they continue to focus on course-level assessment?" However they answer these questions, administrators, faculty, and librarians must remember that the focus of outcomes assessment is on the collective success of institutions and programs of study in developing student abilities in mastering content (evaluation) and in identifying learning goals (assessment). Moving the library's involvement in outcomes assessment to the program and institutional levels enables the library to be a more critical part of classroom learning.

NOTES

1. Kenneth R. Smith, "New Roles and Responsibilities for the University Library: Advancing Student Learning through Outcomes Assessment," 2 (14 pages), accessed June 23, 2012, http://www.arl.org/resources/pubs/mmproceedings/136smith-print.shtml.

2. Ibid.

3. See American Library Association, Association of College and Research Libraries, "Guidelines and Standards" (Chicago: American Library Association), accessed March 24, 2012, http://www.ala.org/acrl/standards.

4. "Outcomes Assessment," *Journal of Academic Librarianship* 28, nos. 1–2 (2002); 28, no. 6 (2002).

5. Oswald M. T. Ratteray, "Information Literacy in Self-Study and Accreditation," *Journal of Academic Librarianship* 28, no. 6 (2002): 368–75.

6. Middle States Commission on Higher Education, *Developing Research & Communication Skills* (Philadelphia: Middle States Commission, 2003). Accessed June 7, 2012, http://www.msche.org/publications/Developing-Skills080111151714.pdf.

7. Middle States Commission on Higher Education, *Student Learning Assessment: Options and Resources* (Philadelphia: Middle States Commission, 2003). The work was later updated in 2007: Middle States Commission on Higher Education, *Student Learning Assessment: Options and Resources*, 2nd ed. (Philadelphia: Middle States Commission, 2007).

8. Peter Hernon and Robert E. Dugan, *An Action Plan for Outcomes Assessment in Your Library American Library Association* (Chicago: American Library Association, 2002).

9. Linda Suskie, *Assessing Student Learning: A Common Sense Guide* (Bolton, MA: Anker Pub. Co., 2004), 9.

10. Linda Suskie, *Assessing Student Learning: A Common Sense Guide*, 2nd ed. (San Francisco: Jossey-Bass, 2009), 4.

11. Peggy L. Maki, *Assessing for Learning: Building a Sustainable Commitment across the Institution* (Sterling, VA: Stylus, 2004), xvii.

12. Peggy L. Maki, *Assessing for Learning: Building a Sustainable Commitment across the Institution*, 2nd ed. (Sterling, VA: Stylus, 2010), xvii, xviii.

13. Ibid., xxii.

14. Ilene F. Rockman and Associates, *Integrating Information Literacy into the Higher Education Curriculum* (San Francisco: Jossey-Bass, 2004).

15. Peter Hernon and Robert E. Dugan, *Outcomes Assessment in Higher Education: Views and Perspectives* (Westport, CT: Libraries Unlimited, 2004); Peter Hernon, Robert E. Dugan, and Candy Schwartz, *Revisiting Outcomes Assessment in Higher Education: Views and Perspectives* (Westport, CT: Libraries Unlimited, 2006).

16. American Library Association, Association of College and Research Libraries, "Assessment Issues," accessed June 23, 2012, http://www.ala.org/acrl/issues/infolit/resources/assess/issues.

17. Laura Saunders, *Information Literacy as a Student Learning Outcome: The Perspective of Institutional Accreditation* (Santa Barbara, CA: Libraries Unlimited, 2011).

18. American Library Association, Association of College and Research Libraries, "Information Literacy Competency Standards for Higher Education" (Chicago: American Library Association, 2000), accessed May 25, 2012, http://www.ala.org/acrl/standards/information literacycompetency.

19. Donald Beagle, "From Learning Commons to Learning Outcomes: Assessing Collaborative Services and Spaces," research bulletin (Boulder, CO: EDUCAUSE Center for Applied Research, 2011), 1, accessed June 23, 2012, http://net.educause.edu/ir/library/pdf/ERB1114.pdf.

20. Ibid., 2.

21. Ibid. 9.

22. See, for instance, Elizabeth Choinski and Michele Emanuel, "The One-Minute Paper: Assessment for One-Shot Library Instruction," *Reference Services Review* 34, no. 1 (2006): 148–55; Patrick Griffis, "Assessment Tool or Edutainment Toy," *Faculty Publications (Libraries)*, Paper 393 (2009), accessed June 23, 2012, http://digitalcommons.library.unlv.edu/lib_articles/393; Tamera Lee, "Exploring Outcomes Assessment: The AAHSL LibQUAL+™ Experience," *Journal of Library Administration* 40, no. 3–4 (2004): 57.

23. Amy E. Mark and Polly D. Boruff-Jones, "Information Literacy and Student Engagement: What the National Survey of Student Engagement Reveals about Your Campus," *College & Research Libraries* 64, no. 6 (November 2003): 480–93.

24. Megan Oakleaf, Michelle S. Millet, and Leah Kraus, "All Together Now: Getting Faculty, Administrators, and Staff Engaged in Information Literacy Assessment," *portal: Libraries and the Academy* 11, no. 3 (July 2011): 831–52; Megan Oakleaf, "Using Rubrics to Assess Information Literacy: An Examination of Methodology and Interrater Reliability," *Journal of the American Society for Information Science and Technology* 60, no. 3 (May 2009): 969–83.

25. Barbara I. Dewey, "Transforming Research Libraries: An Introduction," "From the Selected Works of Barbara I. Dewey, 2010," accessed May 26, 2012, http://works.bepress.com/cgi/viewcontent.cgi?article=1008&context=barbara_dewey&sei-redir=1&referer=http%3A%2F%2Fwww.google.com%2Furl%3Fsa%3Dt%26rct%3Dj%26q%3Dcreation%2Bliteracy%2Bbarbra%2Bdewey%26source%3Dweb%26cd%3D6%26ved%3D0CGQQFjAF%26url%3Dhttp%253A%252F%252Fworks.bepress.com%252Fcgi%252Fviewcontent.cgi%253Farticle%253D1008%2526context%253Dbarbara_dewey%26ei%3D8gPBT-D3MPCe6QGQ65TCCg%26usg%3DAFQjCNGR7Z-NxUvgrsEP9BznZUdstXRn3A#search=%22creation%20literacy%20barbra%20dewey%22.

26. Megan Oakleaf, "Are They Learning? Are We? Learning Outcomes and the Academic Library," *Library Quarterly* 81, no. 1 (January 2011): 61. Before reading this article, readers might first consult Megan Oakleaf, "The Information Literacy Instruction Assessment Cycle: A Guide for Increasing Student Learning and Improving Librarian Instructional Skills," *Journal of Documentation* 65, no. 4 (2009): 539–60.

27. Oakleaf, "Are They Learning? Are We?," 77.

10

---•◦•◦•---

SOME ELEMENTS OF STUDY PROCEDURES

Peter Hernon

The literature on assessment tends to emphasize methods of data collection and to group those methods into two categories: direct and indirect ones. The former refers to methods of observing or reporting what students actually learned, whereas the latter relate the perceptions of students and others about learning experiences, the institution, and service units of the institution (e.g., the library). Of the two, indirect methods are the most commonly used, perhaps because they are easier to employ and because they reflect the responses of larger groups. Student satisfaction, although not associated with learning goals, is often an element that accreditation organizations want institutions, programs, libraries, and faculty to gauge, and they often do so through the use of a survey that inquires about the extent of satisfaction with the institution and the library. However, typically the results are not linked to gap analysis. The purpose of this chapter is to set up the next chapter by explaining two elements of study procedures, namely, research design and data quality (reliability and validity and their counterparts in qualitative research). The chapter also addresses gap analysis, explains student satisfaction, offers relevant metrics applicable to assessment, and highlights research design.

ASSESSMENT

Assessment might occur at the course, program, or institutional level, and the goal is often to monitor learning from the start of the college or university experience to graduation. When faculty and others mention lifelong learning as part of a learning goal, they do not typically mean that they want to take repeated measures over the years since graduation, as it would be very difficult to sort out learning directly attributable to the learning goals guiding student education. Also learning goals change over time. It is more meaningful to determine whether students at the time of graduation have the necessary skills, abilities, and knowledge to be successful in their chosen careers.

OVERVIEW OF RESEARCH DESIGN

Research design, a critical component of research as an inquiry process, like methodology, emerges from the reflective inquiry (problem statement, literature review and theoretical framework, logical structure, and the selection from that structure: objectives, research questions, and hypotheses). In effect, research design is a detailed action plan covering the following:

- Who is studied—the population or a sample. For assessment, the population is known, but the researchers might prefer to study a portion of that population. That portion or sample might be drawn based on a probability or nonprobability sample; the former enables inferences to a population, whereas for the latter, the findings are generalizable only to study participants. A sampling decision relates to the size of the sample and how that sample is determined.

- Design considerations. For assessment, the context of the selection of study participants might be an experimental, quasi-experimental, correlational, descriptive, and so on, framework. Any one of these frameworks might contain many choices and applications. An additional framework might be a case study and focus on a specific target group. It is also possible to isolate or control particular variables, but there is a danger that variables may mask other variables. When that danger might exist, how do those conducting assessment take precautions to lessen the likelihood of contaminated results?

- When will the study be conducted?

- Reliability and validity threats and their qualitative counterparts.

OVERVIEW OF DATA QUALITY

Reliability and validity concerns apply to research design and methodology. Reliability is concerned with replication and the consistency or stability from measurement to measurement for data drawn from the *same* population. Common methods used to test for reliability include test/retest, alternative forms of the instrument, and split halves. For the test/retest method, the same test is administered to the same sample on two different occasions. This approach assumes that there is no substantial change in the construct being measured between the two occasions. The amount of time allowed between measures is critical; the correlation between the two observations depends in part on how much time elapses between the two measurement occasions. The shorter the time gap, the higher the correlation; the longer the time gap, the lower the correlation.

In parallel or alternative forms of reliability, the assessors create two parallel forms. One way to accomplish this is to create a large set of questions that address the same construct and then randomly divide the questions into two sets. The assessors administer both instruments to the same sample of people. The correlation between the two parallel forms is the estimate of reliability. One major problem with this approach is the need to generate a large pool of items that reflect the same construct.

Unlike the other methods, the split-half method can be administered on one occasion. For this method, a test is divided into equivalent parts and the parametric correlation, Pearson's product movement correlation, is computed. That statistic may be adjusted perhaps by using the Spearman–Brown formula. The purpose of doing so is to demonstrate that, indeed, both forms correlate highly to each other.

One final example of a reliability method is inter-score reliability, which refers to the consistency with which different people score the responses to a test or compare student work products with a rubric in a similar way.[1]

Validity refers to the extent to which study findings are generalizable to a population (external validity) or to which the study accurately measures what it purports to measure (internal validity). One threat to internal validity is maturation, which refers to the internal changes of individuals that occur due to passage of time (e.g., the duration of a program of study). Some other types of validity include:

- Face validity, which ascertains that the measure reflects the intended construct under study. To demonstrate face validity, those conducting the assessment show the extent to which they have captured and included relevant theory.

- Construct validity, which ensures that the measure actually measures the construct (e.g., information or visual literacy) and something else. Using a panel of experts familiar with the construct is a way in which this type of validity can be assessed. The experts can examine the items and decide what that specific item is intended to measure.

- Criterion-related validity, which is used to predict future or current performance. It correlates test results with another criterion of interest.

If the reliability and internal validity of the data are limited, so too is the degree to which the findings can be generalized, even within a particular setting.

Qualitative Counterparts

Researchers engaged in qualitative research may not believe that reliability and validity provide an appropriate basis to judge the soundness of qualitative research, and they may prefer the following criteria as better reflecting the underlying assumptions involved in much qualitative research:

- Credibility involves establishing that the results are credible or believable. Trustworthiness is an integral part of credibility. Since from this perspective, the purpose of qualitative research is to describe or understand the phenomena of interest from the participant's perspective, the participants are the only ones who can legitimately judge the credibility of the results.

- Transferability is the extent to which the results can be generalized or transferred to other contexts or settings.

- Dependability emphasizes the need for the researcher to account for the ever-changing context within which research occurs. The researcher describes the changes that occur in the setting and how these changes affected the way the researcher approached the study. This criterion replaces replicability or repeatability, which is concerned with whether researchers obtain the same results when they observe the same thing twice. However, they cannot actually measure the same thing twice. By definition, if they measure something twice, they are measuring two different things.

- Confirmability refers to the extent to which the results could be confirmed or corroborated by others.

OPERATIONALIZING RESEARCH DESIGN
AND DATA QUALITY

At the course level, sample selection is most likely to focus on students in a class, whereas at the program or institutional level, there are more options for selecting students for the determination of their mastery of learning goals. Students might be enrolled in a general education program or the sample might comprise a subset of those students, perhaps sorted by class level. Other choices, applicable to both undergraduate and graduate programs, include:

• Students enrolled in different courses throughout a program of study. Students might be selected from core courses and from electives. They might also be selected based on class level or entry in the program in comparison with those nearing graduation. Another option is to target program majors or minors or to compare students based on the number of credit hours completed.

• Creating a capstone experience and measuring students at the start of a program and during the capstone experience. In this case, student identity might be used to compare pre-test and post-test results; however, those identities must be withheld from scrutiny.

Against the background provided in the previous sections, this section builds from the extensive discussion of research designs, especially experimental ones, and reliability and validity appearing in *Engaging in Evaluation and Assessment Research*.[2] This section will highlight two examples: one applicable to the course level and the other either to the program or institutional level.

Course Level

In Figure 10.1, the first four tables represent two variations of an experimental design relevant to course-level assessment. Those engaged in assessment might want to compare sections of the same course, or they might prefer to ignore sections and to focus on courses. In either case, course-level assessment, as practiced today, focuses on those courses or sections in which the faculties allow librarians a presence. As a result, it is not possible to draw conclusions about all courses in a program. If librarians think the pre-test might sensitize students about the learning goal under review, they might prefer to limit the pre-test to certain courses. Still, there are other validity issues that assessors need to know about and cope with. First, random assignment is not possible, as course-level assessment deals with an intact group, but the results might be the result of individual variations. For instance, if a learning goal relates to quantitative reasoning, some students in the group might be more advanced, and the results might be attributed to the treatment rather than variations within the group. Second, there is no comparison or control group. However, for assessment, the goal is to influence all students and not to withhold treatment from any of them. The critical issue is how aware the assessors are of these issues and what do they do to account for them.

Program/Institutional Level

The remaining tables in Figure 10.1 represent different choices at the program or institutional level. Similar to the other tables, the assessors can apply or withhold

Some Types of Experimental Designs

A. Course Assessment

Course	Pre-test	Treatment	Post-test
Section one	Yes	Yes	Yes
Section two	Yes	Yes	Yes
And so on	Yes	Yes	Yes

B. Course Assessment

Course	Pre-test	Treatment	Post-test
Section one	Yes	Yes	Yes
Section two	No	Yes	Yes
And so on	Yes	Yes	Yes

C. Course Assessment

Course	Pre-test	Treatment	Post-test
One	Yes	Yes	Yes
Two	Yes	Yes	Yes
And so on	Yes	Yes	Yes

D. Course Assessment

Course	Pre-test	Treatment	Post-test
One	Yes	Yes	Yes
Two	No	Yes	Yes
And so on	Yes	Yes	Yes

E. Program/Institutional Assessment

Course	Pre-test	Treatment	Post-test	Pre-test	Treatment	Post-test	So on
One	Yes	Yes	Yes	Yes	Yes	Yes	Yes
Two	Yes	Yes	Yes	Yes	Yes	Yes	Yes
So on	Yes	Yes	Yes	Yes	Yes	Yes	Yes

(Continued)

F. Program/Institutional Assessment

Course	Pre-test	Treatment	Post-test	Pre-test	Treatment	Post-test	So on
One	Yes	Yes	No	Yes	Yes	Yes	Yes
Two	No	Yes	Yes	Yes	No	Yes	Yes
So on	Yes	Yes	Yes	Yes	Yes	Yes	Yes

G. Program/Institutional Assessment

Course	Pre-test	Treatment	Post-test
Required	Yes	Yes	Yes
Required	Yes	Yes	Yes
Required (and so on)	Yes	Yes	Yes

H. Program/Institutional Assessment

Elective Course	Treatment	Post-test	Treatment	Post-test	And so on
One	Yes	Yes	Yes	Yes	Yes
Two	Yes	Yes	Yes	Yes	Yes
Three	Yes	Yes	Yes	Yes	Yes

Figure 10.1 Some Types of Experimental Designs

the pre-test. They might merely use the pre-test for required courses, assuming that students must complete those courses before enrolling in elective courses (table G). As a consequence, there might be no need to reuse the pre-test in subsequent assessments (table H). As an alternative, they might continue to use the pre-test (table E) or to withhold the pre-test on an occasional basis (table F). Still, taking intact groups leads to validity issues associated with the absence of a control group and the lack of random assignment to a group.

As an alternative to any of the approaches outlined in the figure, some colleges and universities have an assessment day where they gather data from a population, for example, all students in a program or enrolled at the institution. In other instances, probability sampling might focus on students within programs and involve some type of evidence gathering from the sample.

Regardless of the research design selected, assessors must recognize that study results might be influenced by internal validity issues, chance, and measurement error. Viewed from another perspective, possible impact (outcome of the treatment as measured via post-test or graduation from one level to the next as indicated in some rubric guiding the program) must take into account the absence of a control group and validity issues (including nonrandom assignment to a course). Further, fluctuations might be attributed to change and measurement error. Since those engaged in assessment may not view course-, program-, or institutional-level assessment as an area of research and publication, they may be willing to tolerate absences associated with the lack of a control group and the validity issues. In such cases, it is important to be cautious in data interpretation.

Sampling Student Work Products

Although the focus of this section and chapter have been on the selection of students, sampling might also be applied to work products—the types of assignments and work they perform to meet course and program requirements. Linda Suskie applies probability sampling to the selection of work products, whether they are found in an e-portfolio or whether they are obtained directly from faculty.[3]

SATISFACTION

Satisfaction is a sense of contentment or a state of mind that students and others have about a particular library (academic or other), and the extent to which their expectations have been met or exceeded over a period of time—perhaps since enrolling at the institution or during a particular visit. In either instance, satisfaction measurement requires a comparison of the actual experience with the expected experience. Such a comparison focuses on the Gaps Model of Service Quality, which offers a framework for identifying services in the forms of the gaps that exceed (or fail to meet) customers' expectations. The model posits five gaps that reflect a discrepancy between customers' expectations and management's perceptions of these expectations (Gap 1); management's perceptions of customers' expectations and service quality specifications (Gap 2); service quality specifications and actual service delivery (Gap 3); actual service delivery and what is communicated to customers about it (Gap 4); and customers' expected service delivery and the perceived service delivered (Gap 5).[4]

Although all of the gaps may hinder an organization or institution in the provision of high-quality services and learning experiences, the fifth gap is the basis most frequently used for a study of satisfaction. Studies of satisfaction examine the discrepancy between customers' expectations of excellence and their perceptions of the actual service delivered. For assessment, the learning experience might serve as a substitute for service and its delivery. Expectations are defined as *desired* wants, the extent to which customers associate a particular attribute with an excellent service provider. They also comprise subjective judgments of service performance.

Given this characterization of satisfaction, any survey that institutions or libraries employ to gauge satisfaction must include questions that enable those doing assessment to measure the extent of the gap. It is not sufficient merely to ask students and others about the extent of their satisfaction with the library infrastructure (facilities, collections, staff, and technology) or their perceived mastery of learning goals. The National Survey of Student Engagement (NSSE) is not a satisfaction instrument; rather, it measures "the amount of time and effort students put into their studies and other educationally purposeful activities" and how institutions deploy their resources and organize "the curriculum and other learning opportunities to get students to participate in activities that decades of research studies show are linked to student learning."[5] NSSE enables institutions to map findings related to student engagement to regional accreditation standards, but it does not measure satisfaction.[6]

Noel-Levitz® "annually publishes national reports summarizing the composite results from campuses using its Satisfaction-Priorities Surveys, including the Student Satisfaction Inventory (SSI), the Institutional Priorities Survey (IPS), the Adult Student Priorities Survey (ASPS), the Adult Learner Inventory (ALI), and the new Parent Satisfaction Inventory (PSI)."[7] Two sample SSI items relate to a library:

1. "Library staff are helpful and approachable"
2. "Library resources and services are adequate"

However, neither these nor the other statements in the various surveys probe a gap or do they connect the statement to learning goals and assessment.

Counting Opinions developed a satisfaction survey in common use in academic and public libraries, which, combines satisfaction with user preferences for information resources, facilities, and technology. As a result, the instrument has value to an academic library interested in measuring the satisfaction of students and others. Figure 10.2 offers a complementary form, one associated with assessment. This could be part of a larger survey, one where students rate the importance of various aspects of the college or university. Those aspects might include, among other things,

• campus appearance
• cost/affordability
• academic reputation
• financial aid
• scheduling of classes at convenient times

Within this context, a satisfaction question might ask students whether they would choose this college or university, all else being equal. Figure 10.2, which is merely illustrative, is arranged in two parts, each of which focuses on the library. The first part examines overall satisfaction and the second focuses on information literacy as a learning goal. It is possible to broaden the concept of information literacy to include visual and other types of literacy. Both sections include questions that enable those engaged in assessment to measure the fifth gap. In the first part, the first four questions actually comprise two sets of questions. Questions 1 and 2 can be compared, as can questions 3 and 4, to measure the gap. The remaining two questions are basic satisfaction-related questions. In the second part, students would answer each question in terms of *importance* and *satisfaction*, thus producing a gap.

With the first part and the two sets of comparative questions, it is possible to calculate the Net Promoter Score, developed by Fred Reichheld of Bain and Company. Measuring customer loyalty, it focuses on the likelihood of students recommending the library, their program of study, or the institution to friends or colleagues. The word *promoter* refers to students who take delight in encouraging others to visit the library and rely on its resources, services, facilities, technology, and staff. In the case of a program or institution, delight refers to encouraging others to enroll.

Student Satisfaction Survey*

	Not important → ← Very important									
Overall, how important is this library to you in receiving a high-quality education?	1	2	3	4	5	6	7	8	9	10
Overall, how satisfied are you with the services of this library?	1	2	3	4	5	6	7	8	9	10
How well do library services compare to your expectations?	1	2	3	4	5	6	7	8	9	10
Overall, how do you rate the quality of those services?	1	2	3	4	5	6	7	8	9	10
Would you recommend the services of this library to others?**	1	2	3	4	5	6	7	8	9	10
How likely are you to reuse the services of this library?	1	2	3	4	5	6	7	8	9	10

Please indicate your level of satisfaction with and the importance of the following services of the library in obtaining a high-quality education	Importance	Satisfaction
a. Recognizing the value and differences of potential resources in a variety of formats (e.g., multimedia, database, websites, data sets, audio/visual, and book—print and e-books)	1 2 3 4 5 6 7 8 9 10	1 2 3 4 5 6 7 8 9 10
b. Differentiating between primary and secondary sources	1 2 3 4 5 6 7 8 9 10	1 2 3 4 5 6 7 8 9 10
c. Locating, screening, and organizing information to complete classroom assignments	1 2 3 4 5 6 7 8 9 10	1 2 3 4 5 6 7 8 9 10
d. Understanding the elements and correct syntax of a citation for a wide range of sources	1 2 3 4 5 6 7 8 9 10	1 2 3 4 5 6 7 8 9 10
e. Examining and comparing information from various sources in order to evaluate reliability, validity, accuracy, authority, timeliness, and point of view or bias	1 2 3 4 5 6 7 8 9 10	1 2 3 4 5 6 7 8 9 10

(Continued)

| f. Comfortable seating and workspace conducive to socializing, studying, and doing class work | 1 2 3 4 5 6 7 8 9 10   1 2 3 4 5 6 7 8 9 10 |
| g. The library represents a safe environment for me | 1 2 3 4 5 6 7 8 9 10   1 2 3 4 5 6 7 8 9 10 |

Figure 10.2   Student Satisfaction Survey

*For questions to ask in a general satisfaction survey, one not connected with assessment, see Peter Hernon and Ellen Altman, *Assessing Service Quality: Satisfying the Expectations of Library Customers* (Chicago: American Library Association, 2010), 137–52. Most of the questions asked in the second section of the draft satisfaction survey were derived from American Library Association, Association of College and Research Libraries, "Objectives for Information Literacy Instruction: A Model Statement for Academic Librarians" (Chicago: Association of College and Research Libraries, 2001), accessed July 10, 2010, http://www.ala.org/acrl/standards/objectivesinformation.

**At the institutional level, a similar question is "I would choose this university again."

The Net Promoter Score (NPS) is the percentage of promoters minus the detractors: those customers who feel so badly treated that they cut back on the frequency of their library use, switch their use to other libraries or competitors, or become lost customers. For a program or institution, detractors are at risk of dropping out or switching institutions. On a 10-point satisfaction scale (e.g., with end points of *extremely unlikely* and *extremely likely*), detractors answer with a number no higher than "6." Customers who mark a "7" or "8" are considered neutral and do not factor into the score. Promoters are those who provide a "9" or "10."

People cannot always provide a meaningful number. If that is the case, it is important to collect qualitative data in which they explain their answer. In some instances, library staff might ask supplementary questions to determine whether the score was due to staff friendliness, approachability, and so on.

For the second set of questions, library staff might consider the use of an *Opportunity Index* to identify issues on which to focus their resources or to continue to persuade students about the importance and relevancy of that issue. Clearly, the index indicates respondent needs that are important to the respondent and not currently satisfied by the library, program, or institution or by the learning goals. In other words, it could offer a new perspective on learning goals.[8] Figure 10.3 presents the steps for calculating this index. (Please note that for any questions that do not relate to parts 1 and 2 included in the instrument, the staff are likely to calculate the mean and the standard deviation—the spread of scores around the mean.)

Research Design

As part of any assessment using the table depicted in Figure 10.1, the post-test might include a short survey adapted from Figure 10.2. An alternative is to include the survey as part of assessment day or to conduct a separate survey independent of formal assessment activities. In such an instance, do librarians time the survey near the administration of the post-test? As they answer this question, they must be aware that they risk a low response rate. Are they willing to settle for such a response rate? Surely, they should not be! However, this gives rise to questions about what they plan to do to generate a response rate of at least 70 percent.

Calculating the Opportunity Index

This index, which complements the Net Promoter Score, compares responses to questions for which respondents indicate both *importance* and *satisfaction*. Importance is the theoretical matter of greatest importance to customers. The Opportunity Index measures the distance between the level of importance and that of satisfaction.

The index is based on the calculation of the mean scores for importance + mean scores for importance – mean scores for satisfaction	*Or* The index is based on the calculation of the mean scores for importance – mean scores for satisfaction + mean scores for importance

Ideally, the gap (the fifth gap in the Gaps Model of Service Quality) should be inconsequential—less than the mean score (steps one–three, the first two questions in Figure 10.2).

From the survey depicted in Figure 10.2, first focus on the first two questions:

1. Overall, how important is this library to you in receiving a high-quality education?
2. Overall, how satisfied are you with the services of this library?

Step one:

Find the mean score for each question; the mean is the sum of all the scores divided by the number of scores

Step two:

Take the mean for question 1 (importance) and add it twice. So, if the mean for that question was 6.133, add 6.133 and 6.133, for a total of 12.266

Step three:

Now look at question 2 and the mean, say it is 4.222. Subtract that value from 12.266. The answer is 8.044

Step four:

We now have a value that we can compare with the questions in the section on the *following services*

(Continued)

Step five:

Find the mean for both "satisfaction" and "importance" for each of the services, repeating steps one–three

Step six:

Array those questions with scores of at least the mean score for step three, questions one and two (highest to lowest). Those service areas comprise the Opportunity Index*

Figure 10.3   Calculating the Opportunity Index

Note: In addition to calculating the Opportunity Index, library managers might also determine the recommendation rate (question 5), by subtracting the percentage of students marking 0–8 from the percentage marking 9, 10; and the reuse rate (question 6), by subtracting the percentage of students marking 0–8 from the percentage marking 9, 10.

*For an example of an Opportunity Index, see Peter Hernon and Joseph R. Matthews, *Listening to the Customer* (Santa Barbara, CA: Libraries Unlimited, 2011), 164.

CONCLUDING THOUGHTS

Except when institutions terminate an educational program, assessment is formative or ongoing, and its purpose is to improve student learning and performance, and to meet formally stated learning goals better. Improvement refers to making adjustments in the content or approach of a course of program. After all, assessment occurs within a planning framework so that any evidence gathered is reviewed with the intention of enhancing student learning.

As this chapter indicates, methods of assessment must be placed within a context. That context is research design, supplemented with a focus on data quality. Both of these areas of research as an inquiry process are critical to judging the evidence that emerges as librarians and others engage in assessment. It is important to avoid a situation in which methodologies are applied and evidence gathered without any consideration of research design and data quality.

Finally, it is important to view the Net Promoter Score an the Opportunity Index as largely comprising evaluation. Their inclusion illustrates that evaluation and assessment might be combined in an effort to improve service performance.

NOTES

1. See Linda Suskie, *Assessing Student Learning: A Common Sense Guide*, 2nd ed. (San Francisco: Jossey-Bass, 2009). In this work, she presents the types of scoring errors and offers strategies to minimize those errors (pp. 44–45).

2. Peter Hernon, Robert E. Dugan, and Danuta A. Nitecki, *Engaging in Evaluation and Assessment Research* (Santa Barbara, CA: Libraries Unlimited, 2011), 85–92.

3. Suskie, *Assessing Student Learning*, 49.

4. For a graphic depiction of the Gaps Model of Service Quality, see Hernon, Dugan, and. Nitecki, *Engaging in Evaluation and Assessment Research*, 63.

5. National Student Engagement Survey, "About NSSE: What Is Student Engagement" (2012), accessed July 10, 2012, http://nsse.iub.edu/html/about.cfm.

6. National Student Engagement Survey, "NSSE Regional Accreditation Toolkit" (2012), accessed July 10, 2012, http://nsse.iub.edu/_/?cid=136.

7. Noel-Levitz™, "National Satisfaction and Priorities Reports" (2012), accessed July 10, 2012), https://www.noellevitz.com/student-retention-solutions/satisfaction-priorities-assessments/student-satisfaction-inventory.

8. For a discussion of the Opportunity Index, see Mark C. Meyer, "White Paper on Customer Loyalty Metrics: A Three-Phase Maturity Model Approach" (Strategy to Value Consulting, 2006), accessed July 12, 2012, http://www.strategytovalue.com/files/Customer_Loyalty_Metrics.pdf.

11

EVIDENCE GATHERING

Candy Schwartz

There are almost as many different methods of gathering evidence relating to student outcomes and student learning outcomes (LOs) as there are outcomes themselves. This chapter will look briefly at evidence for assessing student outcomes and then focus more fully on student LOs. In all cases, it is important to ground the gathering of evidence in a clear understanding of the goals of the assessment and the resources at hand for performing it, with buy-in from the community involved. It is sometimes the case that outcomes assessment is imposed on a set of existing processes and activities, as a way of satisfying an accreditation or stakeholder requirement. This often results in poor implementation, murky data, resentful personnel and students, and little likelihood that the results will lead to significant improvement. Good outcomes assessment that leads to gains in effectiveness or efficiency takes time and labor, and while both are in short supply in academic institutions, the strategic benefits are worth the effort.

STUDENT OUTCOMES

As discussed in Chapter 1, student outcomes assessment is primarily concerned with accountability for the wise expenditure of stakeholder dollars for the greatest effect. Thus, it focuses on evidence of success in activities that have to do with making administrators, governments, families of students, students, and taxpayers, and other stakeholders feel that they are achieving a good return on investment (ROI). These include the following:

- Evidence up through graduation ("Will Johnny or Sue make it through school?")
  - Accessibility (ability to get into a program of study)
  - Student retention rate (first-year, first-term, overall)
  - Transfer rate (incoming and outgoing)
  - Course completion rate

- Overall completion rate (percentage of those who complete degree/certificate by anticipated date)
- Graduation rate
- Number of degrees/certificates awarded
- Time-to-degree/certificate rate
- Credits-to-degree/certificate rate
- Class size
- Diversity in population
- Revenue evidence ("What do taxpayers and the institution spend to provide Johnny or Sue with schooling?")
  - Tuition revenue
  - State/local appropriations
- Post-graduation evidence ("Will Johnny or Sue be successful once he or she has graduated?")
  - Employment placement rate of graduates
  - Acceptance rate of graduates entering advanced studies
  - Licensure achievement rate for graduates in license-based professions
  - Earning potential
  - Student indebtedness
  - Rate of repayment of student loans
- Faculty productivity ("Are the faculty worth what they cost?")
  - Productivity defined in terms of tuition dollars generated
    - Number of courses taught
    - Number of students taught
    - Number of students advised
    - Number of credit-bearing independent studies supervised
  - Productivity defined in terms of luster
    - Number and amount of grants received
    - Number of publications

The kinds of data gathered on individual indicators in this category are typically factual and straightforward—"how many" and "how much." This is unlike student LOs evidence, which tends to be more concerned with "the degree to which," and is much less straightforward. That being said, the data for student outcomes can be difficult to gather. Facts and figures might be embedded in a variety of different campus information systems, administered by personnel with varying degrees of cooperativeness or expertise, and stored in formats that may make manipulation difficult, especially where several different data sets need to be brought together. Some data in this category are not held institutionally and would require research (e.g., post-graduation surveys of alumni regarding employment) and possibly the acquisition and use of external data sets, such as earning potential projections in different industries and professions. Another issue is that data are reported in the aggregate and should not be able to be associated with individuals, but even so, issues of privacy and confidentiality can be raised.

Even assuming that institutional and other required data are readily available, decisions about how to use them may require a very granular or multifaceted approach. To take graduation rate as an example, apart from reporting a total overall graduate rate, it might be necessary to break this down or cross-tabulate it by a variety of different factors, such as program, department, departmental unit, major, ethnic background, gender, family income, age, place of residence, or native language. Employment placement data might be gathered one year out and five years out, or at other pre-determined intervals deemed to be relevant. In some cases, notably in institutions for which certain reporting is required or "highly recommended," complex calculations may come into play. One policy question in the *Complete to Compete* action guide suggests a metric concerned with "certificate and degree completions (weighted by field) per $100,000 of education and related spending by institutions." This is calculated as "ratio of undergraduate degrees and certificates (of at least one year in expected length) awarded per $100,000 of education and related spending . . ., weighted according to median earnings of graduates by degree level (e.g., certificate, associate's, and bachelor's) and field (e.g., science, technology, engineering, and math [STEM]; health; and other)."[1]

This underscores the importance of planning before data gathering. Agreement is needed ahead of time as to the purpose and objectives, which will in turn suggest what will be collected, how data will be sampled, what calculations might be made, and how the results will be reported. This kind of planning is well described in *Engaging in Evaluation and Assessment Research,*[2] which is also a good guide through the assessment research process in general, including insights into what can and cannot be done with different kinds of measurements and how best to present data visually. Superior visual presentations of student outcomes assessment can make convincing statements to stakeholders about success or about the need for resources to bring about improvements.

STUDENT LEARNING OUTCOMES

Student outcomes, as expected, measure ROI in more-or-less monetary terms and largely do not focus on whether or what students actually learned (except perhaps to extrapolate that they learned enough to acquire a job or licensure). Many formal policy documents about the importance of gathering student outcomes usually include a section at some point to the effect that LOs should not be ignored. *Complete to Compete* suggests a few direct and indirect measures of learning,[3] but the direct measures are based mainly on proficiency tests. Teaching staff in academic departments, on the other hand, are typically more concerned about student LOs than ROI, especially as many accrediting bodies look for evidence of student learning. Administrators of academic units are in the perhaps unfortunate position of having to pay attention to both types of outcomes.

Student LOs rarely involve number-crunching and usually elude easy definition. It is challenging to determine whether students have gained what is referred to as deep learning or have acquired abilities in such areas as critical thinking, leadership, ethical behavior, cultural sensitivity, and similar desired characteristics. It is even challenging for faculty to agree on how such characteristics might be manifested. Fortunately, a great deal of research and practice over the past two decades has provided some guidance, but there is no "one size fits all" template for gathering evidence to assess student learning, although standard or best practices are emerging.

Outcomes-based assessment of student learning can take place at any level of an institution, or for that matter, collection of institutions. It is common practice for the syllabi of individual courses to include student LOs. Apart from their intended benefits, such course-level outcomes have a particular advantage in helping to ensure that multiple sections of the same course, taught by different people, result in similar learning, assuming that learning is measured by the same rubrics. Program-level LOs, by contrast, move away from the specifics of individual courses and are intended for use in assessing the impact of a larger unit on student learning. The larger unit might be a department, a major, a special suite of such courses as that might be found in a certificate program, a whole degree program, a whole institution, or the institutions in a state or other aggregation.

The existence of multiple levels of LOs within an institution is common;[4] however, it is not always that case that a logical connection is evident among them. An early adopter faculty member or academic unit might have put LOs into place well before an institution takes on (or is required to take on) outcomes-based learning assessment, and adjustments will have to be made as LOs assessment permeates the larger setting. Like a vision or mission statement, and strategic planning, LOs should be in harmony across an institution, so that assessment activities at any level and in any context reinforce each other and provide evidence of progression through learning stages.

Learning Outcomes Example: University of Hong Kong

The master of science program in library and information management (MScLIM) at the University of Hong Kong shows an integrated LOs framework. To contextualize their efforts, it is important to note the degree of institutional support for LOs assessment. As one element in preparation for government-mandated reforms in education, the University of Hong Kong recently instituted an outcomes-based approach to student learning. Their Centre for the Enhancement of Teaching and Learning provides an impressive collection of assessment resources under the project title AR@HKU (http://ar.cetl.hku.hk/), including discussion of the goals and types of assessment; recommended grading standards; a large glossary of terms with detailed definitions; course templates; comprehensive guidelines and tips for self, peer, large class, and group assessment; an all-encompassing catalog of tools, each with description, purpose, advantages, disadvantages, design tips, marking standards, and web references for follow-up; and an extensive collection of links to assessment websites, publications, journals, and conferences. The AR@HKU frames assessment in Biggs's principle of constructive alignment, which they explain:

> The intended learning outcomes, the learning activities and the assessment tasks in a course/programme must be properly aligned. Thus the intended learning outcomes (what do we want the learners to know?) must be supported by the correct use of learning activities (how will the learners learn?) and the assessment tasks including the languages employed (how will we know the learners have learnt?).[5]

In accordance with this initiative, the MScLIM faculty developed core program learning outcomes (PLOs) for all students and additional PLOs for the three areas of specialization (information management, knowledge management, and libraries). Each module (i.e., course) also has module LOs. Following the templates provided by AR@HKU,[6] the LOs and PLOs permeate each syllabus. A syllabus typically begins with a course description, followed by a grid showing each LO, the related PLO, and which assessment task (assignment) is related to that specific LO. This is followed by an outline of topics that also lists the LOs for each class meeting and a table showing, for each assignment, the mode of assessment (group or individual), the percentage of the grade, and the related LOs. Each assignment is then described in depth, including standards for assessment (this last varies in detail across syllabi).

A program gains from this kind of work in several ways. Assuming that the PLOs and LOs are appropriate and well thought-out, students benefit by having meaningful assignments that are targeted specifically to what the faculty feel is important for students to learn. Also faculty can map LOs to PLOs to ensure that all LOs are covered for all students progressing through the program. Since this program also has a capstone experience, faculty can use the PLOs to drive self-reflection activities and students can use the syllabus PLO to LO mappings to bring appropriate work samples and course experiences into their contemplations. The next step might be for the university to present institution-wide LOs overarching the PLOs—this would reduce inconsistencies that no doubt exist among programs and would be a way to demonstrate to stakeholders that the university is accountable for a basic foundation of learning for all students.

Direct and Indirect Assessment

As described in Chapter 10, LOs can be assessed using indirect and direct measures.[7] Some of the student outcomes evidence listed earlier (e.g., measures related to retention, graduation, and employment) might be used as indirect measures of program-level LOs. While the information gained from these is certainly related to learning, it does not indicate *whether* or *what* students have learned or *how* they have been transformed, but rather indicates whether their education has enabled them to be successful in the marketplace and was worth what it cost. In addition to these kinds of factual data, other indirect measures might include interviews, data on the use of library collections and services, time spent in service learning or doing homework, and surveys intended to elicit perceptions about gained knowledge and skills from faculty, alumni, employers, and students. These indirect measures may reveal a great deal about the environment in which learning is taking place, which is useful in exploring *why* students are learning. End-of-course grades are also not direct measures, as Derek Bruff reminds us:

> Course grades are synthesized over the length of an entire course and often include non-learning measures like participation. Without detailed context and planning, it can be very difficult to match a student's grade in a course to specific program-level learning outcomes. Knowing that a student receives an "A" in a course does not tell you *what* that student has learned.[8]

There are many methods for observing the results of learning directly, including a large number that are appropriate for classroom-level assessment, such as minute papers, directed paraphrasing, RSQC2 (recall, summarize, question, comment, and connect), transfer and apply, and similar.[9] Program-level techniques for assessing LOs usually focus on higher-order phenomena, such as critical thinking, ethical behavior, leadership, information literacy, and effectiveness in communication, and they assess the entire learning experience. They may take into account learning achieved outside of the classroom, including extracurricular activities. Program-level assessment often includes elements of self-reflection and intentional learning; the student is led to consider the learning experience as an integrated whole and to deliberate as to how various aspects of the program led to transformation.

Typical tools used in assessing program-level learning include portfolios (usually electronic), standardized tests (nationally or locally developed), work samples, behavioral observations, and capstone experiences, which might take the form of courses, seminars, independent studies, work projects, and internships. Some of these are individual experiences, some involve groups of students, and juries of internal or external assessors may play a role. A program or institution might use multiple direct measures, of which some might be local and some used across the entire institution. The SALT (Student Assessment of Teaching and Learning) form used by Hope College is mandated for use in every course and is an interesting combination of an old-style course evaluation instrument (e.g., "overall average number of hours you worked per week," and instructor "presented material in a clear and organized manner") with a section that is more attuned to LOs. This latter part begins with "This course helped me enhance the following skills and habits of learning" and then lists 10 items such as "use mathematics to interpret, make inferences, and solve problems," "have intellectual courage and honesty," and "make logical and relevant connections, weigh evidence."[10] Each is scored on a five-point scale, but there is no opportunity for self-reflection, and so what faculty and administrators learn from this will be somewhat limited, though the finding may point to areas that need probing with a different kind of assessment.

Although some methods, especially standardized tests, may serve to evaluate individual students, that is almost incidental to their use in assessment. The point is not to judge the achievement of students, but rather to measure the success of the program in reaching its goals and to determine where improvement is needed. To that end, it might be the case that only a sample of the evidence is examined.

Rubrics

Anyone involved in LOs assessment, even if only at the course level, is familiar with rubrics. A rubric is typically presented as a table identifying an assignment's or activity's component skills and knowledge in the first column and then descriptions of the evidence for varying levels of mastery of each component in remaining columns, numbering from usually three to five. Sometimes the degrees of mastery are associated with grades or points. There are collections of rubrics on the Internet covering almost every trait (the Rubric Bank at the University of Hawaii, http://manoa.hawaii.edu/assessment/resources/rubricbank.htm, is just one example), and there are tools for creating rubrics (e.g., Rubistar, http://rubistar.4teachers.org/, and Teachnology, http://www.teach-nology.com/web_tools/rubrics/).

Rubrics have moved well beyond the classroom and are applied in assessing program-level artifacts and activities. Rubrics are widely available for assessing portfolios, self-refection, service learning, and other similar direct measures of learning. Institution-wide rubrics are also becoming more common. The Association of American Colleges and Universities' (AACU) VALUE (Valid Assessment of Learning in Undergraduate Education) project seeks to "focus the national conversation about student learning on the set of essential learning outcomes that faculty, employers, and community leaders say are critical for personal, social, career, and professional success in this country and in the global environment."[11] Faculty and academic professionals from various campuses developed a set of 15 rubrics that are used to assess LOs in three areas: intellectual and practical skills, personal and social responsibility, and integrative and applied learning. These rubrics are freely available online (http://www.aacu.org/value/rubrics/index_p.cfm?) and are being applied by more than 80 institutions of varying sizes and types around the United States.

Assessment Plan Example: Portland State University

Portland State University's University Studies (UNST) program includes a deeply integrated assessment plan that is embedded in a sequence of courses and activities starting with Freshman Inquiry and ending with Senior Capstone. UNST courses use five rubrics to assess the progress of student learning in four areas: communication (which includes numeracy and competency in use of communication technologies), diversity of human experience, ethics and social responsibility, and inquiry and critical thinking. In the freshman and sophomore years, in addition to portfolio review, students complete prior-learning, early term, and end-or-term assessment surveys. As part of the capstone, faculty prepare portfolios that contain syllabi, assignments, student work samples, and reflections on one of the LOs.

The UNST website (http://www.pdx.edu/unst/) includes the five rubrics, an interactive program map, annual reports as well as reports organized by level and by LO, demographic and social analyses based on data from the prior-learning and other surveys, examples of work, video tutorials, and other types of student, faculty, and administrator support. UNST also runs periodic surveys and focus group interviews to monitor student satisfaction with the processes and functions. It is small wonder that Portland State won the 2012 Council on Higher Education Award for "Outstanding Institutional Practice in Student Learning Outcomes," which stresses that ". . . programs clearly articulate expected student learning outcomes, implement exemplary institutional practices to assess student outcomes by analyzing representative student work, disseminate critical findings and use the data to improve student learning."[12]

LEARNING ANALYTICS

Diane Oblinger defines *analytics* as "the use of data, statistical and quantitative methods, and explanatory and predictive models to allow organizations and individuals to gain insights into and act on complex issues."[13] The application of analytics to higher education, and more specifically to learning, seems to have emerged from a recent confluence of three disparate areas that have all come to maturity at relatively the same time, but did not have much to do with each other: data mining for business intelligence, outcomes assessment, and online learning. Businesses have been using analytics to improve operations for decades—Oblinger suggests that higher education has now taken analytics on because of the sheer volume of computer-stored data, affordable computational capacity, improved techniques for meaningful visualization, and the pressure for accountability.[14] Online learning has been around in one form or another also for decades, but is now managed by complex learning management systems (LMS), which can provide vast quantities of data characterizing student behavior. Lately, especially with the rapid growth of online course offerings at most campuses, and with the development of MOOCs, online learning has become a disruptive force in higher education. LOs assessment has also been a disruptive force, one that has forced the rethinking and restructuring of courses and programs; however, its application to the online learning environment has lagged.[15] These three strands (data mining, online learning, and outcomes assessment) come together in learning analytics.

Everything a student does in an LMS can be (and usually is) logged—every post to a forum, every completed assignment or quiz, every point or grade, every uploaded file or picture, and even the amount of time spent in completing each task or activity. Faculty teaching online courses use relatively simple reports of such data in assessing individual or group student behavior. Learning analytics can do much more with these data, can combine then with data from other campus systems and even social media, and can be used at the program or institution level. Algorithms can analyze the digital trails students take through an LMS, compare students, identify students in trouble, predict that students might have difficulties, suggest, for example, that students who achieved low grades spent x-many hours using the chat room, and so on, and can present those data in visual displays that are easier to interpret than tables of data. Data can be used to detect patterns and develop predictive models, or to support research with specific hypotheses or research questions.[16] Angela van Barneveld, Kimberly E. Arnold, and John P. Campbell provide a good overview of the types of analytics used in higher education, pointing out how differently each type focuses on the constituents: institution (and by extension stakeholders), department, instructor, and learner.[17]

The use of learning analytics is fairly new and is not without controversy. Privacy and confidentiality of course are key issues; trusted data governance and management are a necessary requirement, as is an understanding of the Family Educational Rights and Privacy Act (20 U.S.C. § 1232g; 34 CFR Part 99). Skeptical faculties who feel that numbers are not a good basis for looking at LOs are another barrier, an opinion that is backed by a lack of expertise in sophisticated number-crunching. Writing in 2012, van Barneveld, Arnold, and Campbell identify what is needed for learning analytics (as opposed to academic business analytics) to be ubiquitous and to be perceived as useful: credibility through the development of rigorous tested standards, transformation of faculty, open and accessible scholarship about learning analytics, and an infrastructure to support long-term sustainability with staff expertise.[18]

Donald M. Norris claims that instead of improving business operations, learning analytics has the goal of improving LOs.[19] In fact, much of what learning analytics focuses on is student outcomes rather than student LOs. One of the early adopters, the American Public University System, has a multi-institutional Predictive Analytics Reporting Framework project using predictive analytics to "remove obstacles to student success and reduce problems with student retention,"[20] which are really student outcomes, not LOs. Bruff points out that learning analytics uses data reflecting demographics, academic performance history, and LMS behavior, but while these "say a lot about what students bring to the learning process and what they do during the learning process, . . . they don't really say much about what students are learning or how they're making sense of course material."[21] He suggests that learning analytics could be taken to the next level if used to predict not that one student might have difficulties, but which topics or activities cause problems, what seems to have the greatest effect on skills improvement, and other data that might transform a course. Matthew Prineas and Marie Cini go further:

> As a national movement, however, learning outcomes assessment is concerned mostly with adjustments to curricula and instruction at the program level, generally applying these adjustments to assist future students to achieve at greater levels. To be truly revolutionary, student learning data generated in online technologies must be applied in a systematic way at the program level and in real time, so that students can benefit from ongoing adjustments at the program level—changes in curricula, course sequences, academic requirements, resource allocation, and so on.[22]

CONCLUDING THOUGHTS

A survey of outcomes assessment at close to 3,000 higher education institutions of all types conducted in 2009 by the National Institute for Learning Outcomes Assessment had eight major findings:

1. Most institutions have identified a common set of learning outcomes that apply to all students.
2. Most institutions use a combination of institution-level and program-level assessment approaches.
3. The most common uses of assessment data relate to accreditation.
4. Assessment approaches and uses of assessment results vary systematically by institutional selectivity.
5. Assessment is driven more by accreditation and a commitment to improve than external pressures from government or employers.
6. Most institutions conduct learning outcomes assessment on a shoestring: 20 percent have no assessment staff and 65 percent have two or fewer.
7. Gaining faculty involvement and support remains a major challenge. Campuses would also like more assessment expertise, resources, and tools.
8. Most institutions plan to continue learning outcomes assessment despite budgetary challenges.[23]

Although most of these points are likely to still be true, it seems as though there has been one subtle shift. Although there has been no follow-up survey, it seems that assessment is now driven equally (if not more) by "external pressures," that is, the need to be fiscally accountable to stakeholders. Student outcomes seem to be more important at the institutional level than student LOs, and the lack of understanding of the difference between these two types persists. That being said, progress has certainly been made. A number of universities, colleges, and organizations offer models of best practice and share their processes and findings generously; adoption of LOs assessment has become more systematic at departmental and institutional levels around the country; and the literature and research in the field have matured. Despite frustrations, disappointments, and lack of recognition, more and more faculty and students recognize that the gains are worth the effort.

NOTES

1. National Governors Association, Center for Best Practices. *Complete to Compete: From Information to Action: Revamping Higher Education Accountability Systems* (2011): 18, accessed June 22, 2012, http://www.nga.org/files/live/sites/NGA/files/pdf/1107C2CACTIONGUIDE.PDF.

2. Peter Hernon, Robert E., Dugan, and Danuta A. Nitecki, *Engaging in Evaluation and Assessment Research* (Santa Barbara, CA: Libraries Unlimited, 2011).

3. National Governors Association, Center for Best Practices. *Complete to Compete*.

4. George Kuh and Stanley Ikenberry, *More Than You Think, Less Than We Need: Learning Outcomes Assessment in American Higher Education* (Champaign, IL: National Institute for Learning Outcomes Assessment, 2009), accessed October 25, 2012, http://www.learningoutcomeassessment.org/documents/fullreportrevised-L.pdf.

5. University of Hong Kong, Centre for the Enhancement of Teaching and Learning, *Assessment Drives Learning* (2009), accessed October 25, 2012, http://ar.cetl.hku.hk/obasl.htm.

6. University of Hong Kong, Centre for the Enhancement of Teaching and Learning, *Course Outline Template: Guidelines for Writing Course Outlines* (2010), accessed October 25, 2012, http://ar.cetl.hku.hk/pdf/HKU%20CourseOutlineTemplateV1.1.pdf.

7. A fuller elaboration of direct and indirect measures is found in Peter Hernon and Candy Schwartz, "Applying Student Learning Outcomes to an Educational Program," in *Revisiting Outcomes Assessment in Higher Education*, edited by Peter Hernon, Robert E. Dugan, and Candy Schwartz (Westport, CT: Libraries Unlimited, 2006), 181–98. See especially Figure 10.5, "Outcomes Assessment Measures,"191–92. See also Peter Hernon, "Methods of Data Collection," in *Revisiting Outcomes Assessment in Higher Education*, 135–50; Peter Hernon, "Selecting from the Assessment Tool Chest," in *Outcomes Assessment in Higher Education: Views and Perspectives*, edited by Peter. Hernon and Robert E. Dugan (Westport, CT: Libraries Unlimited, 2004), 149–73.

8. Derek Bruff, "Learning Analytics, Program Assessment, and the Scholarship of Teaching" [web log posting], *Agile Learning* [blog] (July 23, 2012), accessed October 25, 2012, http://derekbruff.org/?p=2273.

9. Thomas A. Angelo and K. Patricia, Cross, *Classroom Assessment Techniques: A Handbook for College Teachers*, 2d ed. (Hoboken, NJ: Wiley, 1993).

10. Hope College, Provost's Office, Student Assessment of Teaching & Learning (2012), accessed October 25, 2012, http://surveys.cs.hope.edu/surveys/create?SurveyName=SALT&CourseID=HOPE&Term=SS10.

11. "The Value Project Overview," *Peer Review* 11, no. 1 (Winter 2009): 4, accessed October 25, 2012, http://www.aacu.org/peerreview/pr-wi09/documents/Peer_Review_Winter_2009.pdf.

12. "2010 CHEA Award for Outstanding Institutional Practice in Student Learning Outcomes," *CHEA Chronicle* 11, no. 1 (February 2010): 2, accessed October 25, 2012, http://www.chea.org/pdf/Chea-Chronicle_Feb2010.pdf.

13. Diane Oblinger, "LET'S Talk . . . Analytics," *Educause Review* 47, no. 4 (2012): 11, accessed October 25, 2012, http://www.educause.edu/ir/library/pdf/ERM1240P.pdf.

14. Ibid.

15. Matthew Prineas and Marie Cini, *Assessing Learning in Online Education: The Role of Technology in Improving Student Outcomes*, NILOA Occasional Paper 12 (Champaign, IL: National Institute for Learning Outcomes Assessment, 2011), accessed October 25, 2012, http://www.learningoutcomeassessment.org/documents/onlineed.pdf.

16. Ibid.

17. Angela van Barneveld, Kimberly E. Arnold, and John P. Campbell, *Analytics in Higher Education: Establishing a Common Language*. Educause Learning Initiative Paper (Washington, DC: Educause, January 2012), accessed October 25, 2012, http://net.educause .edu/ir/library/pdf/ELI3026.pdf.

18. Ibid.

19. Donald M. Norris, *7 Things You Should Know about First-Generation Learning Analytics, Educause Learning Initiative Paper.* Washington, DC: Educause (December 6, 2011), accessed October 25, 2012, http:/www.educause.edu/ir/library/pdf/ELI7079.pdf.

20. Brian Muys, "American Public University System Extends Online Learning Collaboration with WCET for Predictive Analytics Reporting Framework" (August 30, 2012), accessed October 25, 2012, http://www.marketwatch.com/story/american-public-university-system-extends-online-learning-collaboration-with-wcet-for-predictive-analytics-reporting-framework-2012-08-30.

21. Bruff, "Learning Analytics, Program Assessment, and the Scholarship of Teaching."

22. Prineas and Cini, *Assessing Learning in Online Education*, 10.

23. Kuh and Ikenberry, *More Than You Think, Less Than We Need*.

Section IV

CONCLUSION

12

MOVING FORWARD

Peter Hernon and Robert E. Dugan

Anyone reading about higher education and its recovery from the economic crisis realizes that the federal government and states are placing greater emphasis on metrics associated with accountability and economic efficiency. Perusal of the Almanac issue of *Chronicle of Higher Education*[1] and reading Chapters 3, 4, and 6 of this book underscore the national focus on institutional transparency and enabling parents and prospective students to engage in comparison shopping—matching institutions and programs of study to their career expectations, ability to manage the costs of a degree, and projected completion rates. For them, as well as the federal government and states, critical student outcomes thus become:

- Time-to-degree
- Retention rate
- Completion (graduation) rate
- Amount of student indebtedness likely incurred

At least six states, including Indiana and Michigan, link state appropriations to completion rates, and a number of other states are contemplating a similar linkage. Clearly, states want to maximize their investment in higher education—even if it is dwindling—while adding to the workforce of qualified professionals who are unlikely to move elsewhere and who will generate additional tax revenue. Complicating matters, many employers are dissatisfied with the college graduates they hire. They believe that the graduates perform below expectations on learning goals associated with critical thinking and adaptability. They also want "linkage between educational outcomes and workforce development."[2] This finding, together with the expectation of institutional and program accreditation organizations, reinforces the importance of student learning outcomes but within a context framed by student outcomes.

To help parents and prospective students engage in comparison shopping, in October 2011, the federal government required all undergraduate institutions that award federal title IV financial aid to post net-price calculators on their websites to provide estimates of what students would pay to attend.[3],[4] At the same time, the Consumer Financial Protection Bureau (CFPB), established by the Dodd-Frank Wall Street Reform and Consumer Protection Act of 2010, is now "accepting complaints from borrowers having difficulties with their private student loans. The CFPB will assist all borrowers experiencing problems taking out a private student loan, repaying their private student loan, or managing a student loan that has gone into default and may have been referred to a debt collector."[5]

All of these activities create pressures for colleges and universities as they cope with the aftermath of the economic recession and continue to seek additional economic efficiencies through the closing or consolidation of academic programs, place increased reliance on adjunct instructors, and offer more online courses to attract a global population, especially one of adult learners. One means of curbing expenses pertains to bookstores and libraries, namely, wanting to expand student use of electronic textbooks. However, e-textbooks are not always as inexpensive as some stakeholders assume.

GRADUATION RATE

The importance of graduation is underscored by the pledge of the Association of Public and Land-Grant Universities and the American Association of State Colleges and Universities, which represent approximately 500 public four-year colleges. Known as "Project Degree Completion," the institutions are promising to help 60 percent of adults earn a college degree by 2025. The goal is to increase the number of baccalaureate-degree holders by 3.8 million by 2025. To achieve this goal, the colleges are considering strategies such as "reaching out to former students who took courses at the colleges but did not complete their degrees, collaborating more closely with elementary and secondary schools and community colleges, limiting the number of credits needed for certain majors, and providing more-intensive academic advising."[6] Undoubtedly, the colleges want to renew their partnership with government and see the partnership as one way to reduce regulations or increase financial support.

A NEW PERSPECTIVE

In a report limited to one state, *The Earning Power of Graduates from Tennessee's Colleges and Universities, College Measures* quantifies the value of a degree by focusing on starting salaries and casts the purpose of an education in narrow terms: job creation and workforce needs of a state, and not on becoming a so-called educated person, defined as someone well-read and grounded in the liberal arts. Students and their parents can monitor wage differences by major and view an education in terms of initial and perhaps potential earnings. At the same time, governors such as the one in Florida can seek to allocate state budgets to fields that are likely to lead to good paying jobs and away from fields that do not serve "the state's vital interest." Also students might be forewarned about careers that pay low wages and will result in a longer time needed to erase student indebtedness.[7] This new perspective adds other metrics to student outcomes, namely, those associated with earnings, and appeal to an increasing number of states.

OUTCOME OF NATIONAL ELECTION, 2012

As we write this chapter in the fall, 2012, it seems safe to predict that the November, 2012, election should not alter the general trends documented in previous chapters. The concern about the rising cost of a college degree will remain while alternatives to traditional education (i.e., the presence of community colleges and vocational training, online universities and online education, for-profit universities) will thrive, despite the criticism they concentrate on student enrollment rate and not retention and graduates rates, and they inadequately prepare graduates to enter the workforce and engage in lifelong learning. The Obama administration, however, would continue its crackdown on for-profit colleges and universities whereas the Republicans see them as competitors to traditional institutions and oppose efforts to regulate them. The Democrats favor expanded access to higher education and regard higher education as vital to national competitiveness and to being part of the middle class. They also want the United States to have the world's highest proportion of college graduates by 2020.

College affordability remains a central issue and employers will continue to push for a better educated workforce, thereby pressuring colleges and universities to raise their expectations that a college education cannot be equated with remedial education. Student aid remains an issue of contention, as Republicans reject the federal government as the guarantor of student loans and do not want it to stand between students and the private sector. They want private lenders and banks, rather than the federal government, to issue federally subsidized college loans. ". . . [A] cut in federal financial aid would increase the burden on students and families in the short term, and there is no hard evidence that it would curb tuition increases down the road."[8] The Democrats want the federal government to continue to play a critical role; however, they want some changes to the process and improved repayment options.

Republicans, as reflected in their party platform of 2008 and 2012, view faculty as liberal and engaged in political indoctrination. Intellectual intolerance, they maintain, has no place in places of higher education and the intellectual exchange of ideas. Absent from the platforms is mention of quality, as that topic remains for accreditation organizations and employers to shape.[9] As shown in previous chapters, for government and some others, educational quality is the same as completion rate. Although they differ, their combination simplifies accountability, as the Lumina Foundation proposes.

TRANSPARENCY

One indicator of quality control is institutional and program accreditation. As Laura Saunders found when she examined the homepages of colleges and universities, many do not make their self-studies publicly available.[10] In 2012, the Western Association of Schools and Colleges (WASC), one of the six regional higher education accreditation organizations, announced that it will regularly make all of its accreditation reports available to the public. In doing so, WASC provides stakeholders with additional information on colleges and universities. However, as Andrew P. Kelly and Mark Schneider note,

> As anyone who has ever read an accreditation report can tell you, making these documents public will do little to help prospective students in the near

term. You need a higher education glossary and a helping of patience to even begin to decipher the jargon. Even then, the results are often difficult to interpret, and almost impossible to use in a comparative way.[11]

Typically, when the review process uncovers areas where institutions and programs need to improve, those results are not routinely made public. Most colleges and universities simply announce that they have passed; in some instances, a news item reports that a college or university—or program—lost or is "on probation" or "at risk" of losing its accreditation. "Otherwise, all accredited schools bear the same seal of approval, whether they have a sterling record of success or a troubled history."[12] Kelly and Schneider think that WASC's new policy is

> rhetorically important for what it signals to the insular, risk-averse, and often defensive culture of higher education. The days of hiding behind accreditation and benefiting from its imprimatur will slowly come to an end. Demands for better information about higher education quality and value—whether defined in terms of student learning, labor market outcomes, or return on investment—are growing from the statehouse to the White House.[13]

CUSTOMER SATISFACTION

Student learning goals can be set at the course, program, or institutional level. Regardless, these focus on learning (knowledge, skills, abilities, attitude, and disposition, and ways of knowing), attainment, and development. Such goals are often viewed in the context of behaviors (employment, further education, career mobility, and income) as well as student satisfaction.[14] The Accrediting Commission of the Distance Education and Training Council, in a document requesting public comment, underscores the importance of student learning goals and completion rates (for courses and programs), but sees the importance of "students taking the course as additional indicators of student success and satisfaction"—satisfaction with the instructional and educational services provided.[15] As a further explanation, the Commission maintains that;

> Student satisfaction can range from whether the course materials were current and comprehensive to whether grading services were prompt and fair and if faculty members have performed adequately. Student expressions of satisfaction are normally attained through institution surveys, but an institution can also gather and present data such as unsolicited testimonials, referrals of other students, and repeat enrollments in new or subsequent courses. . . . The students' expression of their own satisfaction is another form of evidence used to document outcome achievement.[16]

To determine student satisfaction, some institutions use surveys designed to measure student satisfaction at the program or institutional level. At the course level, they often rely on course evaluations, which are not designed to measure satisfaction (defined in terms of gap analysis as the difference between ideal expectations and the actual experience).

As librarians explore assorted metrics, be they input, output, or outcome metrics, they should not forget to collect and analyze data that deal with customer satisfaction. Academic and public libraries using LibPAS, developed by Counting Opinions, have an instrument that measures the gap while reporting data about customer information-seeking preferences. However, that instrument does not apply to learning. Some libraries mistakenly use LibQUAL+™ to gauge satisfaction, when in fact that instrument measures service quality, a concept that is the antecedent to satisfaction.[17]

Another Perspective

Alumni Factor, which offers a perspective on 177 institutions (see https://www .alumnifactor.com/), completes rankings of student satisfaction by reporting the satisfaction of those who graduated with a baccalaureate degree. It includes responses to questions such as:

- If you had it to do all over again, would you choose to attend your alma mater?
- Do you think the education you received there, was a good value?
- Would you recommend your alma mater to a student who was considering it?

Additional questions make it clear that the focus is on what students gained from their education, mainly a career and an income. A subset of respondents was "asked about their intellectual and social development, as well as their 'overall happiness.'"[18] This college guide appears to consider educational outcomes in terms of variables such as students' preparation for their first job since graduation and their salary (net worth). In summary, a set of new metrics might be known as alumni metrics. To date, we are unaware of an institution that uses such metrics except to report on fund-raising and to monitor alumni engagement in the institution and their program of study.

STATUS QUO

It is common for libraries to engage in change management, with the change being incremental and, in some instances, dramatic. Rush Miller argues that "it is not a time for retrenchment and timidity but for expansion and boldness for academic libraries. The library that thrives, even in the midst of a recession, will be the one which seizes the opportunity to redesign itself for the future." He adds, "We cannot allow anything to deter us from creating the future for libraries that will maintain our relevance to the academic mission of our universities."[19] A number of libraries are adapting a similar perspective and actively work with academic departments on data curation, educating students in the use of digital data and digital archives, assuming new roles in open access publishing, and focusing special collections in areas where they can take on new roles and responsibilities (e.g., collecting primary sources on human rights and creating partnerships with human rights organizations).

Despite these activities, academic librarians tend to maintain a status quo relationship in meeting the expectations of institutional and program accreditation organizations; the only exception involves fulfilling those standards that speak specifically to the library's collection. When librarians participate in student learning outcomes, they tend to focus exclusively on information literacy and a role in those courses to which faculty will permit entry. They might apply a data collection instrument that measures mastery of all facets of information literacy at the course level. There is little, if any, participation with faculty as partners in shaping those facets of information literacy most important to students majoring in a subject or area of knowledge. Instead of merely advocating for a classroom presence, librarians are now calling for a credit course on information literacy, perhaps for students enrolled in an English course.[20] The purpose is to reach more students, but this falls short of engaging in instruction on a cooperative basis with faculty throughout a general education program or with departmental majors throughout their undergraduate experience.

It seems that, when library directors offer a vision for the future of the academic library, they do not include the expectations of accreditation organizations as a component of that vision. They see their institutional role in other areas and probably do not want to divert resources to the learning process beyond the course level, except perhaps for an online course open to students beyond one course or section. They may be content to develop library guides that student across disciplines and programs can use as needed. Playing a direct instructional role at the program and institutional levels likely requires the hiring of more professionals knowledgeable about educational and learning pedagogy as well as assessment research, and implies the ability to partner with teaching faculty in the setting of learning goals, the measurement of student progress in achieving those goals, and making adjustments in the teaching and learning process as needed.

CONCLUDING THOUGHTS

Outcomes assessment encompasses both student outcomes and student learning outcomes, with government emphasizing one and others perhaps emphasizing the other or a combination of student outcomes and student learning outcomes. Nonetheless, both types of outcomes are becoming more complicated and more disconnected from each other. The two really should be interconnected. Government stakeholders are emphasizing affordability, transparency, completion, and retention as student outcomes. However, quality as an important student outcome is dependent on a better understanding and measuring of student learning outcomes. When quality is discussed, it might be only in regard to a separation from remedial education; given the weakness of a high school education and higher education having to engage in remedial education, stakeholders see remedial education as a precursor to an educated graduate. This remedial focus on quality frequently ignores values (being ethical) and attitudes (work ethic), which are also important student learning outcomes. Along with a set of workforce-ready skills and abilities, employers expect personal and professional values and attitudes. Furthermore, quality, when associated with credit completions as in Tennessee's implementation of its 2010 Complete College Act, is also directly linked to performance funding; it is feared that course expectations might be lowered as greater pressure is applied to course instructors expected to pass students along in order to retain state funding.[21] To the dismay of educators, student learning outcomes are becoming lost in the noise of affordability, completion, and debt. Stakeholders want higher education to graduate students faster and cheaper. And while they have said "better," they mean it in the context of workforce readiness. Faster, cheaper, and graduated are becoming proxies for quality. However, faster, cheaper, and graduated do not necessarily equate to "skilled, with values" or "educated" in the past context of those words' societal and cultural meaning.

While public dollar investment in higher education decreases, the demand for accountability increases. "Do more with less" while at the same time, "report more and measure more" is the usual refrain. Higher education is seen as a major contributor to the economy, but it is simultaneously subjected to increasing oversight and regulation. The commercial sector would battle these constraints, but the higher education institutions do not. Why? The answer may be that higher education is still dependent on public dollars and not yet comfortable with severing the public assistance cord from the demands for accountability. Perhaps senior higher education administrators are concerned that they may fail to reflect their own message. For example, higher education wants *helicopter parents* (a term for parents who pay extremely close attention to their child's daily education and communicate directly with instructors as well as being actively involved in the selection of the right institution for their child) to let their children mature while in college. And yet, those in higher education do not seem to be able or willing to give up the same chord of dependence for which they chastise the parents. The focus is less on quality as reflected through any assessment of learning (e.g., student learning outcomes) and more on accountability, institutional efficiency, and the immediate need of individuals to contribute to greater economic productivity. Clearly, some major stakeholders and those in higher education have a different perspective on what comprises an educated person, and the gulf between both perspectives is widening.

NOTES

1. "Almanac 2012–13," *Chronicle of Higher Education* LIX, no. 1 (August 31, 2012), entire issue.

2. Anthony S. Bieda, *Closing the Gap between Career Education & Employer Expectations: Implications for America's Unemployment Rate* (Washington, DC: Accrediting Council for Independent Colleges and Schools, 2011): 6, accessed August 18, 2012, http://www.acics.org/events/content.aspx?id=4718.

3. Sara Lipka, "A Shaper Focus on Cost and Whether Students Graduate," *Chronicle of Higher Education* LIX, no. 1 (August 31, 2012): 30.

4. Both the College Board and the National Center for Education Statistics, Department of Education, also maintain net price calculators; see http://netpricecalculator.collegeboard.org/; http://nces.ed.gov/ipeds/netpricecalculator/.

5. Student loans have now surpassed credit cards as the largest source of unsecured consumer debt. Millions of students turn to private loans to pay for college when scholarships and federal student loans do not cover the full costs. But unlike federal student loans, private student loans do not generally have the same borrower protections such as military deferments, discharges upon death, or income-based repayment plans. ". . . Among the complaints that the Bureau anticipates receiving: difficulties making full payment; confusing advertising or marketing terms; billing disputes; deferment and forbearance issues; and debt collection and credit reporting problems." See U.S. Consumer Financial Protection Bureau, "Press Release: Consumer Financial Protection Bureau Now Taking Private Student Loan Complaints" (March 5, 2012), accessed August 21, 2012, http://www.consumerfinance.gov/pressreleases/consumer-financial-protection-bureau-now-taking-private-student-loan-complaints/.

6. Eric Kelderman, "Public Colleges Pledge to Raise Number of Graduates, and Seek Help in Doing So," *Chronicle of Higher Education* (October 2, 2012), accessed October 2, 2012, http://chronicle.com/article/Public-Colleges-Pledge-to/134812/?cid=pm&utm_source=pm&utm_medium=en.

7. Dan Berrett, "All about the Money," *Chronicle of Higher Education* LIX, no. 4 (September 21, 2012): A1, A4, A6. See also Beckie Supiano, "Students Need Better Data on Earnings and Other College Outcomes, Senators Say," *Chronicle of Higher Education* LIX, no. 5 (September 28, 2012): A15.

8. Adeshina Emmanuel, "Private Sector Role Is at Heart of Campaigns' Split on College Costs," *New York Times* (September 8, 2012): A9.

9. Peter T. Ewell, *Accreditation and Student Learning Outcomes: A Proposed Point of Departure*, CHEA Occasional Paper (Washington, DC: Council for Higher Education Accreditation, 2001), accessed August 22, 2012, http://www.chea.org/pdf/EwellSLO_Sept2001.pdf.

10. Laura Saunders, *Information Literacy as a Student Learning Outcome: The Perspective of Institutional Accreditation* (Santa Barbara, CA: Libraries Unlimited, 2011).

11. Andrew P. Kelly and Mark Schneider, "Small Step for Quality Control," *Inside Higher Ed* (July 31, 2012), accessed August 3, 2012, http://www.insidehighered.com/views/2012/07/31/accreditors-bold-strike-greater-college-transparency-essay#.UFSv-W4T33U.email.

12. Ibid.

13. Ibid.

14. Distance Education and Training Council, Accrediting Commission, "Policy on Student Achievement and Satisfaction" (Washington, DC: Distance Education and Training Council, 2012), 2, 4, accessed August 18, 2012, http://www.detc.org/actions/comment/june2012/1%20-%20C.14.%20Policy%20on%20Student%20Achievement.pdf.

15. Ibid.

16. Ibid., 6.

17. See Peter Hernon and Ellen Altman, *Assessing Service Quality: Satisfying the Expectations of Library Customers*, 2nd ed. (Chicago: American Library Association, 2010).

18. Eric Hoover, "New Player in the College-Rankings Game Mines Alumni Opinions," *Chronicle of Higher Education* LIX, no. 3 (September 14, 2012): A29.

19. Rush Miller, "Damn the Recession, Full Speed Ahead," *Journal of Library Administration* 52, no. 1 (2012): 3, 17.

20. See, for instance, Yvonne Mery, Jill Newby, and Ke Peng, "Why One-Short Information Literacy Sessions Are Not the Future of Instruction: A Case for Online Credit Courses," *College & Research Libraries* 73, no. 4 (July 2012): 366–77.

21. Eric Kelderman, "With State Support Now Tied to Completion, Tennessee Colleges Must Refocus," *Chronicle of Higher Education* LIX, no. 6 (October 5, 2012): A16, A18.

Appendix

HIGHER EDUCATION ORGANIZATIONS, ASSOCIATIONS, AND CENTERS WITH RESPONSIBILITIES, ACTIVITIES, AND/OR RESEARCH RELATED TO OUTCOMES

ORGANIZATION/ ASSOCIATION/ CENTER	WEBSITE ADDRESS	DESCRIPTION
The Accrediting Commission for Community and Junior Colleges [WASC]	http://www.accjc .org/	Accredits associate degree-granting institutions in the Western region of the United States under the Western Association of Schools and Colleges
The Accrediting Commission for Senior Colleges and Universities [WASC]	http://www .wascsenior.org/	A regional postsecondary accrediting agency of the Western Association of Schools and Colleges
Accrediting Council for Independent Colleges and Schools	http://www.acics .org/	The U.S. DOE- and CHEA-recognized national accrediting organization of degree-granting institutions, accrediting professional, technical, and occupational programs and institutions offering certificates, diplomas, and degrees from the associate's through the master's
Achieve	http://achieve.org/	Independent, bipartisan, nonprofit education reform organization
ACT	http://www.act.org/	Provides research and solutions that provide administrators with data and tools to inform institutional initiatives

(Continued)

ORGANIZATION/ ASSOCIATION/ CENTER	WEBSITE ADDRESS	DESCRIPTION
Adult College Completion Network	http://adultcollege completion.org/	Unites organizations and agencies working to increase college completion by adults with prior college credits but no degree in a collaborative learning network
Advisory Committee on Student Financial Assistance (U.S. DOE)	http://www2.cd.gov/ about/bdscomm/ list/acsfa/edlite-index.html	An independent and bipartisan source of advice and counsel on student financial aid policy to both Congress and the secretary of education
American Association for Higher Education and Accreditation	http://www.aahea .org/	Provides accreditation to more than 20 disciplines of higher education
American Association of Colleges for Teacher Education	http://www.aacte .org/	National alliance of educator preparation programs supported by programs in data gathering, policy analysis, and professionals issues
American Association of Colleges of Nursing	http://www.aacn .nche.edu/	Serves the public interest by setting standards, providing resources, and developing the leadership capacity of member schools to advance nursing education, research, and practice
American Association of Collegiate Registrars and Admissions Officers	http://www.aacrao .org/	Promote higher education and further the professional development of members working in admissions, enrollment management, financial aid, institutional research, records, registration, scheduling, academic standards, and student progress
American Association of Community Colleges	http://www.aacc .nche.edu/	Primary advocacy organization for the nation's two-year degree-granting institutions
American Association of State Colleges and Universities	http://aascu.org/	Higher education association of public colleges, universities, and systems dedicated to research and creativity that advances their regions' economic progress and cultural development
American Association of University Professors	http://www.aaup .org/aaup	Purpose is to advance academic freedom and shared governance, to define fundamental professional values and standards for higher education, and to ensure higher education's contribution to the common good

ORGANIZATION/ ASSOCIATION/ CENTER	WEBSITE ADDRESS	DESCRIPTION
American Association of University Women	http://www.aauw .org/	Advances equity for women and girls through advocacy, education, philanthropy, and research
American College Personnel Association	http://www2 .myacpa.org/	Supports and fosters college student learning through the generation and dissemination of knowledge, which informs policies, practices, and programs for student affairs professionals and the higher education community
American Conference of Academic Deans	http://www.acad-edu .org/	A membership-driven organization committed to the ideals of a liberal education that provides academic leaders with the resources they need to excel in their field
The American Council of Trustees and Alumni	http://www.goacta .org/	Independent, nonprofit organization supporting a liberal arts education, upholding high academic standards, safeguarding the free exchange of ideas on campus, and ensuring a high-quality college education at an affordable price
American Council on Education	http://www.acenet .edu/	Foster collaboration and partnerships within and outside the higher education community to help colleges and universities address the challenges of the 21st century
American Dental Education Association	http://www.adea .org/Pages/ default.aspx	National organization representing academic dentistry that determines best practices for dental education and encourages changes in dental education programs through advocacy
American Educational Research Association	http://aera.net/	International professional organization with the primary goal of advancing educational research and its practical application
American Enterprise Institute for Public Policy Research	http://www.aei.org	Producing research in several key policy areas including respect and support for the power of free enterprise and a strong defense centered on smart international relations, and opportunity for all

(Continued)

ORGANIZATION/ ASSOCIATION/ CENTER	WEBSITE ADDRESS	DESCRIPTION
The American Indian College Fund	http://www .collegefund.org/	Disburses scholarships for American Indian students seeking to better their lives through higher education and provides funding support for tribal college needs ranging from capital support to cultural preservation activities
American Indian Higher Education Consortium	http://www.aihec .org/index.cfml	Provides leadership and influences public policy on American Indian higher education issues through advocacy, research, and program initiatives
American Institutes for Research	http://www.aei.org	Research and evaluation work identify successful practices to increase educational access and to coordinate K-12 preparation with postsecondary needs
American Library Association	http://www.ala.org/	Professional organization that provides leadership for the development, promotion, and improvement of library and information services and the profession of librarianship in order to enhance learning and ensure access to information for all
American Society for Engineering Education	http://www.asee .org/	A nonprofit organization of individuals and institutions committed to furthering education in engineering and engineering technology through policies, programs, and advocacy
Association for Institutional Research	http://www.airweb .org/	Supports quality data and decisions for higher education through forums, institutes, and workshops
Association for Non-Traditional Students in Higher Education	http://www.antshe .org/	An international partnership of students, academic professionals, institutions, and organizations whose mission is to encourage and coordinate support, education, and advocacy for the adult learner
Association for the Advancement of Sustainability in Higher Education	http://www.aashe .org/	Provides resources, professional development, and a network of support to enable institutions of higher education to model and advance sustainability

ORGANIZATION/ ASSOCIATION/ CENTER	WEBSITE ADDRESS	DESCRIPTION
Association for the Study of Higher Education	http://www.ashe .ws/	Promotes collaboration among its members and others engaged in the study of higher education through research, conferences, and publications
Association of Academic Health Centers	http://www.aahcdc .org/	Nonprofit organization that seeks to advance the nation's health and well-being through vigorous leadership of the nation's academic health centers
Association of American Colleges and Universities	http://www.aacu .org/	National association reinforces the commitment to liberal education at both the national and local levels and to help individual colleges and universities keep the quality of student learning at the core of their work
Association of American Law Schools	http://www.aals .org/	Nonprofit educational association to improve the legal profession through professional development programs, an annual meeting, and as legal education's principal representative to the federal government
Association of American Medical Colleges	https://www.aamc .org/	Its programs and services strengthen the world's most advanced medical care by supporting the entire spectrum of education, research, and patient care activities conducted by member institutions
Association of American Universities	http://www.aau .edu/	Focuses on issues of research-intensive universities, including funding for research, research and education policy, and graduate and undergraduate education
Association of Catholic Colleges and Universities	http://www.accunet .org/	Help member institutions strengthen their stated Catholic mission and to foster collaboration among Catholic colleges and universities
Association of College and Research Libraries	http://www.ala.org/ acrl/	Professional association dedicated to enhancing the ability of academic library and information professionals to serve the information needs of the higher education community and to improve learning, teaching, and research

(Continued)

ORGANIZATION/ ASSOCIATION/ CENTER	WEBSITE ADDRESS	DESCRIPTION
Association of College and University Telecommunications Administrators	http://www.acuta .org/wcm/acuta/	Support higher education information communications technology professionals in contributing to the achievement of the strategic mission of their institution
Association of Community College Trustees	http://www.acct .org/	Nonprofit educational organization of governing boards, representing elected and appointed trustees who govern community, technical, and junior colleges
Association of Governing Boards of Universities and Colleges	http://agb.org/	Serves the interests and needs of academic governing boards, boards of institutionally related foundations, and campus CEOs and other senior-level campus administrators on issues related to higher education governance and leadership
Association of Higher Education Facilities Officers	http://www.appa .org/	Professional association for administrators of the physical plants of institutions of higher education
Association of Independent Colleges of Art and Design	http://aicad.org/	Nonprofit consortium of art schools that helps to strengthen the member colleges and to inform the public about the members and the value of studying art and design
Association of Jesuit Colleges and Universities	http://www.ajcunet .edu/	National voluntary service organization to provide an excellent education to develop competent, compassionate, and committed leaders in the service of the church and society
Association of Private Sector Colleges and Universities	http://www.career .org/	Source of information and public policy recommendations that promote access to career education and the importance of workforce development
Association of Public and Land-grant Universities	https://www.aplu .org/	Undertakes the responsibility to identify certain issues that affect public higher education and, as appropriate, suggest ways for involvement on such issues

ORGANIZATION/ ASSOCIATION/ CENTER	WEBSITE ADDRESS	DESCRIPTION
Association of Research Libraries	http://www.arl.org/	Advances the goals of its members by providing leadership in public and information policy, fostering the exchange of ideas and expertise, and facilitating the emergence of new roles for research libraries
Association of University Technology Managers	http://www.autm .net/home.htm	Membership organization of more than 350 universities, research institutions, teaching hospitals, and government agencies as well as hundreds of companies involved with managing and licensing innovations derived from academic and nonprofit research
Association on Higher Education and Disability	http://www.ahead .org/	Professional membership organization for individuals involved in the development of policy and in the provision of services to meet the needs of persons with disabilities involved in all areas of higher education
Bill & Melinda Gates Foundation	http://www .gatesfoundation .org/Pages/home .aspx	The Postsecondary Success Strategy aims to increase the number of young adults who complete postsecondary education
The Brookings Institution	http://www .brookings.edu/	Nonprofit public policy organization conducting independent research to provide innovative, practical recommendations
Business-Higher Education Forum	http://www.bhef .com/	Organization of business and higher education executives dedicated to advancing solutions to the U.S. education and workforce challenges, conducting research to create solutions and to identify strategies and policy reforms
Campus Compact	http://www .compact.org/	National coalition of college and university presidents promoting public and community service, helping campuses forge community partnerships, and providing resources for faculty seeking to integrate civic and community-based learning into the curriculum

(Continued)

ORGANIZATION/ ASSOCIATION/ CENTER	WEBSITE ADDRESS	DESCRIPTION
The Campus Computing Project	http://www .campuscomputing .net/	Continuing study of the role of computing, e-learning, and information technology in American higher education
Carnegie Foundation for the Advancement of Teaching	http://www .carnegiefoundation .org/	An independent policy and research center for improving teaching and learning
The Center for American Progress	http://www .americanprogress .org/	Liberal think tank addressing such 21st-century challenges as energy, national security, economic growth and opportunity, immigration, education, and health care
The Center for College Affordability and Productivity	http://centerfor collegeaffordability .org/	Is dedicated to researching the rising costs and efficiency in higher education, and to facilitate dialogue on the issues facing the higher education institutions with the public, policymakers, and the higher education community
Center for Community College Student Engagement	http://www.ccsse .org/center/	Conducts a collection of national surveys including the Community College Survey of Student Engagement (CCSSE), and the Survey of Entering Student Engagement (SENSE), among others
The Center for Education Reform	http://www .edreform.com/	Seeks structural and sustainable changes that can improve educational opportunities by improving the accuracy and quality of discourse and decisions about education reform
Center for Higher Education Policy Analysis (at University of Southern California)	http://www.usc .edu/dept/chepa/	Uses multiple publication formats, conference and school presentations, and electronic communication to inform the discussion regarding the future of higher education
Center for International Higher Education (at Boston College)	http://www.bc.edu/ research/cihe/	Publishes book series and sponsors occasional conferences on key issues in higher education and engages in research on higher education in international perspective

ORGANIZATION/ ASSOCIATION/ CENTER	WEBSITE ADDRESS	DESCRIPTION
Center for Postsecondary Research (at Indiana University)	http://cpr.iub.edu/ index.cfm	Promotes student success and institutional effectiveness through research and service to postsecondary institutions and related agencies
Center for Research on Education, Diversity & Excellence (at UC-Berkeley)	http://crede .berkeley.edu/	Promotes research by university faculty and graduate students focused on improving the education of students whose ability to reach their potential is challenged by language or cultural barriers, race, geographic location, or poverty
Center for Studies in Higher Education (at UC-Berkeley)	http://cshe.berkeley .edu/	Multidisciplinary research and policy center on higher education oriented to California, the nation, and comparative international issues
Center for the Study of Education Policy (Illinois State University)	http://centereducation policy.illinoisstate .edu/	Collects and organizes information, conducts research, and brings the results of research into the everyday world of school administrators, governmental leaders, and higher education policymakers
Center for the Study of Higher Education (at Penn State University)	http://www.ed.psu .edu/educ/cshe	Conducts theory-based research that informs efforts to improve higher education policy and practice
Center for Urban Education (at University of Southern California)	http://cue.usc.edu/	Leads socially conscious research and develops tools needed for institutions of higher education to produce equity in student outcomes
Center on Education and the Workforce (at Georgetown University)	http://cew .georgetown.edu/	An independent, nonprofit research and policy institute that studies the link between education, career qualifications, and workforce demands
Center on Education Policy and Workforce Competitiveness (at University of Virginia)	http://curry.virginia .edu/research/ centers/cepwc	Provide research and exchange of ideas to inform the design of education policy targeted to improving educational outcomes and the economic competitiveness of American workers in an increasingly globalized world

(Continued)

ORGANIZATION/ ASSOCIATION/ CENTER	WEBSITE ADDRESS	DESCRIPTION
Coalition of Higher Education Assistance Organizations	http://www.coheao .com/	A partnership of colleges, universities, and organizations dedicated to promoting the federal campus-based loan programs and other student financial services with updates through newsletters, webinars, and annual conferences
Coalition of Urban and Metropolitan Universities	http://www .cumuonline.org/	Mission to use their campuses in education, research, and service to enhance the communities in which they are located through conferences, a journal, research projects, and the creation of a policy agenda
College and University Professional Association for Human Resources	http://www.cupahr .org/	Provides knowledge, resources, advocacy, and connections to achieve organizational and workforce excellence in higher education human resources
The College Board	http://www .collegeboard.org/	Provide resources, tools, and services to students, parents, colleges, and universities in the areas of college planning, recruitment and admissions, financial aid, and retention
College Choices for Adults	http://www.college choicesforadults .org/	Consumer database to help adult learners choose an online program; includes program-level learning outcomes
Collegiate Learning Assessment	http://www.collegiate learningassessment .org/	Helps institutions improve undergraduate education through assessment, professional development, best practices, and collaboration
Commission on Institutions of Higher Education	http://cihe.neasc .org/	A regional postsecondary accrediting agency of the New England Association of Schools and Colleges
Committee on Education and the Workforce, U.S. House of Representatives	http://edworkforce .house.gov/	Oversees programs that affect hundreds of millions of Americans—from school teachers and small business owners to students and retirees

ORGANIZATION/ ASSOCIATION/ CENTER	WEBSITE ADDRESS	DESCRIPTION
Community College Research Center (at Columbia University)	http://ccrc .tc.columbia.edu/	Conducts research on the major issues affecting community colleges in the United States and contributes to the development of practice and policy that expands access to higher education and promotes success for all students
Complete College America	http:// completecollege .org/	National nonprofit works with states to increase the number of Americans with quality career certificates or college degrees
Consortium for Higher Education Benchmarking Analysis	http://cheba.com/	Provides a forum for the exchange of performance measurements and benchmarking data for all levels of higher education around the world
Consortium for North American Higher Education Collaboration	http://www .conahec.org/ conahec/index.jsp	Advises and connects institutions interested in establishing or strengthening academic collaborative programs in North America
Consortium of Liberal Arts Colleges	http://www .liberalarts.org/	Not-for-profit organization to explore and promote the use of information technology among its members including an annual conference and representation of the interests of liberal arts institutions on information technology issues at the national level
Consortium on Financing Higher Education	http://web.mit .edu/cofhe/	Organization of 31 private liberal arts colleges; its data collection, research, and policy analysis focus primarily on matters pertaining to undergraduate access, affordability, and assessment
Council for Adult and Experiential Learning	http://cael.org/ home	Supports ways to link learning from an individual's work and life experiences to their educational goals
Council for Advancement and Support of Education	http://www.case .org/	Professional association serving educational institutions and advancement professionals who work on their behalf in alumni relations, communications, development, marketing, and allied areas

(Continued)

ORGANIZATION/ ASSOCIATION/ CENTER	WEBSITE ADDRESS	DESCRIPTION
Council for Aid to Education	http://cae.org/	Focused on improving quality and access in higher education for public university systems; manages the Collegiate Learning Assessment (CLA), a national effort to assess the quality of undergraduate education by directly measuring student learning outcomes
Council for Christian Colleges and Universities	http://www.cccu .org/	A nonprofit international association of intentionally Christian colleges and universities to help member institutions transform lives through programs and services
Council for Higher Education Accreditation	http://www.chea .org/	An association of degree-granting colleges and universities that is an advocate and institutional voice for self-regulation of academic quality through accreditation by recognizing institutional and programmatic accrediting organizations
Council for Opportunity in Education	http://www.coenet .us/	Nonprofit organization dedicated to furthering the expansion of college opportunities for low-income, first-generation students, and students with disabilities throughout the United States
Council for the Accreditation of Educator Preparation	http://www.caepsite .org/	Through the consolidation of NCATE and TEAC, CAEP will serve as a single accreditor for reform, innovation, and research in educator preparation by the end of 2012
Council of Graduate Schools	http://www.cgsnet .org/	Mission is to advance graduate education in order to ensure the vitality of intellectual discovery and to promote an environment that cultivates rigorous scholarship
Council of Independent Colleges	http://www.cic .edu/	National service organization for all small and mid-sized, independent, liberal arts colleges and universities focuses on providing seminars, workshops, and programs

ORGANIZATION/ ASSOCIATION/ CENTER	WEBSITE ADDRESS	DESCRIPTION
The Council of State Governments	http://www.csg .org/	Nonpartisan organization that brings state leaders together to share ideas, foster innovation in state government, and highlight examples of how ingenuity and leadership are transforming the way state government serves residents
The Council on Governmental Relations	http://www.cogr .edu/	An association of research universities that provides advice and information to its membership and makes certain that federal agencies understand academic operations and the impact of proposed regulations on colleges and universities
Council on Undergraduate Research	http://www.cur .org/	Mission is to support and promote high-quality undergraduate student–faculty collaborative research and scholarship
Data Quality Campaign	http://dataquality campaign.org/	National, collaborative effort to encourage and support state policymakers to improve the availability and use of high-quality education data to improve student achievement
Digital Promise	http://www .digitalpromise .org/	An independent nonprofit organization created through the federal HEO Act of 2008 to support a research and development program about the capacity of information and digital technologies to improve all levels of learning and education
Education Commission of the States	http://www.ecs .org/	Keep policymakers informed by gathering, analyzing, and disseminating information about current and emerging issues, trends, and innovations in state educational postsecondary policy and system designs
Education Finance Council	http://www.efc.org/	Association representing the nation's nonprofit and state agency student finance organizations and dedicated to the single purpose of making college more affordable

(Continued)

ORGANIZATION/ ASSOCIATION/ CENTER	WEBSITE ADDRESS	DESCRIPTION
Education Sector	http://www .educationsector .org/	Nonprofit, nonpartisan organization; the goal of its higher education work is to improve learning and graduation outcomes for students attending nonelite colleges
Education Trust	http://www.edtrust .org/	Promotes high academic achievement for all students at all levels— pre-kindergarten through college
Educational Policy Institute	http://www .educationalpolicy .org/	Conducts research that can assist federal, state, and local policymakers with research, conferences, and workshops
Educational Testing Service	http://www.ets.org/	A nonprofit that advances quality and equity in education by creating assessments based on rigorous research
EDUCAUSE	http://www .educause.edu/	Nonprofit association whose mission is to advance higher education by promoting the intelligent use of information technology
Excelencia in Education	http://edexcelencia .org/	Links research, policy, and practice to inform policymakers and institutional leaders who in turn promote policies and practices that support higher educational achievement for Latino and all students
Foundation for Independent Higher Education	http://www.fihe .org/	Secures financial resources; develops collaborative programs within its network and with other organizations; and is a primary voice of independent higher education to corporate and philanthropic communities
Fund for the Improvement of Postsecondary Education (U.S. DOE)	http://www2 .ed.gov/about/ offices/list/ope/ fipse/index.html	Supports innovative projects that propose significant reforms and improvements in the U.S. postsecondary education and have the potential to serve as national models for reform
The Heartland Institute	http://heartland.org	Discover, develop, and promote free-market solutions to social and economic problems, including higher education, through research publications and newspapers

ORGANIZATION/ ASSOCIATION/ CENTER	WEBSITE ADDRESS	DESCRIPTION
Higher Education Research Institute (at UCLA)	http://www.heri .ucla.edu/index .php	Informs educational policy and promotes institutional improvement through an increased understanding of higher education and its impact on college students
The Higher Learning Commission	http://www.ncahlc .org/	A regional postsecondary accrediting agency of the North Central Association of Colleges and Schools
Hispanic Association of Colleges and Universities	http://www.hacu .net/hacu/default .asp	Represents colleges and universities committed to Hispanic higher education success in the United States, Puerto Rico, Latin America, Spain, and Portugal
Hispanic College Fund	http://hispanicfund .org/index.php	National nonprofit organization providing educational, scholarship, and mentoring programs to students
The Institute for College Access and Success	http://www.ticas .org/index.php	Seeks to improve the processes and public policies that can pave the way to successful educational outcomes for students and for society through nonpartisan research, analysis, and advocacy
Institute for Higher Education Leadership and Policy (at CSU-Sacramento)	http://www.csus .edu/ihelp/	Nonprofit organization that has an emphasis on community colleges to enhance leadership and policy for higher education in California and the nation through research and services for policymakers, practitioners, and educators
Institute for Higher Education Policy	http://www.ihep .org/	Increases access and success in postsecondary education through research and programs that inform decision makers who shape public policy and support economic and social development
Institute for Public Policy and Social Research (at Michigan State University)	http://www.ippsr .msu.edu/default .asp	Develops research-based policy education initiatives, forums, events, and publications

(Continued)

ORGANIZATION/ ASSOCIATION/ CENTER	WEBSITE ADDRESS	DESCRIPTION
Institute of Education Sciences (U.S. DOE)	http://www2 .ed.gov/about/ offices/list/ies/ index.html	The research arm of the U.S. DOE encompassing the National Center for Education Statistics, the National Center for Education Evaluation and Regional Assistance, the National Center for Education Research, and the National Center for Special Education Research
The Institute of Higher Education (at University of Georgia)	http://ihe.uga.edu/	Committed to advancing higher education policy, management, and leadership through research, graduate education, and outreach at the campus, state, national, and international levels
Institute on Education and the Economy (at Columbia University)	http://www .tc.columbia.edu/ centers/iee/	Conducts a program of research and policy analysis and provides intellectual leadership on the implications of changes in the economy and labor markets for all levels of our education and training systems
Integrated Postsecondary Education Data System (U.S. DOE)	http://nces.ed.gov/ ipeds/	The primary source for data on colleges, universities, and technical and vocational postsecondary institutions in the United States
Intercollegiate Studies Institute	http://www.isi.org/ homepage.aspx	A nonprofit, nonpartisan, educational organization to further in college students an understanding of the values and institutions that sustain a free and humane society through its program of lectures, conferences, publications, and fellowships
International Association of Universities	http://www.iau-aiu .net/	UNESCO-based worldwide association of higher education institutions bringing together institutions and organizations from some 120 countries for reflection and action on common concerns in higher education

ORGANIZATION/ ASSOCIATION/ CENTER	WEBSITE ADDRESS	DESCRIPTION
International Center for Academic Integrity (at Clemson University)	http://www .academicintegrity .org/	A consortium through which information about academic integrity is shared, and successful policies, enforcement procedures, sanctions, research, curricular materials, and education/ prevention programs are discussed
The International Comparative Higher Education Finance and Accessibility Project	http://gse.buffalo .edu/org/IntHigher EdFinance/	University of Buffalo program of research and information dissemination looking at the worldwide shift of the burden of higher education costs from governments and taxpayers to parents and students
Internet Course Exchange	http://wiche.edu/ ice	Enables students, through their home institutions, to access online courses and programs offered by other four-year and two-year ICE member institutions
Jobs for the Future	http://www.jff.org/	Identifies, develops, and promotes education and workforce strategies by improving the pathways leading from high school to college to family-sustaining careers
The Learning Alliance (at the University of Pennsylvania)	http://www .thelearningalliance .info/index.php	Provides access to expertise, current educational research, market data, and leadership support services to presidents of accredited, nonprofit two- and four-year colleges and universities
Lumina Foundation	http://www .luminafoundation .org/	A private, independent foundation dedicated exclusively to increase students' access to and success in postsecondary education
Mid-continent Research for Education and Learning	http://www.mcrel .org/	Researchers and education consultants working together to provide educators with research-based practical guidance on the issues and challenges facing K–16 education

(Continued)

215

ORGANIZATION/ ASSOCIATION/ CENTER	WEBSITE ADDRESS	DESCRIPTION
Middle States Association of Colleges and Schools	http://www .middlestates.org/	A regional accrediting agency; postsecondary is the responsibility of the Commission on Higher Education
Middle States Commission on Higher Education	http://www.msche .org/	A regional postsecondary accrediting agency of the Middle States Association of Colleges and Schools
Midwestern Higher Education Compact	http://www .mhec.org/ MHECHomePage	Enhancing member states' ability to maximize higher education opportunity and performance through collaboration and resource sharing
NAFSA: Association of International Educators	http://www.nafsa .org/	Nonprofit professional association that advances public policies supporting a broad public dialogue about the value and importance of international education
NASPA: Student Affairs Administrators in Higher Education	http://www.naspa .org/	Association for the advancement of the student affairs profession by providing programs and services that cultivate student learning and success aligned with the mission of colleges and universities
National Academic Advising Association	http://www.nacada .ksu.edu/	Promotes and supports academic advising to enhance the educational development of students by providing a forum for discussion, debate, and the exchange of ideas and publications
The National Academy for Academic Leadership (at Syracuse University)	http://www.the nationalacademy .org/	Provides consultation and planning services on campuses and offer rigorous courses, workshops, and seminars tailored to the needs of institutions and individual professionals
National Assessment of Adult Literacy	http://nces.ed.gov/ naal/	Sponsored by the National Center for Education Statistics (NCES), NAAL is the nation's most comprehensive measure of adult literacy

ORGANIZATION/ ASSOCIATION/ CENTER	WEBSITE ADDRESS	DESCRIPTION
National Association for College Admission Counseling	http://www .nacacnet.org/ Pages/default.aspx	Advocates and supports ethical and professional practice in helping students transition to postsecondary education through publications and media resources
National Association for Equal Opportunity in Higher Education	http://www.nafeo .org/community/ index.php	Not-for-profit umbrella organization of the nation's Historically Black Colleges and Universities (HBCUs) and Predominantly Black Institutions (PBIs)
National Association of College and University Attorneys	http://www.nacua .org/	Purpose is to enhance legal assistance to colleges and universities by educating attorneys and administrators as to the nature of campus legal issues
National Association of College and University Business Officers	http://www.nacubo .org/	Nonprofit organization representing the interests of chief administrative officers; provides seminars, information programs, research, and information concerning government activities affecting higher education
National Association of Colleges and Employers	http://www .naceweb.org/ home.aspx	Connects campus recruiting and career services professionals, and provides best practices, trends, research, professional development, and conferences
National Association of Independent Colleges and Universities	http://www.naicu .edu/	Represents private colleges and universities on such policy issues with the federal government as those affecting student aid, taxation, and government regulation
National Association of State Student Grant and Aid Programs	http://www.nassgap .org/index.aspx	Promotes, strengthens, and encourages high standards in the administration and operation of postsecondary student grant and aid programs
National Association of Student Financial Aid Administrators	http://www.nasfaa .org/	Supports the professional development of financial aid administrators; advocates for public policies and programs that increase student access and success; and serves as a forum for student financial aid issues

(Continued)

ORGANIZATION/ ASSOCIATION/ CENTER	WEBSITE ADDRESS	DESCRIPTION
The National Association of System Heads	http://nashonline.org/	Association that serves as a forum for the exchange of views and information of the chief executives of the 52 colleges and university systems of public higher education
National Center for Academic Transformation	http://thencat.org/	Independent nonprofit organization dedicated to the effective use of information technology to improve student learning outcomes and reduce the cost of higher education
National Center for Education Evaluation and Regional Assistance (U.S. DOE)	http://ies.ed.gov/ncee/index.asp	Conducts and disseminates the results of unbiased large-scale evaluations of education programs and practices supported by federal funds; provides research-based technical assistance to educators and policymakers
National Center for Education Research (U.S. DOE)	http://ies.ed.gov/ncer/index.asp	Supports rigorous research that addresses the nation's most pressing education needs, from early childhood to adult education
National Center for Educational Statistics (U.S. DOE)	http://nces.ed.gov/	The primary federal entity for collecting and analyzing data related to education in the United States and other nations
National Center for Higher Education Management Systems	http://www.nchems.org/	Mission is to improve strategic decision making in higher education for states and institutions in the United States and abroad
The National Center for Postsecondary Research (at Columbia University)	http://postsecondaryresearch.org/	Focuses on measuring the effectiveness of programs designed to help students make the transition to college and master the basic skills needed to advance to a degree
National Center for Public Policy and Higher Education	http://www.highereducation.org/	Independent, nonprofit, nonpartisan organization prepares analyses of policy issues regarding opportunity and achievement in higher education institutions

ORGANIZATION/ ASSOCIATION/ CENTER	WEBSITE ADDRESS	DESCRIPTION
The National Center on Education and the Economy	http://www.ncee .org/	Not-for-profit organization engaged in policy analysis and development that works at the local, state, and national levels to develop proposals for building the United States's world-class education and training system
National College Access Network	http://www .collegeaccess.org/ NCAN/Default .aspx	Unites the key organizations dedicated to increasing college access and success, especially those students underrepresented in postsecondary education, to enter and complete college
National Collegiate Athletic Association	http://www.ncaa .org/	Governs competition in a fair, safe, equitable, and sportsmanlike manner, and to integrate intercollegiate athletics into higher education so that the educational experience of the student-athlete is paramount
The National Conference of State Legislatures	http://www.ncsl .org/	Bipartisan organization that provides research, technical assistance, and opportunities for policymakers to exchange ideas on the most pressing state issues
National Council of University Research Administrators	http://www.ncura .edu/content/	Advances the field of research administration through education and professional development programs and the sharing of knowledge and experience
National Governors Association	http://www.nga .org/cms/home .html	Governors identify priority issues and deal collectively with matters of public policy and governance at the state and national levels
National Initiative for Leadership and Institutional Effectiveness (at NC State University)	http://ced.ncsu .edu/lpahe/nilie/ index.html	Provides support to enhance leadership development and improve institutional effectiveness through research, information sharing, and consulting services
National Institute for Learning Outcomes Assessment	http://learningout comeassessment .org/	Assists institutions and others in discovering and adopting promising practices in the assessment of college student learning outcomes

(Continued)

ORGANIZATION/ ASSOCIATION/ CENTER	WEBSITE ADDRESS	DESCRIPTION
National Postsecondary Education Cooperative (U.S. DOE)	http://nces.ed.gov/ npec/	A voluntary organization that encompasses all sectors of the postsecondary education community with a major interest in postsecondary education data collection
National Science Board	http://www.nsf .gov/nsb/	Recommends and encourages the pursuit of national policies for the promotion of research and education in science and engineering
National Society for Experiential Education	http://www.nsee .org/	Nonprofit membership association of educators, businesses, and community leaders for the development and improvement of experiential education programs nationwide
National Student Clearinghouse Research Center	http://research .studentclearing house.org/index .html	Studies on student enrollment and transfer behavior, persistence, outcomes, best practices, and case studies
National Survey of Student Engagement (at Indiana University)	http://nsse.iub.edu/	Annually collects and reports on information about student participation in programs and activities, providing an estimate of how undergraduates spend their time and what they gain from attending college
New England Association of Schools and Colleges	http://cihe.neasc .org/	A regional accrediting agency; postsecondary is the responsibility of the Commission on Institutions of Higher Education
The New England Board of Higher Education	http://www.nebhe .org/	Promotes greater educational opportunities and services for the residents of New England
The New England Resource Center for Higher Education (at UMass-Boston)	http://www.nerche .org/	Research projects, programs, and activities draw on the practitioner perspective to improve practice and to inform and influence policy, moving from the local to regional and national levels

ORGANIZATION/ ASSOCIATION/ CENTER	WEBSITE ADDRESS	DESCRIPTION
New Leadership Alliance for Student Learning and Accountability	http://newleader shipalliance.org/	Advocacy-focused organization supporting efforts to move the higher education community toward gathering, reporting on, and using evidence to improve student learning in American undergraduate education
Nonprofit Leadership Alliance	http://www .humanics.org/	Workforce development organization that certifies diverse, work-ready talent for the nonprofit sector, thereby assuring the talent exists to meet the increasing leadership needs of the nonprofit sector
North Central Association Commission on Accreditation and School Improvement	http://www.ncacasi .org/	Its Office of Postsecondary Education is responsible for the accountability of schools with postsecondary certificate-granting designation in accordance with federal regulations
North Central Association of Colleges and Schools	http://www.north centralassociation .org/index.htm	A regional accrediting agency; postsecondary is the responsibility of the Higher Learning Commission
The Northwest Commission on Colleges and Universities	http://www.nwccu .org/	A regional postsecondary accrediting agency
Office of Postsecondary Education (U.S. DOE)	http://www2 .ed.gov/about/ offices/list/ope/ index.html	Formulates federal postsecondary education policy and administers programs that address critical national needs in support of our mission to increase access to quality postsecondary education
Office of Vocational and Adult Education (U.S. DOE)	http://www2 .ed.gov/about/ offices/list/ovae/ index.html	Administers, coordinates programs that are related to adult education and literacy, career, and technical education, and community colleges
Organisation for Economic Co-operation and Development	http://www.oecd .org/home/	Provides a forum for world governments to measure productivity; analyzes and compares data to predict future trends; looks at issues and recommend policies designed to make the lives of ordinary people better

(Continued)

221

ORGANIZATION/ ASSOCIATION/ CENTER	WEBSITE ADDRESS	DESCRIPTION
Peabody Center for Education Policy (at Vanderbilt University)	http://peabody .vanderbilt.edu/ peabody_center_ for_education_ policy.xml	A research and policy development agency devoted to understanding and advancing education reform across K–12 and higher education arenas through research through publications, national forums, and conferences
Public Agenda	http://www .publicagenda.org/	Public opinion research and public engagement organization focused on ensuring that the public's views are represented in decision making
Public Policy Institute of California	http://www.ppic .org/main/home .asp	Informs and improves public policy in California through independent, objective, nonpartisan research on major social, economic, and political issues including higher education
Rockefeller Institute of Government (at the SUNY-Albany)	http://www .rockinst.org/	Enhances the capacities of state governments and the federal system to deal effectively with the nation's domestic challenges including education
Rocky Mountain Association for Institutional Research	http://rmair.org/	Advances institutional research knowledge and expertise to improve institutions of higher education and holds meetings during which research findings and methods are exchanged
Society for College and University Planning	http://www.scup .org/page/index	Is a community of higher education leaders responsible for, or are involved in, the integration of planning on campuses and for the professionals who support them
Southeastern Universities Research Association	http://sura.org/ home/index.html	One focus is its information technology efforts on initiatives in network infrastructure and applications development that enable collaborative research
Southern Association of Colleges and Schools	http://www.sacs .org/	A regional accrediting agency; postsecondary is the responsibility of the Southern Association of Colleges and Schools Commission on Colleges

ORGANIZATION/ ASSOCIATION/ CENTER	WEBSITE ADDRESS	DESCRIPTION
The Southern Association of Colleges and Schools Commission on Colleges	http://www.sacscoc .org/	A regional postsecondary accrediting agency of the Southern Association of Colleges and Schools
Southern Regional Education Board	http://www.sreb .org/	Nonprofit, nonpartisan organization that works with 16 member states to improve public pre-K-12 and higher education
Stanford Institute for Higher Education Research	http://siher .stanford.edu/	Sponsored research projects that examine contemporary higher education planning and policy issues from a range of analytical perspectives, including those of social scientists and policy audiences
State Higher Education Executive Officers	http://www.sheeo .org/	Serves statewide coordinating and governing boards in developing and sustaining excellent systems of higher education
The State Higher Education Policy Center	http://www.nchems .org/about/shepc .php	The named shared facility for collaborations of the National Center for Higher Education Management Systems, State Higher Education Executive Officers Association, and the Western Interstate Commission for Higher Education (WICHE)
State Higher Education Policy Database	http:// higheredpolicies .wiche.edu/ content/policy/ index	Provides policymakers, education leaders and consumers, and practitioners with an inventory of state-level policies and resources in key policy issue areas related to student achievement, access, and success
The Steinhardt Institute for Higher Education Policy (at New York University)	http://steinhardt .nyu.edu/sihep/	Supports research and dialogue that enhance the understanding of higher education as an institution that both reflects and influences social, cultural, racial, and economic difference

(Continued)

ORGANIZATION/ ASSOCIATION/ CENTER	WEBSITE ADDRESS	DESCRIPTION
Student Organization of North America	http://www .conahec.org/ conahec/sona/ EN_student_ organization/ EN_main.html	Organization is a nongovernmental, politically independent and nonprofit organization of students promoting cross-cultural relations, respect, and understanding across Canada, the United States, and Mexico
Teacher Education Accreditation Council	http://www.teac .org/	Teacher education program accreditor; merging with NCATE into the Council for the Accreditation of Educator Preparation by the end of 2012
Thurgood Marshall College Fund	http://www.thurgood marshallfund.net/	Aims to increase access, retention, and graduation rates of students attending their schools by providing student scholarships, grants to support faculty with research projects, and policy advocacy that benefits the students attending Fund member-schools
UNESCO: United Nations Educational, Scientific and Cultural Organization	http://www.unesco .org/new/en/	UNESCO's education sector facilitates partnerships to strengthen national educational leadership and to serve as a clearinghouse for ideas
United Negro College Fund	http://www.uncf .org/	Known for its scholarship program; the organization also has a research institute to impact public policy and improve local education practice
University Professional and Continuing Education Association	http://upcea.edu/	Advances university professional continuing education through programs, publications, conferences, institutes, seminars, and public advocacy
Voluntary System of Accountability	http:// voluntarysystem .org/index.cfm	An initiative by public 4-year universities to supply comparable information on the undergraduate student experience to constituencies through the College Portrait
Washington Higher Education Secretariat	http://www.whes .org/	Serves as a voluntary forum for chief executive officers of national higher education associations

ORGANIZATION/ ASSOCIATION/ CENTER	WEBSITE ADDRESS	DESCRIPTION
WestEd	http://www.wested.org/	A research, development, and service agency, works with education and other communities to promote excellence, achieve equity, and improve learning for children, youth, and adults
Western Academic Leadership Forum	http://www.wiche.edu/forum	Community of regional colleagues and leaders who inform and learn from one another, collaborate on projects for mutual benefit, and annually bring in experts on timely topics
The Western Alliance for Community College Academic Leaders	http://www.wiche.edu/alliance	Academic leaders at community colleges and technical schools and at systems and state governing and coordinating boards exchange ideas and information, share resources and expertise, and collaborate on regional initiatives
Western Association of Graduate Schools	http://www.wagsonline.org/	Considers mutual problems among the member institutions relating to graduate studies and research
Western Association of Schools and Colleges	http://www.wascweb.org/	A regional accrediting agency; postsecondary is the responsibility of the Accrediting Commission for Senior Colleges and Universities
Western Governors' Association	http://westgov.org/	An independent, nonprofit organization that identifies and addresses key policy and governance issues including higher education
Western Interstate Commission for Higher Education (WICHE)	http://www.wiche.edu/	Works to improve access to higher education and ensure student success through student exchange programs, regional initiatives, and research and policy work
WICHE Cooperative for Educational Technologies	http://wcet.wiche.edu/	Accelerates the adoption of effective practices and policies, advancing excellence in technology-enhanced teaching and learning in higher education

(Continued)

225

ORGANIZATION/ ASSOCIATION/ CENTER	WEBSITE ADDRESS	DESCRIPTION
Women's College Coalition	http://www .womenscolleges .org/	An association of women's colleges and universities that are two- and four-year, public and private, religiously affiliated and secular; is engaged in research and advocacy about the benefits of a women's college education in the 21st century

BIBLIOGRAPHY

ARTICLES

"Almanac 2012–13." *Chronicle of Higher Education* LIX, no. 1 (August 31, 2012), entire issue.

Baum, Sandy. "The New Higher Education Act: Where It Comes Up Short," *Chronicle of Higher Education* 54, no. 48 (August 8, 2008): A19.

Bell, Steven J. "Bringing Back the Faculty: The Evolution of the Faculty Commons in the Library," *Library Issues: Briefings for Faculty and Administrators* 31, no. 4 (March 2011): 1–4.

Berrett, Dan. "All about the Money," *Chronicle of Higher Education* LIX, no. 4 (September 21, 2012), A1, A4, A6.

Blumenstyk, Goldie. "For-Profit Colleges Compute Their Own Gradation Rates," *Chronicle of Higher Education* LVIII, no. 27 (March 9, 2012): A14.

Bodi, Sonia. "Critical Thinking and Bibliographic Instruction: The Relationship," *Journal of Academic Librarianship* 14, no. 3 (1988): 150–54.

Cameron, Kim. "Measuring Organizational Effectiveness in Institutions of Higher Education," *Administrative Science Quarterly* 23, no. 4 (December 1978): 624–32.

Choinski, Elizabeth, and Michele Emanuel. "The One-Minute Paper: Assessment for One-Shot Library Instruction," *Reference Services Review* 34, no. 1 (2006): 148–55.

"Do Graduation Rates Matter?" *Chronicle of Higher Education* LVIII, no. 27 (March 9, 2012): A1.

Emmanuel, Adeshina. "Private Sector Role Is at Heart of Campaigns' Split on College Costs," *New York Times* (September 8, 2012): A9.

Emmons, Mark, and Frances C. Wilkinson. "The Academic Library Impact on Student Persistence," *College & Research Libraries* 72, no. 2 (March 2011), 128–49.

Gratch-Lindauer, Bonnie. "Comparing the Regional Accreditation Standards: Outcomes Assessment and Other Trends," *Journal of Academic Librarianship*, 28, no. 1/2 (2002): 14–26.

"A Guide to the College Completion Site," *Chronicle of Higher Education* LVIII, no. 27 (March 9, 2012): A11.

Hoover, Eric. "New Player in the College-Rankings Game Mines Alumni Opinions," *Chronicle of Higher Education* LIX, no. 3 (September 14, 2012): A29.

Kelderman, Eric. "With State Support Now Tied to Completion, Tennessee Colleges Must Refocus," *Chronicle of Higher Education* LIX, no. 6 (October 5, 2012): A16, A18.

Kramer, Lloyd A., and Martha B. Kramer. "The College Library and the Drop-out," *College & Research Libraries* 29, no. 4 (1968): 310–12.

Lee, Tamera. "Exploring Outcomes Assessment: The AAHSL LibQUAL+™ Experience," *Journal of Library Administration* 40, no. 3–4 (2004): 49–58.

Mark, Amy E., and Polly D. Boruff-Jones. "Information Literacy and Student Engagement: What the National Survey of Student Engagement Reveals about Your Campus," *College & Research Libraries* 64, no. 6 (November 2003): 480–93.

Mehaffy, George L. "Medieval Models, Agrarian Calendars, and 21st-Century Imperatives," *Teacher-Scholar: The Journal of the State Comprehensive* University 2, no. 1 (Fall 2010): 4–20.

Mery, Yvonne, Jill Newby, and Ke Peng. "Why One-Short Information Literacy Sessions Are Not the Future of Instruction: A Case for Online Credit Courses," *College & Research Libraries* 73, no. 4 (July 2012): 366–77.

Mezick, Elizabeth M. "Return on Investment: Libraries and Student Retention." *Journal of Academic Librarianship* 33, no. 5 (2007): 561–66.

Miller, Rush. "Damn the Recession, Full Speed Ahead," *Journal of Library Administration* 52, no. 1 (2012): 3–17.

Miller, Charles. "The New Higher Education Act: Where It Comes Up Short," *Chronicle of Higher Education* 54, no. 48 (August 8, 2008): A19.

Morgan, Julie Margetta. "Consumer-Driven Reform of Higher Education: A Critical Look at New Amendments to the Higher Education Act," *Journal of Law and Policy* 17, no. 2 (2009): 531–78.

Nassirian, Barmak. "The New Higher Education Act: Where It Comes Up Short," *Chronicle of Higher Education* 54, no. 49 (August 8, 2008): A19.

Oakleaf, Megan. "Are They Learning? Are We? Learning Outcomes and the Academic Library," *Library Quarterly* 81, no. 1 (January 2011): 61–82.

Oakleaf, Megan. "The Information Literacy Instruction Assessment Cycle: A Guide for Increasing Student Learning and Improving Librarian Instructional Skills," *Journal of Documentation* 65, no. 4 (2009): 539–60.

Oakleaf, Megan. "Using Rubrics to Assess Information Literacy: An Examination of Methodology and Interrater Reliability," *Journal of the American Society for Information Science and Technology* 60, no. 3 (May 2009): 969–83.

Oakleaf, Megan, Michelle S. Millet, and Leah Kraus. "All Together Now: Getting Faculty, Administrators, and Staff Engaged in Information Literacy Assessment," portal: *Libraries and the Academy* 11, no. 3 (July 2011): 831–52.

"Outcomes Assessment" [entire issue], *Journal of Academic Librarianship* 28, nos. 1–2 (2002); 28, no. 6 (2002).

Powell, Brett A., Diane S. Gilleland, and L. Carolyn Pearson. "Expenditures, Efficiency, and Effectiveness in U.S. Undergraduate Higher Education: A National Benchmark Model," *Journal of Higher Education* 83, no. 1 (January/February 2012): 103–27.

Ratteray, Oswald M. T. "Information Literacy in Self-Study and Accreditation," *Journal of Academic Librarianship* 28, no. 6 (2002): 368–76.

Saunders, Laura. "Regional Accreditation Organizations' Treatment of Information Literacy: Definitions, Collaboration, and Assessment," *Journal of Academic Librarianship*, 33, no. 3, (2007): 317–26.

Scheppach, Raymond C. "The New Higher Education Act: Where It Comes Up Short," *Chronicle of Higher Education* 54, no. 48 (August 8, 2008): A19.

Selingo, Jeff. "The Rise and Fall of the Graduation Rate," *Chronicle of Higher Education* LVIII, no. 27 (March 9, 2012): A10, A12.

Shireman, Robert. "The New Higher Education Act: Where It Comes Up Short," *Chronicle of Higher Education* 54, no. 48 (August 8, 2008): A19.

Simpson, John B. "In a Crisis, Our Nation Must Have an Ambitious Education Strategy," *Chronicle of Higher Education* (March 20, 2009): A72.

Supiano, Beckie. "Students Need Better Data on Earnings and Other College Outcomes, Senators Say," *Chronicle of Higher Education* LIX, no. 5 (September 28, 2012): A15.

Supiano, Beckie, and Elyse Ashburn. "With New Lists, Federal Government Moves to Help Consumers and Prod Colleges to Limit Price Increases," *Chronicle of Higher Education* (June 30, 2011): A17–A18.

Wilder, Stanley. "Library Jobs and Student Retention," *College & Research Libraries News* 51 no. 11 (1990): 1035–38.

BOOKS

Anderson, Lorin W., and David R. Krathwohl, eds. *A Taxonomy for Learning, Teaching, and Assessment: A Revision of Bloom's Taxonomy of Educational Objectives.* New York: Longman, 2001.

Angelo, Thomas A., and Cross, K. Patricia. *Classroom Assessment Techniques: A Handbook for College Teachers,* 2nd ed. Hoboken, NJ. Wiley, 1993.

Arum, Richard, and Josipa Roska. *Academically Adrift: Limited Learning on College Campuses.* Chicago: University of Chicago Press, 2010.

Arum, Richard, Esther Cho, Jeannie Kim, and Josipa Roksa. *Documenting Uncertain Times: Postgraduate Transitions of the Academically Adrift Cohort.* New York: Social Science Research Council, 2012.

Bloom, Benjamin Samuel. *The Taxonomy of Educational Objectives: The Classification of Educational Goals.* New York: D. McKay Co., 1956.

Bloom, Benjamin Samuel, ed. *The Taxonomy of Educational Objectives: Cognitive Domain.* New York: David McKay Co., 1956.

Dugan, Robert E., Peter Hernon, and Danuta A. Nitecki. *Viewing Library Metrics from Different Perspectives: Inputs, Outputs and Outcomes.* Santa Barbara, CA: Libraries Unlimited, 2009.

Hernon, Peter, and Robert E. Dugan, ed. *An Action Plan for Outcomes Assessment in Your Library American Library Association.* Chicago: American Library Association, 2002.

Hernon, Peter, and Ellen Altman. *Assessing Service Quality: Satisfying the Expectations of Library Customers.* Chicago: American Library Association, 2010.

Hernon, Peter, and Robert E. Dugan, ed. *Outcomes Assessment in Higher Education: Views and Perspectives.* Westport, CT: Libraries Unlimited, 2004.

Hernon, Peter, Robert E. Dugan, and Danuta A. Nitecki. *Engaging in Evaluation and Assessment Research.* Santa Barbara, CA: Libraries Unlimited, 2011.

Hernon, Peter, Robert E. Dugan, and Candy Schwartz, ed. *Revisiting Outcomes Assessment in Higher Education: Views and Perspectives.* Westport, CT: Libraries Unlimited, 2006.

Hersch, Richard, and Richard Keeling. *We're Losing Our Minds: Rethinking American Higher Education.* New York: Keeling and Associates, LLC, 2012.

Kelly, Maurie Caitlin, and Andrea Kross, ed. *Making the Grade: Academic Libraries and Student Success.* Chicago: Association of College and Research Libraries, 2002.

Krathwohl, David R., Benjamin S. Bloom, and Bertram B. Masia. *Taxonomy of Educational Objectives: Handbook II: Affective Domain.* New York: David McKay Co., 1964.

Maki, Peggy L., ed. *Assessing for Learning: Building a Sustainable Commitment across the Institution.* Sterling, VA: Stylus Publishing, 2004.

Maki, Peggy L., ed. *Assessing for Learning: Building a Sustainable Commitment across the Institution,* 2nd ed. Sterling, VA: Stylus Publishing, 2010.

Middaugh, Michael F. *Planning and Assessment in Higher Education: Demonstrating Institutional Effectiveness.* San Francisco: Jossey-Bass, 2010.

Rockman, Ilene F., and Associates. *Integrating Information Literacy into the Higher Education Curriculum.* San Francisco: Jossey-Bass, 2004.

Saunders, Laura. *Information Literacy as a Student Learning Outcome: The Perspective of Institutional Accreditation.* Santa Barbara, CA: Libraries Unlimited, 2011.

Sullivan, Teresa A., Christopher Mackie, William F. Massy, and Esha Sinha, ed. *Panel on Measuring Higher Education Productivity: Conceptual Framework and Data Needs.* Washington, DC: National Academies Press, 2012.

Suskie, Linda. *Assessing Student Learning: A Common Sense Guide.* Bolton, MA: Anker Pub. Co., 2004.

Suskie, Linda. *Assessing Student Learning: A Common Sense Guide*, 2nd ed. San Francisco, CA: Jossey-Bass, 2009.

DISSERTATIONS

Saunders, Laura. *Information Literacy as a Student Learning Outcome: As Viewed from the Perspective of Institutional Accreditation*, PhD diss. Boston: Simmons College, 2010, UMI Number: 3452631.

GOVERNMENT PUBLICATIONS

Aud, W. Hussar, G. Kena, K. Bianco, L. Frohlich, J. Kemp, and L. Tahar. *The Condition of Education 2011.* Washington, DC: U.S. Department of Education, 2011. Accessed June 7, 2012, http://nces.ed.gov/programs/coe/pdf/coe_er2.pdf.

California State University. "Higher Education Opportunities Act (HEOA): Textbook Information Provision," n.d. Accessed February 12, 2012, http://als.csuprojects.org/heoa.

Jones, Elizabeth A. *National Assessment of College Student Learning: Identifying College Graduates' Essential in Writing, Speech and Listening, and Critical Thinking.* Washington, DC: National Center for Education Statistics, 1995.

Kansas State University, Office of Assessment. "Measures, Rubrics, and Tools for Assessing Student Learning Outcomes." Manhattan, KS: Kansas State University, 2008. Accessed June 25, 2012, http://www.k-state.edu/assessment/plans/measures/index .htm.

Massachusetts Department of Higher Education. "The Vision Project." Boston: Massachusetts Department of Higher Education, 2011. Accessed March 26, 2012, http://www.mass.edu/currentinit/vpwhatsnew.asp.

Mocker, Donald W., and George E. Spear. *Lifelong Learning: Formal, Informal, and Self-Directed.* Washington, DC: National Institute of Education, 1982. Accessed June 14, 2012, http://eric.ed.gov/PDFS/ED220723.pdf.

National Advisory Committee on Institutional Quality and Integrity. *NACIQI Draft Report: Higher Education Accreditation Reauthorization Policy Recommendations*, February 8, 2012. Accessed May 10, 2012, http://www2.ed.gov/about/bdscomm/list/naciqi-dir/naciqi_draft_final_report.pdf.

Obama, President Barack. *Blueprint for an America Built to Last* (January 24, 2012). Accessed April 18, 2012, http://www.whitehouse.gov/sites/default/files/blueprint_for_an_america_built_to_last.pdf.

Obama, President Barack. "National Information Literacy Awareness Month," 2009. Accessed May 10, 2012, http://www.whitehouse.gov/the_press_office/Presidential-Proclamation-National-Information-Literacy-Awareness-Month.

Obama, President Barack. "Remarks by the President in State of the Union Address" (January 24, 2012). Accessed April 18, 2012, http://www.whitehouse.gov/the-press-office/2012/01/24/remarks-president-state-union-address.

Obama, President Barack. "Remarks by the President on the American Graduation Initiative" (July 14, 2009). Accessed on July 4, 2012, http://www.whitehouse.gov/the_press_office/Remarks-by-the-President-on-the-American-Graduation-Initiative-in-Warren-MI/.

Organization for Economic Cooperation and Development. *Education at a Glance: Summary of Key Findings*, 2009. Accessed June 7, 2012, http://www.oecd.org/datao ecd/40/60/43634212.pdf.

Schumer, Senator Charles E. "Schumer Announces Passage of Higher Education Bill with His Provisions to Protect Upstate NY Families and College Students from Soaring Tuition and Textbook Costs" (August 1, 2008). Accessed February 12, 2012, http://schumer.senate.gov/new_website/record.cfm?id=301891.

Texas A & M University. "Measuring the Pursuit of Teaching, Research, & Service Excellence," accessed May 18, 2012, https://accountability.tamu.edu/.

U.S. Consumer Financial Protection Bureau. "Press Release: Consumer Financial Protection Bureau Now Taking Private Student Loan Complaints" (March 5, 2012). Accessed August 21, 2012, http://www.consumerfinance.gov/pressreleases/ consumer-financial-protection-bureau-now-taking-private-student-loan-complaints/.

U.S. Department of Education. *A Test of Leadership: Charting the Future of U.S. Higher Education*. Washington, DC: Department of Education, 2006. Accessed June 7, 2012, http://www2.ed.gov/about/bdscomm/list/hiedfuture/reports/pre-pub-report.pdf.

U.S. Department of Education, National Center for Education Statistics. Net Price Calculator, http://nces.ed.gov/ipeds/netpricecalculator/.

U.S. Department of Education, National Center for Education Statistics. *Enhancing the Quality and Use of Student Outcome Data: Final Report of the NPEC Working Group on Student Outcomes from a Data Perspective*. Washington, DC: National Center for Education Statistics, 1997. Accessed March 24, 2012, http://nces.ed.gov/ pubs97/97992.pdf.

U.S. Department of Education, National Center for Education Statistics. "National Assessment of Adult Literacy." Accessed May 9, 2012, http://nces.ed.gov/naal/kf_dem_ edu.asp.

U.S. Department of Education, Office of Postsecondary Education. "State Assessment Policy Analysis." Accessed June 20, 2012, http://www.stanford.edu/group/ncpi/ unspecified/assessment_states/stateReports.html.

U.S. Department of Labor. *What Work Requires of School*. Washington, DC: Department of Labor, 1991. Accessed June 12, 2012, http://wdr.doleta.gov/SCANS/whatwork/ whatwork.pdf.

U.S. Department of the Treasury. *New Report from Treasury, Education Departments: The Economic Case for Higher Education* (June 21, 2012). Accessed July 12, 2012, http:// www.treasury.gov/press-center/press-releases/Documents/The%20Economics% 20of%20Higher%20Education_REPORT%20CLEAN.pdf.

University of Arkansas. "OpenUA." Accessed July 15, 2012, http://openua.uark.edu/.

The University of Texas System. "Welcome to the UT System Dashboard." Accessed May 26, 2012, http://www.utsystem.edu/osm/dashboard/homepage.html.

University of West Florida Libraries, Office of the Dean of Libraries. "Information . . . ." Pensacola, FL: University of West Florida Libraries, 2012. Accessed March 26, 2012, http://libguides.uwf.edu/office-of-dean-of-libraries.

University of West Florida Libraries, Office of the Dean of Libraries. "Institutional Return on Investment," 2012. Accessed June 21, 2012, http://libguides.uwf.edu/content .php?pid=188487&sid=2184200.

University of West Florida Libraries, Office of the Dean of Libraries. "Student Return on Investment," 2012. Accessed June 21, 2012, http://libguides.uwf.edu/content .php?pid=188487&sid=2183215.

Voluntary System of Accountability®. "About the College Portrait," n.d. Accessed March 26, 2012, http://www.voluntarysystem.org/index.cfm?page=about_cp; accessed June 21, 2012, http://www.voluntarysystem.org/index.cfm?page=about_cp.

Voluntary System of Accountability®. "Methodology for Calculating the Success and Progress Rate," accessed June 21, 2012, http://www.voluntarysystem.org/docs/ cp/SP_Methodology.pdf.

White House. "College Scorecard." Washington, DC: White House, 2012. Accessed March 27, 2012, July 15, 2012, http://www.whitehouse.gov/issues/education/higher-education/college-score-card.

White House, Office of the Press Secretary. "Fact Sheet: President Obama's Blueprint for Keeping College Affordable and within Reach for All Americans" (January 27, 2012). Accessed February 18, 2012, http://www.whitehouse.gov/the-press-office/2012/01/27/fact-sheet-president-obama-s-blueprint-keeping-college-affordable-and-wi.

Zurkowski, Paul B. *The Information Service Environment Relationships and Priorities.* Washington, DC: National Commission on Library and Information Science, 1974.

PUBLICATIONS OF ACCREDITATION ORGANIZATIONS

Council for Higher Education. "2011 CHEA Awards." Washington, DC: Council for Higher Education, 2011. Accessed March 26, 2012, http://www.chea.org/chea%20award/CA_2011.02-B.html; http://www.chea.org/2012_CHEA_Award.html.

Ewell, Peter T. *Accreditation and Student Learning Outcomes: A Proposed Point of Departure,* CHEA Occasional Paper. Washington, DC: Council for Higher Education Accreditation, 2001. Accessed August 22, 2012, http://www.chea.org/pdf/EwellSLO_Sept2001.pdf.

Middle States Commission on Higher Education. *Assessing Student Learning and Institutional Effectiveness: Understanding Middle States Expectations.* Philadelphia: Middle States Commission on Higher Education, 2005.

Middles States Commission on Higher Education. *Developing Research and Communication Skills: Guidelines for Information Literacy in the Curriculum.* Philadelphia: Middle States Commission on Higher Education, 2003. Accessed June 7, 2012, http://www.msche.org/publications/Developing-Skills080111151714.pdf.

Middle States Commission on Higher Education. *Student Learning Assessment: Options and Resources.* Philadelphia: Middle States Commission, 2003, 2007.

Southern Association of Colleges and Schools Commission on Colleges. *Criteria for Accreditation.* Decatur, GA: Southern Association of Colleges and Schools Commission on Colleges, 1998.

REPORTS

American Council of Trustees and Alumni. *Becoming an Educated Person: Toward a Core Curriculum for College Students.* Washington, DC: ACTA, 2003. Accessed June 10, 2012, http://www.goacta.org/publications/downloads/BEPFinal.pdf.

American Council of Trustees and Alumni. "What Will They Learn," 2012. Accessed June 10, 2012, http://www.whatwilltheylearn.com/.

American Council of Trustees and Alumni. *Why Accreditation Doesn't Work and What Policymakers Can Do about It.* Washington, DC: American Council of Trustees and Alumni, 2007.

Association of American Colleges & Universities and Council for Higher Education. "A Statement of Principles, Commitments to Action." Washington, DC: Association of American Colleges & Universities and Council for Higher Education, 2009.

Beagle, Donald. "From Learning Commons to Learning Outcomes: Assessing Collaborative Services and Spaces," research bulletin. Boulder, CO: EDUCAUSE Center for Applied Research, 2011. Accessed June 23, 2012, http://net.educause.edu/ir/library/pdf/ERB1114.pdf.

The Boyer Commission on Educating Undergraduates in the Research University. *Reinventing Undergraduate Education: A Blueprint for America's Research Universities.* Stony Brook, NY: State University of New York, 1998. Accessed June 10, 2012, http://www.niu.edu/engagedlearning/research/pdfs/Boyer_Report.pdf.

Lumina Foundation for Education. *College Productivity: Four Steps to Finishing First.* Indianapolis: Lumina Foundation, n.d. Accessed June 22, 2012, http://www.lumina foundation.org/publications/Four_Steps_to_Finishing_First_in_Higher_Education .pdf.

Lumina Foundation. *Degree Qualifications Profile.* Washington, DC: Lumina Foundation, 2011. Accessed June 7, 11, 2012, http://www.luminafoundation.org/publications/ The_Degree_Qualifications_Profile.pdf.

Marcucci, Pamela, and Alex Usher. *2011 in Review: Global Changes in Tuition Fee Policies and Student Assistance.* Toronto: Higher Education Strategy Associates, 2012. Accessed June 7, 2012, http://higheredstrategy.com/wp-content/uploads/2012/03/YIR2012.pdf.

The National Advisory Committee on Institutional Quality and Integrity. "NACIQI Draft Final Report: Higher Education Accreditation Reauthorization Policy Recommendations" (February 8, 2012). Accessed May 16, 2012, http://www2.ed.gov/ about/bdscomm/list/naciqi-dir/naciqi_draft_final_report.pdf.

National Governors Association, Center for Best Practices. "Access and Compliance," 2010. Accessed June 21, 2012, http://www.nga.org/cms/home/nga-center-for-best-practices/center-issues/page-edu issues/col2-content/main-content-list/access-and-completion.html.

National Governors Association, Center for Best Practices. *Complete to Compete: From Information to Action: Revamping Higher Education Accountability Systems,* 2011. Accessed June 22, 2012, http://www.nga.org/files/live/sites/NGA/files/ pdf/1007COMMONCOLLEGEMETRICS.PDF.

National Governors Association, Center for Best Practices. "Issue Brief: Measuring Student Achievement at Postsecondary Institutions," 2009. Accessed June 21, 2012, http:// www.nga.org/files/live/sites/NGA/files/pdf/0911MEASURINGACHIEVEMENT .PDF.

Project on Accreditation and Assessment. *Taking Responsibility for the Quality of the Baccalaureate Degree.* Washington, DC: Association of American Colleges and Universities, 2004.

Social Program Evaluators and Consultants, Inc. *Year One Evaluation of Lumina Foundation's Higher Education Productivity Work in Seven States.* Detroit, MI: Social Program Evaluators and Consultants, Inc, 2011. Accessed June 22, 2012, http://www.specassociates.org/docs/Year%20One%20Evaluation%20of%20Lumina%20 Foundation's%20HE%20Productivity%20Work%20in%20Seven%20States.pdf.

Swing, Randy L. and Christopher S. Coogan. *Valuing Assessment: Cost-benefit Considerations,* NILOA Occasional Paper no.5. Urbana, IL: University of Illinois and Indiana University, National Institute for Learning Outcomes Assessment, 2010. Accessed June 21, 2012, http://www.learningoutcomeassessment.org/occasionalpaperfive.htm.

WEB RESOURCES

ACRLMetrics. Accessed June 23, 2012, http://www.acrlmetrics.com.

Albitz, Rebecca S. "The What and Who of Information Literacy and Critical Thinking in Higher Education," *portal: Libraries and the Academy* 7, no. 1 (2007): 97–109. Accessed June 12, 2012 Project MUSE.

Alverno College, College Educational Research and Evaluation Office. "Learning Outcomes Studies Educational Research and Evaluation" (2012). Accessed June 25, 2012, http://www2.alverno.edu/for_educators/ere_research.html.

American Library Association. "Presidential Committee on Information Literacy: Final Report," 1989. Accessed May 10, 2012, http://www.ala.org/acrl/publications/ whitepapers/presidential.

American Library Association, Association of College and Research Libraries. "ACRL Visual Literacy Competency Standards for Higher Education," 2011. Accessed June 11, 2012, http://www.ala.org/acrl/standards/visualliteracy.

American Library Association, Association of College and Research Libraries. "Assessment Issues." Accessed June 23, 2012, http://www.ala.org/acrl/issues/infolit/resources/assess/issues.

American Library Association, Association of College and Research Libraries. "Guidelines and Standards." Chicago: Association of College and Research Libraries, 2012. Accessed March 24, 2012, http://www.ala.org/acrl/standards.

American Library Association, Association of College and Research Libraries. "Information Literacy Competency Standards for Anthropology and Sociology Students," 2008. Accessed June 11, 2012, http://www.ala.org/acrl/standards/anthro_soc_standards.

American Library Association, Association of College and Research Libraries. "Information Literacy Competency Standards for Journalism Students and Professionals," 2011. Accessed June 11, 2012, http://www.ala.org/acrl/sites/ala.org.acrl/files/content/standards/il_journalism.pdf.

American Library Association, Association of College and Research Libraries. "Information Literacy Competency Standards for Higher Education," 2000. Accessed May 10, 25, 2012, June 11, 2012, http://www.ala.org/acrl/standards/informationliteracycompetency.

American Library Association, Association of College and Research Libraries. "Objectives for Information Literacy Instruction: A Model Statement for Academic Librarians," Chicago: Association of College and Research Libraries, 2001. Accessed July 10, 2010, http://www.ala.org/acrl/standards/objectivesinformation.

American Library Association, Association of College and Research Libraries. "Political Science Research Competency Guidelines," 2008. Accessed June 11, 2012, http://www.ala.org/acrl/sites/ala.org.acrl/files/content/standards/PoliSciGuide.pdf.

American Library Association, Association of College and Research Libraries. "Psychology Information Literacy Standards," 2010. Accessed June 11, 2012, http://www.ala.org/acrl/standards/psych_info_lit.

American Library Association, Association of College and Research Libraries. "Information Literacy Competency Standards for Science and Technology," 2006. Accessed June 11, 2012, http://www.ala.org/acrl/standards/infolitscitech.

American Library Association, Association of College and Research Libraries. "Information Literacy Competency Standards for Teacher Education," 2011. Accessed June 11, 2012, http://www.ala.org/acrl/sites/ala.org.acrl/files/content/standards/ilstandards_te.pdf.

American Library Association, Association of College and Research Libraries. "Research Competency Guidelines for Literatures in English," 2007. Accessed June 11, 2012, http://www.ala.org/acrl/standards/researchcompetenciesles.

American Library Association, Association of College and Research Libraries. "Standards for Libraries in Higher Education." Chicago: Association of College and Research Libraries, 2011. Accessed March 26, 2012, http://www.ala.org/acrl/standards/standardslibraries.

Anderson, Patrick B. "UW System Students Facing Greater Debt," *LaCrosseTribune.com* (March 11, 2012). Accessed June 15, 2012, http://lacrossetribune.com/news/local/report-ranks-uw-l-among-most-selective-in-uw-system/article_62b96232-375d-11e1-bfa4-0019bb2963f4.html.

Asimov, Nanette. "Yee Bill Is 2nd Effort to Cap CSU Executive Pay," *SFGate* (January 14, 2012). Accessed May 29, 2012, http://www.sfgate.com/cgi-bin/article.cgi?f=/c/a/2012/01/13/BAB71MPBCV.DTL#ixzz1wGRRsuIP.

Associated Press [unidentified contributed author]. "College Presidents Wary of Obama Cost-Control Plan," Thecabin.net: Log Cabin Democrat (January 28, 2012). Accessed February 18, 2012, http://thecabin.net/news/2012-01-28/college-presidents-wary-obama-cost-control-plan#.UQkhYB2Yu9E.

Association of American Colleges and Universities. *College Learning for the New Global Century*. Washington, DC: Association of American Colleges & Universities, 2007. Accessed June 7, 2012, http://www.aacu.org/leap/documents/GlobalCentury_final.pdf.

Association of American Colleges and Universities. *An Introduction to LEAP*. Washington, DC: AACU, n.d. Accessed June 10, 2012, http://www.aacu.org/leap/documents/Introduction_to_LEAP.pdf.

Association of American Colleges and Universities. "Leap States Initiative." Washington, DC: Association of American Colleges and Universities, 2012. Accessed March 26, 2012, http://www.aacu.org/about/index.cfm.

Association of American Colleges and Universities. *The LEAP Vision for Learning: Outcomes, Practices, Impact, and Employers' Views*. Washington, DC: Association of American Colleges & Universities, 2011. Accessed June 7, 2012, http://www.aacu.org/leap/documents/leap_vision_summary.pdf.

Association of American Colleges and Universities. "Statement on Liberal Learning," 1998. Accessed June 10, 2012, http://www.aacu.org/About/statements/liberal_learning.cfm.

Barker, Tim. "Colleges to Prove Worth for State Funds," *stltoday.com* (April 17, 2012). Accessed May 26, 2012, http://www.stltoday.com/news/local/education/colleges-to-prove-worth-for-state-funds/article_fc67a932-685c-5435-a2b6-133fd9deec95.html.

Basu, Kaustuv. "And the Livin' Is Easy?" *Inside Higher Ed* (March 27, 2012). Accessed May 29, 2012, http://www.insidehighered.com/news/2012/03/27/newspaper-op-ed-sets-debate-over-faculty-workload-and-faculty-bashing.

Bennett, William J. "Do We Need a Revolution in Higher Education?" *CNN* (June 13, 2014). Accessed June 14, 2012, http://www.cnn.com/2012/06/13/opinion/bennett-higher-education/index.html.

Berrett, Dan. " 'Adrift' in Adulthood: Students Who Struggled in College Find Life Harsher after Graduation," *Chronicle of Higher Education* (January 25, 2012). Accessed May 26, 2012, http://chronicle.com/article/Adrift-inadulthood-/130444/.

Bieda, Anthony S. *Closing the Gap between Career Education & Employer Expectations: Implications for America's Unemployment Rate*. Washington, DC: Accrediting Council for Independent Colleges and Schools, 2011. Accessed August 19, 2012, http://www.acics.org/events/content.aspx?id=4718.

Biemiller, Lawrence. "While Tuition Revenue Climbs, Discounts Do Too, Moody's Says," *Chronicle of Higher Education* (January 4, 2012). Accessed June 16, 2012, http://chronicle.com/article/while-tuition-revenue-climbs/130210/.

Blumenstyk, Goldie. "College Officials Welcome Obama's Focus on Higher-Education Costs, but Raise Some Concerns," *Chronicle of Higher Education* (January 30, 2012). Accessed February 18, 2012, http://chronicle.com/article/Obama-Puts-College-Costs-Front/130503.

Blumenstyk, Goldie. "Obama Calls for Control of College Costs and Renewed Support for Higher Education," *Chronicle of Higher Education* (January 27, 2012). Accessed February 18, 2012, http://chronicle.com/article/Obama-Calls-for-Control-of/130496.

Board of Trustees, Minnesota State Colleges and Universities. "Accountability Dashboard." Accessed July 15, 2012, http://www.mnscu.edu/board/accountability/index.html.

Breivik, Patricia S. "Information Literacy and the Engaged Campus," *AAHE Bulletin* 53 (2000): 3–6. Accessed June 7, 18, 2012, http://www.aahea.org/articles/nov2000_1.htm.

Breivik, Patricia S. "21st Century Learning and Information Literacy," *Change* 37, no.2 (2005): 20–27. Accessed June 12, 2012, EBSCO.

Bruce, Christine, Hilary Hughes, and Mary M. Somerville. "Supporting Informed Learners in the Twenty-First Century," *Library Trends* 60, no. 3 (2012): 522–45. Accessed June 14, 2012, Project MUSE.

Bruff, Derek. "Learning Analytics, Program Assessment, and the Scholarship of Teaching [web log posting]," *Agile Learning* [blog] (July 23, 2012), accessed October 25, 2012, http://derekbruff.org/?p=2273.

Carey, Kevin. " 'Academically Adrift': The News Gets Worse and Worse," *Chronicle of Higher Education* (February 12, 2012). Accessed on May 26, 2012, http://chronicle.com/article/academically-adrift-the/130743/.

Carey, Kevin. "Belt Tightening on College Costs," NPR (January 10, 2012). Accessed February 17, 2012, http://www.npr.org/2012/01/10/144953645/new-republic-belt-tightening-on-college-costs.

Carey, Kevin. "MIT Mints a Valuable New Form of Academic Currency," *Chronicle of Higher Education* (January 22, 2012). Accessed May 28, 2012, http://chronicle.com/article/MIT-mints-a-valuable-new-form/130410/.

Carlson, Scott. "Outlook for Higher Education Remains Mixed, Moody's Says," *Chronicle of Higher Education* (January 23, 2012). Accessed May 28, 2012, http://chronicle.com/article/outlook-for-higher-education/130434/.

Carlson, Scott. "Self-Sufficient, with a Hand from the Government," *Chronicle of Higher Education* (August 29, 2012). Accessed September 10, 2012, http://chronicle.com/blogs/decision2012/2012/08/29/self-sufficient-with-a-hand-from-the-government/.

Carnevale, Anthony P., Nicole Smith, and Jeff Strohl. *Help Wanted: Projections of Jobs and Education Requirements through 2018*. Washington, DC: Georgetown University: Center on Education and the Workforce, n.d. Accessed June 7, 10, 2012, http://www9.georgetown.edu/grad/gppi/hpi/cew/pdfs/FullReport.pdf.

Cavanaugh, John C. "Accreditation in an Era of Open Resources," *Inside Higher Ed* (December 14, 201). Accessed May 26, 2012, http://www.insidehighered.com/views/2011/12/14/cavanaugh-essay-how-accreditation-must-change-era-open-resources.

The Chronicle of Higher Education College Completion Website. Accessed June 23, 2012, http://getideas.org/resource/the-chronicle-of-higher-education-college-complete-website/.

Clark, Larra, and Marijke Visser. "Digital Literacy Takes Center Stage," *Library Technology Reports* 47, no. 6 (2011): 38–42. Accessed June 14, 2012, EBSCO.

College Board, Net Price Calculator, http://netpricecalculator.collegeboard.org/.

College Board Advocacy & Policy Center. *Trends in College Pricing 2011*. New York: College Board Advocacy & Policy Center, 2011. Accessed March 26, 2012, http://trends.collegeboard.org/sites/default/files/College_Pricing_2011.pdf.

Council of Independent Colleges. "CIC Endorses ACRL Information Literacy Competency Standards," *Independent Online Newsletter*. Accessed June 7, 2012, http://www.cic.edu/publications.

Crawford, Amanda J. "Governors Call for Linking University Financing to Performance," *Bloomberg* (July 15, 2011). Accessed on May 26, 2012, http://www.bloomberg.com/news/2011-07-15/u-s-governors-push-performance-based-support-for-colleges-1-.html.

DeFour, Matthew. "UW System to Offer New 'Flexible Degree' Program," *Wisconsin State Journal* (June 19, 2012). Accessed June 20, 2012, http://host.madison.com/news/local/education/university/uw-system-to-offer-new-flexible-degree-program/article_a8b6ba54-ba1c-11e1-85a7-001a4bcf887a.html.

deMause, Neil. "The Soaring Cost of College Has Multiple Causes and No Easy Solution," *Village Voice* (January 4, 2012). Accessed June 18, 2012, http://www.villagevoice.com/

2012–01–04/news/the-soaring-cost-of-college-has-multiple-causes-and-no-easy-solution/.

Democratic National Committee. "Moving America Forward: 2012 Democratic National Platform" (September 2012). Accessed September 9, 2012, http://assets.dstatic.org/dnc-platform/2012-National-Platform.pdf.

Deslatte, Melinda. "UL System Leader Urges Reworking of College Cuts," *Bloomberg Businessweek* (June 12, 2012). Accessed June 13, 2012, http://www.businessweek.com/ap/2012-06/D9VBL3C80.htm.

de Vise, Daniel. "New Momentum for the Three-Year Degree?," *Washington Post* (May 30, 2012). Accessed June 16, 2012, http://www.washingtonpost.com/blogs/college-inc/post/new-momentum-for-the-three-year-degree/2012/05/30/gJQAh6801U_blog.html.

Dewey, Barbara I. "Transforming Research Libraries: An Introduction," "From the Selected Works of Barbara I. Dewey, 2010). Accessed May 26, 2012, http://works.bepress.com/cgi/viewcontent.cgi?article=1008&context=barbara_dewey&sei-redir=1&referer=http%3A%2F%2Fwww.google.com%2Furl%3Fsa%3Dt%26rct%3Dj%26q%3Dcreation%2Bliteracy%2Bbarbra%2Bdewey%26source%3Dweb%26cd%3D6%26ved%3D0CGQQFjAF%26url%3Dhttp%253A%252F%252Fworks.bepress.com%252Fcgi%252Fviewcontent.cgi%253Farticle%253D1008%2526context%253Dbarbara_dewey%26ei%3D8gPBT-D3MPCe6QGQ65TCCg%26usg%3DAFQjCNGR7Z-NxUvgrsEP9BznZUdstXRn3A#search=%22creation%20literacy%20barbra%20dewey%22.

Distance Education and Training Council, Accrediting Commission. "Policy on Student Achievement and Satisfaction." Washington, DC: Distance Education and Training Council, 2012. Accessed August 18, 2012, http://www.detc.org/actions/comment/june2012/1%20-%20C.14.%20Policy%20on%20Student%20Achievement.pdf.

Dougherty, Kevin, and Rebecca Natow. *The Demise of Higher Education Performance Funding Systems in Three States* (May 2009). Accessed on May 26, 2012, http://ccrc.tc.columbia.edu/DefaultFiles/SendFileToPublic.asp?ft=pdf&FilePath=c:\Websites\ccrc_tc_columbia_edu_documents\332_694.pdf&fid=332_694&aid=47&RID=694&pf=Publication.asp?UID=694.

Dougherty, Kevin, and Vikash Reddy. *The Impacts of State Performance Funding Systems on Higher Education Institutions: Research Literature Review and Policy Recommendations* (December 2011). Accessed May 26, 2012, http://ccrc.tc.columbia.edu/DefaultFiles/SendFileToPublic.asp?ft=pdf&FilePath=c:\Websites\ccrc_tc_columbia_edu_documents\332_1004.pdf&fid=332_1004&aid=47&RID=1004&pf=Publication.asp?UID=1004.

Eaton, Collin. "Colleges' Data on Student Learning Remain Largely Inaccessible, Report Says," *Chronicle of Higher Education* (November 21, 2011). Accessed May 26, 2012, http://chronicle.com/article/Colleges-data-on-students/129853/.

Eaton, Judith S. "Accreditation and the Federal Future of Higher Education," *Academe Online* (September–October 2010). Accessed February 17, 2012, http://www.aaup.org/AAUP/pubsres/academe/2010/SO/feat/eato.htm.

Eaton, Judith S. "The Higher Education Opportunity Act of 2008: What Does It Mean and What Does It Do?" Washington, DC: Council for Higher Education Accreditation, 4, no. 1 (October 30, 2008). Accessed February 12, 2012, http://www.chea.org/ia/IA_2008.10.30.html.

"Editorial: Reining in College Tuition," *New York Times* (February 3, 2012). Accessed February 18, 2012, http://www.nytimes.com/2012/02/04/opinion/reining-in-college-tuition.html.

Editorial Board. "Editorial: Tuition Cost Shift Hurts State's Future," *StarTribune* (May 29, 2012). Accessed June 16, 2012, http://www.startribune.com/opinion/editorials/155494335.html.

Editorial Board. "Restore Public Funding of Universities," *Traverse City Record-Eagle* (May 19, 2012). Accessed June 19, 2012, http://record-eagle.com/opinion/x1321933601/Restore-public-funding-of-universities/print.

Editorial Board. "Welcome Trend in College Tuition," *New York Times* (March 5, 2012). Accessed June 16, 2012, http://www.nytimes.com/2012/03/06/opinion/welcome-trend-in-college-tuition.html.

Elmborg, James. "Critical Information Literacy: Implications for Instructional Practice," *Journal of Academic Librarianship* 32, no.2 (2006): 192–99. Accessed June 13, 2012, Science Direct.

"ETS® Proficiency Profile and the Voluntary System of Accountability (VSA). Accessed June 21, 2012, http://www.ets.org/proficiencyprofile/about/vsa.

Fain, Paul. "Heard but Not Seen," *Inside Higher Ed* (August 30, 2012). Accessed September 10, 2012, http://www.insidehighered.com/news/2012/08/30/student-debt-and-profit-issues-largely-absent-tampa.

Fain, Paul. "Not Quite Complete," *Inside Higher Ed* (March 27, 2012). Accessed May 26, 2012, http://www.insidehighered.com/news/2012/03/27/lumina-reports-slow-progress-completion-push.

Fain, Paul. "Pell Spending Levels Off," *Inside Higher Ed* (September 7, 2012). Accessed September 10, 2012, http://www.insidehighered.com/news/2012/09/07/pell-spending-declines-despite-growth-grant-recipients.

Fain, Paul. "Price of Success," *Inside Higher Ed* (January 16, 2012). Accessed on May 26, 2012, http://www.insidehighered.com/news/2012/01/16/improving-graduation-rates-job-one-city-colleges-chicago.

Field, Kelly. "College Groups React to Obama's Higher-Education Budget with Praise and Caution," *Chronicle of Higher Education* (February 13, 2012). Accessed February 19, 2012, http://chronicle.com/article/College-Groups-React-With/130775/.

Field, Kelly. "Obama Highlights Education's Role in Reaching National Policy Goals," *Chronicle of Higher Education* (January 25, 2012). Accessed February 17, 2012, http://chronicle.com/article/Obama-Puts-Focus-on-Colleges/130447/.

Field, Kelly. "State of the Union Speech Leaves Many Questions Unanswered," *Chronicle of Higher Education* (January 25, 2012). Accessed February 17, 2012, http://chronicle.com/article/State-of-the-Union-Speech/130464/.

Fischer, Karin. "Crisis of Confidence Threatens Colleges," *Chronicle of Higher Education* (May 15, 2011). Accessed May 28, 2012, http://chronicle.com/article/a-crisis-of-confidence/127530/.

Fischer, Bill. "Disruption: Coming Soon to a University near You," *Forbes* (January 19, 2012). Accessed May 28, 2012, http://www.forbes.com/sites/billfischer/2012/01/19/disruption-coming-soon-to-a-university-near-you/.

Friis, Jan. CHEA Update: "Accreditation and the Higher Education Opportunity Act of 2008" (September 19, 2008). Accessed February 12, 2012. http://www.chea.org/Government/HEAUpdate/CHEA_HEA45.html.

Gardner, Lee. "In Scant References to Higher Ed, Ryan Digs at Obama," *Chronicle of Higher Education* (August 30, 2012), accessed September 10, 2012, http://chronicle.com/blogs/decision2012/2012/08/30/in-scant-references-to-higher-ed-ryan-digs-at-obama/.

Gasman, Marybeth. "Yes, Faculty Members Work Hard Enough!" *Chronicle of Higher Education* (March 30, 2012). Accessed May 29, 2012, http://chronicle.com/blogs/innovations/yes-faculty-members-work-hard-enough/32070/.

Gordon, Larry. "More College Freshmen See Getting Good Job as Key Goal, Poll Finds," *Los Angeles Times* (January 26, 2012). Accessed May 26, 2012, http://articles.latimes.com/2012/jan/26/local/la-me-0126-freshman-20120126.

Grasgreen, Allie. "Alumni Adrift," *Inside Higher Ed* (January 25, 2012). Accessed on May 26, 2012, http://www.insidehighered.com/news/2012/01/25/next-phase-academically-adrift-research-links-low-cla-scores-unemployment.

Griffis, Patrick. "Assessment Tool or Edutainment Toy," *Faculty Publications (Libraries)*, Paper 393 (2009). Accessed June 23, 2012, http://digitalcommons.library.unlv.edu/lib_articles/393.

Guarasci Richard. "The Crisis in Higher Education: How Civic Engagement Can Save Higher Education (Part I)," (June 27, 2012) *Huff Post*. Accessed July 20, 2012, http://www.huffingtonpost.com/richard-guarasci/civic-engagement-programs_b_1630919.html.

Hamilton, Reeve. "Outcomes-Based Higher Ed Funding Plans Move Forward," *Texas Tribune* (March 20, 2012). Accessed May 26, 2012, http://www.texastribune.org/texas-education/higher-education/outcomes-based-higher-ed-funding-plans-moving-forw/.

Hamilton, Reeve. "Texas State University System Has $10,000 Degree Plan," *Texas Tribune* (July 12, 2012). Accessed July 20, 2012, http://www.texastribune.org/texas-education/higher-education/texas-state-university-system-unveils-10000-degree/.

Harnisch, Thomas L. *Performance-Based Funding: A Re-Emerging Strategy in Public Higher Education Financing* (June 2011). Accessed May 26, 2012, http://www.congressweb.com/aascu/docfiles/Performance_Funding_AASCU_June2011.pdf.

Harris, Amy Julia. "Task Force Sets Plan to Increase College Completion," *Charlestown Gazette* (June 1, 2012). Accessed June 13, 2012, http://wvgazette.com/News/201206010169.

Hefling, Kimberly. "Obama's Tougher-Stance Question on Higher Education: What Are People Getting for Their Money?" GrandForksHerald.com (February 20, 2012). Accessed February 25, 2012, http://www.grandforksherald.com/event/article/id/230002/.

Helderman, Rosalind S. "Obama Signs Executive Order to Protect Troops from For-Profit College Deceptive Practices," *Washington Post* (April 27, 2012), accessed September 22, 2012, http://www.washingtonpost.com/blogs/44/post/2012/04/27/gIQAYV3ilT_blog.html.

Hope College, Provost's Office. Student Assessment of Teaching & Learning, 2012. Accessed October 25, 2012, http://surveys.cs.hope.edu/surveys/create?SurveyName=SALT&CourseID=HOPE&Term=SS10.

The Institute for a Competitive Workforce. *Leaders & Laggards: A State-by-State Report Card on Public Postsecondary Education* (June 2012). Accessed July 4, 2012, http://icw.uschamber.com/reportcard/files/Leaders-and-Laggards-2012.pdf.

Jacobs, Heidi L.M. "Information Literacy and Reflective Pedagogical Practice," *Journal of Academic Librarianship* 34, no. 3 (2008): 256–62. Accessed June 14, 2012, Science Direct.

Jankowski, Natasha A., and Staci J. Provezis. *Making Student Learning Evidence Transparent: The State of the Art* (November 2011). Accessed May 26, 2012, http://www.learningoutcomesassessment.org/documents/TransparencyOfEvidence.pdf.

Jaschik, Scott. "Western Accreditor Adopts Reforms on Academic Quality," *Inside Higher Ed* (November 15, 2011). Accessed on May 26, 2012, http://www.insidehighered.com/quicktakes/2011/11/15/western-accreditor-adopts-reforms-academic-quality.

Jelski, Daniel. "A Free College Education for All," *Forbes* (January 19, 2012). Accessed June 16, 2012, http://www.forbes.com/sites/ccap/2012/01/19/a-free-college-education-for-all/.

Johnson, Corey M., Elizabeth Blakesley Lindsay, and Scott Walter. "Learning More about How They Think: Information Literacy Instruction in a Campus-Wide Critical Thinking Project," *College & Undergraduate Libraries* 15, nos. 1–2 (2008): 231–54. Accessed June 14, 2012, EBSCO.

June, Audrey Williams. "Professors Seek to Reframe Salary Debate," *Chronicle of Higher Education* (April 8, 2012). Accessed May 29, 2012, http://chronicle.com/article/faculty-group-says/131432/.

Kahlenberg, Richard. "A Better Way to Evaluate Colleges—and Improve Education?" *Chronicle of Higher Education* (April 8, 2012). Accessed May 26, 2012, http://chronicle.com/blogs/innovations/a-better-way-to-evaluate-colleges-and-improve-education/32156.

Kahn Academy. "About Khan Academy." Accessed August 10, 2012, http://www.khanacademy.org/about.

Kelderman, Eric. "Federal Officials Penalize 2 States for College-Spending Cuts," *Chronicle of Higher Education* (March 14, 2012). Accessed June 18, 2012, http://chronicle.com/article/us-penalizes-2-states-for/131150/.

Kelderman, Eric. "In Accreditation Proposal, Panel Pleases neither Reformers nor Status Quo Advocates," *Chronicle of Higher Education* (April 13, 2012). Accessed May 1, 2012, http://chronicle.com/article/In-Accreditation-Proposals/131561/.

Kelderman, Eric. "Public Colleges Pledge to Raise Number of Graduates, and Seek Help in Doing So," *Chronicle of Higher Education* (October 2, 2012), accessed October 2, 2012, http://chronicle.com/article/Public-Colleges-Pledge-to/134812/?cid=pm&utm_source=pm&utm_medium=en.

Kelderman, Eric. "State and Local Spending on Higher Education Reached a New 25-Year Low in 2011," *Chronicle of Higher Education* (March 16, 2012), Accessed June 18, 2012, http://chronicle.com/article/statelocal-spending-onr/131221/.

Kelderman, Eric. "State Student-Aid Grants Should Focus on Completion, Not Just Merit, Report Says," *Chronicle of Higher Education* (May 8, 2012). Accessed June 14, 2012, http://chronicle.com/article/state-student-aid-grants/131821.

Kelderman, Eric. "States Push Even Further to Cut Spending on Colleges," *Chronicle of Higher Education* (January 22, 2012). Accessed June 18, 2012, http://chronicle.com/article/States-Push-Even-Further-to/130416/.

Keller, Rudi. "Higher Education Leaders Describe Effect of State Cuts," *Columbia Daily Tribune* (February 2, 2012). Accessed June 16, 2012, http://www.columbiatribune.com/news/2012/feb/02/higher-education-leaders-describe-effect-of-state/.

Kelly, Andrew P., and Mark Schneider. "Small Step for Quality Control," *Inside Higher Ed* (July 31, 2012). Accessed August 3, 2012, http://www.insidehighered.com/views/2012/07/31/accreditors-bold-strike-greater-college-transparency-essay#.UFSv-W4T33U.email.

Kiley, Kevin. "A Cap on Pay (and Bad Press)," *Inside Higher Ed* (January 26, 2012). Accessed May 29, 2012, http://www.insidehighered.com/news/2012/01/26/california-state-approves-cap-salary-increases-incoming-president.

Kiley, Kevin. "Performance Anxiety," *Inside Higher Ed* (December 16, 2011). Accessed May 26, 2012. Accessed July 8, 2012, http://www.insidehighered.com/news/2011/12/16/indiana-revamps-performance-funding-focusing-first-year-completion.

Kuh, George, and Stanley Ikenberry. *More Than You Think, Less Than We Need: Learning Outcomes Assessment in American Higher Education.* Champaign, IL: National Institute for Learning Outcomes Assessment, 2009. Accessed October 25, 2012, http://www.learningoutcomeassessment.org/documents/fullreportrevised-L.pdf.

Kurbanoglu, S. Serap. "Self-Efficacy: A Concept Closely Linked to Information Literacy and Lifelong Learning," *Journal of Documentation* 59, no. 6 (2003): 645–56. Accessed June 14, 2012, Emerald.

Lederman, Doug. "ACE Panel Calls for Sustaining but Changing Regional Accreditation," *Inside Higher Ed* (June 7, 2012). Accessed on June 12, 2012, http://www.insidehighered.com/news/2012/06/07/ace-panel-calls-sustaining-changing-regional-accreditation.

Lederman, Doug. "College Isn't So Unaffordable," *Inside Higher Ed* (July 12, 2012). Accessed July 20, 2012, http://www.insidehighered.com/news/2012/07/12/report-college-isnt-really-so-unaffordable.

Lederman, Doug. "Dissecting Obama's Message," *Inside Higher Ed* (February 26, 2009). Accessed May 9, 2012, http://www.insidehighered.com/news/2009/02/26/oneyear.

Lederman, Doug. "Firms to Offer Standardized Tests to Individuals through StraighterLine," *Inside Higher Ed* (January 20, 2012). Accessed June 16, 2012, http://www.insidehighered.com/quicktakes/2012/01/20/firms-offer-standardized-tests-individuals-through-straighterline.

Lederman, Doug. "Fixing Accreditation, From the Inside," *Inside Higher Ed* (May 13, 2011). Accessed May 9, 2012, http://www.insidehighered.com/news/2011/05/13/higher_ed_group_creates_panel_to_weigh_new_future_for_accreditation.

Lederman, Doug. "HEA: A Huge, Exacting Accountability Bill," *Inside Higher Ed* (August 1, 2008). Accessed February 12, 2012, http://www.insidehighered.com/news/2008/08/01/hea.

Lederman, Doug. "Quality Assurance, Rearranged," *Inside Higher Ed* (October 31, 2011). Accessed February 19, 2012, http://www.insidehighered.com/news/2011/10/31/us-panels-ideas-revamping-higher-ed-accreditation.

Lederman, Doug. "State Support Slumps Again," *Inside Higher Ed* (January 23, 2012). Accessed June 18, 2012, http://www.insidehighered.com/news/2012/01/23/state-funds-higher-education-fell-76–2011–12.

Levy, David C. "Do College Professors Work Hard Enough?" *Washington Post* (March 23, 2012). Accessed May 29, 2012, http://www.washingtonpost.com/opinions/do-college-professors-work-hard-enough/2012/02/15/gIQAn058VS_story.html.

Lewin, Tamar. "Mixed Reviews of Obama Plan to Keep Down College Costs," *New York Times* (January 27, 2012). Accessed February 18, 2012, http://www.nytimes.com/2012/01/28/education/obamas-plan-to-control-college-costs-gets-mixed-reviews.html.

Lindsay, Thomas K. "Fool for Higher Education," *Inside Higher Ed* (May 17, 2012). Accessed June 15, 2012, http://www.insidehighered.com/views/2012/05/17/us-should-curtail-student-loans-help-taxpayers-and-students-essay.

Lipka, Sara. "Engineering Majors Hit the Books More Than Business Majors Do, Survey Finds," *Chronicle of Higher Education* (November 17, 2011). Accessed on May 26, 2012, http://chronicle.com/article/who-hits-the-books-more-study/129806/.

Longley, Robert. "College Degree Nearly Doubles Annual Earnings," *About.com US Government Info*. Accessed June 21, 2012, http://usgovinfo.about.com/od/censusandstatistics/a/collegepays.htm.

The Lumina Foundation, "About Us." Accessed July 4, 2012, http://www.luminafoundation.org/about_us/.

Ma, Jennifer, and Sandy Baum. Advocacy & Policy Center of the College Board, *Trends in College Pricing 2011* (2011). Accessed July 19, 2012, http://trends.collegeboard.org/sites/default/files/analysis-brief-trends-by-state-july-2012.pdf.

Mack, Julie. "U.S. Colleges Put Low Priority on Student Learning, Say Authors of 'We're Losing Our Minds'," *mlive.com* (May 20, 2012). Accessed May 26, 2012, http://www.mlive.com/education/index.ssf/2012/05/us_colleges_put_low_priority_o.html.

Mackey, Thomas P., and Trudi E. Jacobson. "Reframing Information Literacy as a Metaliteracy," *College & Research Libraries* 72, no. 1 (2011): 62–78. Accessed June 14, 2012, EBSCO.

Maffly, Brian. "U. of Utah Graduation Rate Sags in Face of Poor College Readiness," *Salt Lake Tribune* (November 30, 2011). Accessed May 26, 2012, http://archive.sltrib.com/article.php?id=18260596&itype=storyID.

Maguire Associates. "The Higher Education Opportunity Act of 2008 and the Net Price Calculator: Turning the Act into Action," *Insights for a Challenging Economy* 2, no. 4 (n.d.). Accessed February 16, 2012, http://www.maguireassoc.com/resource/insights_bulletin_vol2_4.html.

Massy, William F. "Metrics for Efficiency and Effectiveness in Higher Education: Completing the Completion Agenda," paper produced with support from the Lumina Foundation, n.d. Accessed June 22, 2012, http://www.sheeo.org/annualmeeting/Metrics%20for%20Efficiency%20and%20Effectiveness%20in%20Higher%20Education.pdf.

McClatchy, Tony Pugh. "Some Private Colleges Offering Deals for Students," *New Hampshire SentinelSource.com* (May 20, 2012). Accessed June 19, 2012, http://www.sentinelsource.com/features/education/some-private-colleges-offering-deals-for-students/article_bdd10238–84d8–59d7–9e13–3e92823908e2.html.

McCleery, Bill. "More Hoosiers Need College Degrees, Commission Says," *Indianapolis Star* (March 11, 2011). Accessed May 26, 2012, http://www.courier-journal.com/article/20120310/news02/303100054/.

Megan Oakleaf—Publications." 2012. Accessed June 25, 2012, http://meganoakleaf.info/publications.html.

Meyer, Mark C. "White Paper on Customer Loyalty Metrics: A Three-phase Maturity Model Approach" (Strategy to Value Consulting, 2006). Accessed July 12, 2012, http://www.strategytovalue.com/files/Customer_Loyalty_Metrics.pdf.

Moltz, David. "Looking Ahead to 2013," *Inside Higher Ed* (December 3, 2010). Accessed February 19, 2012, http://www.insidehighered.com/news/2010/12/03/naciqi.

Mortenson, Tom. "Reverse Tactic of Shifting Costs to Students," *Gazette* (March 18, 2012). Accessed June 16, 2012, http://thegazette.com/2012/03/18/reverse-tactic-of-shifting-costs-to-students/.

Muys, Brian. "American Public University System Extends Online Learning Collaboration with WCET for Predictive Analytics Reporting Framework" (August 30, 2012), accessed October 25, 2012, http://www.marketwatch.com/story/american-public-university-system-extends-online-learning-collaboration-with-wcet-for-predictive-analytics-reporting-framework-2012-08-30.

The National Leadership Council for Liberal Education & America's Promise. *College Learning for the New Global Century* (2007). Accessed May 26, 2012, http://www.aacu.org/leap/documents/GlobalCentury_final.pdf.

National Student Engagement Survey. "About NSSE: What Is Student Engagement" (2012). Accessed July 10, 2012, http://nsse.iub.edu/html/about.cfm.

National Student Engagement Survey. "NSSE Regional Accreditation Toolkit" (2012). Accessed July 10, 2012, http://nsse.iub.edu/_/?cid=136.

Neal, Anne D. "Asking Too Much (and Too Little) of Accreditors," *Inside Higher Ed* (November 12, 2010). Accessed February 19, 2012, http://www.insidehighered.com/views/2010/11/12/neal.

Nelson, Libby A. "At the White House Roundtable," *Inside Higher Ed* (December 6, 2011). Accessed February 17, 2012, http://www.insidehighered.com/news/2011/12/06/obama-meeting-focuses-cost-affordability-productivity.

Nelson, Libby A. "'Gainful Comes to the Nonprofits,'" *Inside Higher Ed* (January 30, 2012). Accessed February 18, 2012, May 9, 2012, http://www.insidehighered.com/news/2012/01/30/obama-higher-education-plan-signals-policy-shift.

Nelson, Libby A. "No Overhaul of Accreditation," *Inside Higher Ed* (December 19, 2011). Accessed February 19, 2012, http://www.insidehighered.com/news/2011/12/19/committee-higher-ed-accreditation-composing-its-final-report.

Nelson, Libby A. "The Obama Agenda," *Inside Higher Ed* (September 2, 2012). Accessed September 10, 2012, http://www.insidehighered.com/news/2012/09/04/higher-education-plays-role-democratic-platform.

Nelson, Libby A. "Pell Grants in the Spotlight," *Inside Higher Ed* (September 5, 2012). Accessed September 9, 2012, http://www.insidehighered.com/news/2012/09/05/higher-ed-first-night-democratic-national-convention.

Nelson, Libby A. "Price Back in the Spotlight," *Inside Higher Ed* (December 1, 2011). Accessed February 17, 2012, http://www.insidehighered.com/news/2011/12/01/congress-duncan-focus-rising-college-prices.

Nelson, Libby A. "A Summer without Pell," *Inside Higher Ed* (August 2, 2012). Accessed August 4, 2012, http://www.insidehighered.com/news/2012/08/02/colleges-worry-about-elimination-summer-pell-grant.

Nelson, Libby A. "A Symbolic, but Pleasing, Budget," *Inside Higher Ed* (February 14, 2012). Accessed February 19, 2012, http://www.insidehighered.com/news/2012/02/14/obama-proposes-increase-education-spending.

Nelson, Libby A. "Warnings of Unintended Consequences: Obama Plan to Tie Tuition Prices to Aid Eligibility Draws Criticism," *Inside Higher Ed* (January 26, 2012). Accessed February 17, 2012, http://www.insidehighered.com/news/2012/01/26/obama-plan-tie-tuition-prices-aid-eligibility-draws-criticism.

Nelson, Libby A. "What We Don't Know about Debt," *Inside Higher Ed* (May 18, 2012). Accessed June 15, 2012, http://www.insidehighered.com/news/2012/05/18/what-we-dont-know-about-college-student-debt.

Nisperos, Neil. "Public Universities Expand Web Education Offerings," *Sun* (San Bernardino and the Inland Empire) (May 27, 2012). Accessed June 18, 2012, http://www.sbsun.com/ci_20714014/public-universities-expand-web-education-offerings.

Noel-Levitz™. "National Satisfaction and Priorities Reports" (2012). Accessed July 10, 2012), https://www.noellevitz.com/student-retention-solutions/satisfaction-priorities-assessments/student-satisfaction-inventory.

Oakleaf, Megan. *The Value of Academic Libraries.* Chicago: Association of College and Research Libraries, 2010. Accessed June 7, 2012, http://www.ala.org/acrl/sites/ala.org.acrl/files/content/issues/value/val_report.pdf.

"Obama Campaign Emphasizes College Affordability," *Inside Higher Ed* (August 22, 2012). Accessed September 10, 2012, http://www.insidehighered.com/quicktakes/2012/08/22/obama-campaign-emphasizes-college-affordability.

Oblinger, Diane. "LET'S Talk . . . Analytics," *Educause Review* 47, no. 4 (2012): 10–13. Accessed October 25, 2012, http:/www.educause.edu/ir/library/pdf/ERM1240P.pdf.

Olson, Gary A. "How Not to Measure Faculty Productivity," *Chronicle of Higher Education* (December 7, 2011). Accessed May 26, 2012, http://chronicle.com/article/how-not-to-measure-faculty/130015/.

Owusu-Ansah, Edward K. "Debating Definitions of Information Literacy: Enough Is Enough," *Library Review* 54, no. 6 (2005): 366–74. Accessed June 14, 2012, Emerald.

Padilla, Jose. "Opportunity Knocks, and Knocks Hard: The Higher Education Opportunity Act of 2008," The Office of the General Counsel, DePaul University (winter 2008–2009). Accessed February 16, 2012, http://generalcounsel.depaul.edu/news_and_events/news/archivedNews_5_1962_1463.html.

Pant, Meagan. "Public Colleges Told to Outline 3-Year Grad Plan," *Dayton Daily News* (July 9, 2012). Accessed July 17, 2012, http://www.daytondailynews.com/news/public-colleges-told-to-outline-3-year-grad-plan-1402608.html.

Paulson, Amanda. "Student Debt: What's Been Driving College Costs So High, Anyway?" *Christian Science Monitor* (June 6, 2012). Accessed June 14, 2012, http://www.csmonitor.com/USA/Education/2012/0606/Student-debt-What-s-been-driving-college-costs-so-high-anyway.

Pelletier, Stephen G. "Stewardship in an Era of Constraint," *Public Purpose* (summer 2011). Accessed May 1, 2012, http://www.aascu.org/uploadedFiles/AASCU/Content/Root/MediaAndPublications/PublicPurposeMagazines/Issue/11summer_stewardship.pdf.

Pérez-Peña, Richard. "Trying to Find a Measure for How Well Colleges Do," *New York Times* (April 7, 2012). Accessed May 26, 2012, http://www.nytimes.com/2012/04/08/education/trying-to-find-a-measure-for-how-well-colleges-do.html.

Pinhel, Rute. "Higher Education Opportunity Act of 2008." Accessed February 12, 2012, http://www.cga.ct.gov/2008/rpt/2008-R-0470.htm.

Potter, Claire. "What a Real Education Policy Would Look Like." *Chronicle of Higher Education* (January 27, 2012). Accessed February 18, 2012, http://chronicle.com/blognetwork/tenuredradical/2012/01/extra-extra-the-white-house-announces-another-federal-education-non-policy/.

Pounds, Marcia Heroux. "Most Florida Jobs Don't Require Bachelor's Degree," *Sun Sentinel* (January 21, 2012). Accessed May 26, 2012, http://articles.sun-sentinel.com/2012-01-21/business/fl-bachelor-degree-florida-20120116_1_job-fairs-annual-openings-fort-lauderdale-job.

Prineas, Matthew, and Cini, Marie. *Assessing Learning in Online Education: The Role of Technology in Improving Student Outcomes*, NILOA Occasional Paper 12. Champaign, IL: National Institute for Learning Outcomes Assessment, 2011. Accessed October 25, 2012, http://www.learningoutcomeassessment.org/documents/onlineed.pdf.

"Prior-Learning Assessment Confers a Semester's Worth of Credits, Study Finds," *Chronicle of Higher Education* (September 7, 2011). Accessed July 17, 2012, http://chronicle.com/blogs/ticker/prior-learning-confers-a-semesters-worth-of-credits-study-says/36003.

Project SAILS. Homepage. Accessed June 25, 2012, https://www.projectsails.org/.

Quinterno, John. *The Great Cost Shift: How Higher Education Cuts Undermine the Future Middle Class*, (2012). Accessed June 18, 2012, http://www.demos.org/sites/default/files/publications/thegreatcostshift_0.pdf.

Rampell, Catherine. "Where the Jobs Are, the Training May Not Be," *New York Times* (March 1, 2012). Accessed June 18, 2012, http://www.nytimes.com/2012/03/02/business/dealbook/state-cutbacks-curb-training-in-jobs-critical-to-economy.html.

Republican National Committee. "We Believe in America: 2012 Republican Party Platform" (August 2012). Accessed September 9, 2012, http://www.gop.com/wp-content/uploads/2012/08/2012GOPPlatform.pdf.

Rich, Motoko. "Private Sector Gets Job Skills; Public Gets Bill," *New York Times* (January 7, 2012). Accessed June 16, 2012, http://www.nytimes.com/2012/01/08/business/states-pay-to-train-workers-to-companies-benefit.html?pagewanted=all.

Ritchel, Matt. "Wasting Time Is the New Divide in Digital Era," *New York Times* (May 29, 2012). Accessed June 14, 2012, http://www.nytimes.com/2012/05/30/us/new-digital-divide-seen-in-wasting-time-online.html?pagewanted=all.

Rivera, Carla. "Keys to College Students' Success Often Overlooked, Report Says," *Los Angeles Times* (November 28, 2011). Accessed May 26, 2012, http://articles.latimes.com/2011/nov/28/local/la-me-college-retention-20111129.

Roush, Matt. "Kettering Offers Fixed Tuition Guarantee for 10 Semesters," *CBS Detroit* (March 13, 2012). Accessed June 16, 2012, http://detroit.cbslocal.com/2012/03/13/kettering-offers-fixed-tuition-guarantee-for-10-semesters/.

Selingo, Jeff. "Fixing College" (Opinion Pages), *New York Times* (June 25, 2012). Accessed June 27, 2012, http://www.nytimes.com/2012/06/26/opinion/fixing-college-through-lower-costs-and-better-technology.html?_r=1.

Selingo, Jeff. "MOOC's Aren't a Panacea, but That Doesn't Blunt Their Promise." *Chronicle of Higher Education* (July 11, 2012). Accessed July 17, 2012, http://chronicle.com/blogs/next/2012/07/11/moocs-arent-a-panacea-but-that-doesnt-blunt-their-promise/.

Selingo, Jeff. "Taking Some of the Guesswork Out of the Value-of-College Question," *Chronicle of Higher Education* (February 20, 2012). Accessed May 26, 2012, http://chronicle.com/blogs/next/2012/02/20/taking-some-of-the-guesswork-out-of-the-value-of-college-question/.

Selingo, Jeff. "The Value Gap," *Chronicle of Higher Education* (January 11, 2012). Accessed May 28, 2012, http://chronicle.com/blogs/next/2012/01/11/the-value-gap/.

Silverleib, Alan, and Tom Cohen. "Obama Unveils Plan to Control College Costs," *CNN Politics* (January 27, 2012). Accessed February 18, 2012, http://www.cnn.com/2012/01/27/politics/obama-trip/index.html.

Simon, Stephanie, and Stephanie Banchero. "Putting a Price on Professors," *Wall Street Journal* (October 22, 2010). Accessed May 26, 2012, http://online.wsj.com/article/SB10001424052748703735804575536322093520994.html.

Skelton, George. "Let's Make Textbooks Affordable," *Los Angeles Times* (December 12, 2011). Accessed June 16, 2012, http://articles.latimes.com/2011/dec/12/local/la-me-cap-textbooks-20111212.

Smith, Kenneth R. "New Roles and Responsibilities for the University Library: Advancing Student Learning through Outcomes Assessment." Accessed June 23, 2012, http://www.arl.org/resources/pubs/mmproceedings/136smith˜print.shtml.

Smith, Mitch. "Textbook Alternative," *Inside Higher Ed* (May 10, 2012). Accessed June 16, 2012, http://www.insidehighered.com/news/2012/05/10/university-minnesota-compiles-database-peer-reviewed-open-source-textbooks.

Spradlin, Courtney. "UCA, Higher Education Major Players in Local Economy," *thecabin.net* (March 3, 2012). Accessed June 19, 2012, http://thecabin.net/news/local/2012-03-03/uca-higher-education-major-players-local-economy#.UQklJB2Yu9E.

Stratford, Michael. "Aid for Students and Veterans Gets a Spotlight at Democrats' Convention," *Chronicle of Higher Education* (September 5, 2012). Accessed September 10, 2012, http://chronicle.com/blogs/decision2012/2012/09/05/aid-for-students-and-veterans-gets-a-spotlight-at-democrats-convention/.

Stratford, Michael. "Democratic Platform Advocates More Higher Education and Attacks Romney on For-Profits," *Chronicle of Higher Education* (September 4, 2012), accessed September 10, 2012, http://chronicle.com/blogs/decision2012/2012/09/04/democratic-platform-advocates-more-higher-ed-and-attacks-romney-on-for-profits/.

Stratford, Michael. "On Republican Convention's Last Night, Fleeting Nods to Student Debt," *Chronicle of Higher Education* (August 31, 2012). Accessed September 10, 2012, http://chronicle.com/blogs/decision2012/2012/08/31/on-republican-conventions-last-night-fleeting-nods-to-student-debt/.

Stripling, Jack. "Unconventional Wisdom," *Inside Higher Ed* (December 10, 2010). Accessed May 26, 2012, http://www.insidehighered.com/news/2010/12/10/productivity.

Supiano, Beckie. "Aid Experts and Officials Question President's College-Affordability Plans," *Chronicle of Higher Education* (January 30, 2012). Accessed February 18, 2012, http://chronicle.com/article/Aid-ExpertsOfficials/130502/.

Swanson, Troy. "Applying a Critical Pedagogical Perspective to Information Literacy Standards," *Community and Junior College Libraries*, 12, no. 4 (2004): 65–78. Accessed June 14, 2012, EBSCO.

Thomason, Andrew. "12 Percent Increase in State Higher Education Funding Goes to Pensions," *Rock River Times* (January 25, 2012). Accessed June 19, 2012, http://rockrivertimes.com/2012/01/25/12-percent-increase-in-state-higher-education-funding-goes-to-pensions/.

Tugman, Lindsey. "University Expenditures Now Available Online." Accessed July 15, 2012, http://www.todaysthv.com/news/story.aspx?storyid=216749.

"2010 CHEA Award for Outstanding Institutional Practice in Student Learning Outcomes," *CHEA Chronicle* 11, no. 1 (February 2010), 1–3. Accessed October 25, 2012, http://www.chea.org/pdf/Chea-Chronicle_Feb2010.pdf.

University of Hong Kong, Centre for the Enhancement of Teaching and Learning. *Assessment Drives Learning* (2009). Accessed October 25, 2012, http://ar.cetl.hku.hk/obasl.htm.

University of Hong Kong, Centre for the Enhancement of Teaching and Learning. *Course Outline Template: Guidelines for Writing Course Outlines* (2010). Accessed October 25, 2012, http://ar.cetl.hku.hk/pdf/HKU%20CourseOutlineTemplateV1.1.pdf.

"The Value Project Overview," *Peer Review* 11, no. 1 (2009): 4–7. Accessed October 25, 2012, http://www.aacu.org/peerreview/pr-wi09/documents/Peer_Review_Winter_2009.pdf.

van Barneveld, Angela, Kimberly E Arnold, and John P. Campbell. *Analytics in Higher Education: Establishing a Common Language, Educause Learning Initiative Paper.* Washington, DC: Educause, January 2012. Accessed October 25, 2012, http://net.educause.edu/ir/library/pdf/ELI3026.pdf.

Vedder, Richard. "Beware: Alternative Certification Is Coming," *Chronicle of Higher Education* (January 23, 2012). Accessed May 28, 2012, http://chronicle.com/blogs/innovations/beware-alternative-certification-is-coming/31369.

Vedder, Richard. "Obama, Higher-Education Costs, and Student Aid," *Chronicle of Higher Education* (January 30, 2012). Accessed June 14, 2012, http://chronicle.com/blogs/innovations/obama-higher-education-costs-and-student-aid/31432.

Walters, Garrison. "It's Not So Easy: The Completion Agenda and the States," *Liberal Education* 98, no. 1 (Winter 2012). Accessed on May 26, 2012, http://www.aacu.org/liberaleducation/le-wi12/walters.cfm.

Weiner, John M. "Is There a Difference between Critical Thinking and Information Literacy? A Systematic Review 2000–2009," *Journal of Information Literacy* 5, no. 2 (2011): 81–92. Accessed June 14, 2012, EBSCO.

Will, George F. "'Higher Education Bubble' Is About to Burst," *BostonHerald.com* (June 10, 2012). Accessed June 18, 2012, http://bostonherald.com/news/opinion/op_ed/view.bg?articleid=1061137890.

Wilmath, Kim. "Tuition Hike Means USF Students Paying for Greater Share of Their Education Than State," *Tampa Bay Times* (April 20, 2012). Accessed June 16, 2012, http://www.tampabay.com/news/education/college/tuition-hike-means-usf-students-paying-for-greater-share-of-their/1225959.

Young, Elise. "Another State to Assess Skills," *Inside Higher Ed* (July 9, 2012). Accessed July 17, 2012, http://www.insidehighered.com/news/2012/07/09/wisconsin-seeks-competency-based-degree-program-without-help-western-governors.

Young, Jeffrey R. "'Badges' Earned Online Pose Challenge to Traditional College Diplomas," *Chronicle of Higher Education* (January 8, 2012). Accessed May 28, 2012, http://chronicle.com/article/badges-earned-online-pose/130241/.

Young, Jeffrey R. "5 Universities to Test Bulk-Purchasing of E-Textbooks in Bid to Rein in Costs," *Chronicle of Higher Education* (January 18, 2012), accessed June 16, 2012, http://chronicle.com/article/5-universities-to-test/130373.

Young, John W. "Validity of the Measure of Academic Proficiency and Progress (MAPP)," 2007. Accessed June 21, 2012, http://www.ets.org/s/mapp/pdf/5018.pdf.

Young, Elise, and Libby A. Nelson. "'Hall of Shame,' Year Two," *Inside Higher Ed* (June 13, 2012). Accessed June 18, 2012, http://www.insidehighered.com/news/2012/06/13/education-department-focuses-state-role-cost-increases-annual-lists.

Zimmerman, Jonathan. "Are College Students Learning?" *Los Angeles Times* (January 31, 2012). Accessed May 26, 2012, http://articles.latimes.com/2012/jan/31/opinion/la-oe-zimmerman-are-college-students-learning-20120131.

Zirkel, Perry A., and Jean Johnson. "Buying the Professor a BMW," *Inside Higher Ed* (December 16, 2011). Accessed June 18, 2012, http://www.insidehighered.com/views/2011/12/16/essay-explores-rising-college-prices-and-whether-professors-benefit.

INDEX

ABOUT THE EDITORS AND CONTRIBUTOR

ROBERT E. DUGAN is the dean of libraries at the University of West Florida (Pensacola, FL; rdugan@uwf.edu). Prior to assuming this position, he had been at Suffolk University, Boston; Wesley College, Dover, DE; and Georgetown University, Washington, DC. He has also worked in state and public libraries during his nearly 40 year career. He is the coauthor of 10 books, including the award winning *Viewing Library Metrics from Different Perspectives* (2009).

PETER HERNON is a professor at Simmons College (Graduate School of Library and Information Science, Boston) and the principal faculty member for the doctoral program, Managerial Leadership in the Information Professions. He received his PhD degree from Indiana University, Bloomington, is the 2008 recipient of the Association of College and Research Libraries' (ACRL) award for Academic/Research Librarian of the Year, is the coeditor of *Library & Information Science Research*, and has taught, conducted workshops, and/or delivered addresses in 10 countries (Canada, Denmark, England, Finland, France, Greece, New Zealand, Norway, Portugal, and South Africa). He is the author or coauthor of 54 books, including the award winning *Federal Information Policies in the 1980s* (1985), *Assessing Service Quality* (1998), and *Viewing Library Metrics from Different Perspectives* (2009).

CANDY SCHWARTZ is a professor in the Graduate School of Library and Information Science at Simmons College, Boston, where she teaches in the area of information organization, digital libraries, and metadata. She received her doctorate from Syracuse University, Syracuse, New York, and has received national service and teaching awards from the American Society for Information Science & Technology (ASIS&T). She is the author of *Sorting out the Web* (2001), coauthor of *Records Management and the Library* (1993), coeditor of *Revisiting Outcomes Assessment in Higher Education* (2006), and has chapters in several books and articles in journals such as the *Journal of Academic Librarianship, Journal of the American Society for Information Science,* and *Library Trends.* She is also the coeditor of *Library & Information Science Research.*

LAURA SAUNDERS is assistant professor in the Graduate School of Library and Information Science at Simmons College, Boston, MA. Her published works have appeared in journals such as *College & Research Libraries* and the *Journal of Academic Librarianship. Information Literacy as a Student Learning Outcome* (Libraries Unlimited, 2011) is based on her dissertation completed at Simmons College.